I0138677

SEPAHDAR

Fathollah Khan Akbar

A Biography

COMPILED AND EDITED BY

GOLI AKBAR KASHANI

MAGE PUBLISHERS

MAGE PUBLISHERS INC

Index: Victoria George

LIBRARY OF CONGRESS CATALOGING-IN-PUBLICATION DATA
Available at the Library of Congress

HARDCOVER EDITION, INCLUDING INDEX
ISBN: 978-1-949445-64-0

VISIT MAGE ONLINE: WWW.MAGE.COM
EMAIL: AS@MAGE.COM

In memory of my father,
Mohsen Akbar

CONTENTS

Preface **ix**

The Akbar Family Tree **xxxi**

A Note on the Text and Acknowledgments **xxxii**

Early Years **1**

The Constitutional Revolution **23**

Cooperation with Constitutional Cabinets **61**

Vosuq al-Dowleh's First Cabinet **79**

Prime Minister **115**

Sepahdar's First Cabinet **137**

Britain's Ultimatum and the Collapse of the Cabinet **149**

Prime Minister Again **175**

The Coup **191**

The Rise of Sardar Sepah and the Fall of the Qajar Dynasty **207**

Final Years **223**

Appendix **229**

Bibliography **243**

Index **251**

PREFACE

I

A year ago, my two daughters gave me a surprise gift bought from Shapero Rare Books on New Bond Street in London. A first edition *The History of the Life of Nader Shah, King of Persia*, published in 1770, the book is indeed rare. The author, William Jones, a British civil servant in Calcutta, was commissioned by King Christian VII of Denmark in 1768 to chronicle the life of the Persian king Nader Shah Afshar. As Nader Shah had been assassinated just twenty-one years before Jones wrote the book, many of his contemporaries were still alive and able to provide eyewitness accounts of his life and reign.

Eyewitness accounts can provide invaluable and new insights that can breathe life into history. Still, such personal accounts, particularly the oral histories passed down from generation to generation, change over time. It is thus imperative to record and preserve such accounts before too much time passes.

Just as Nader Shah rose from obscurity to become one of Iran's great rulers at a critical time for the country, so too did Reza Shah Pahlavi, who came to power a hundred years ago following a coup d'état in 1921, when Iran once again was on the brink of collapse. While none of those who witnessed the events of 1921 are still alive and able to describe what happened during that time, documents, memoirs, and oral reports passed down from that period all contribute to the rich history of this era and its key figures.

One such individual was my paternal grandfather, Fathollah Khan Akbar, Sepahdar A'zam, known simply as Sepahdar (Commander).[1] This book is a historical biography of Sepahdar, prime minister under Ahmad Shah Qajar during the 1921 coup d'état, who took the reins of a country on the verge of ruin, albeit for a short period only, and navigated it through a perfect storm. Accepting the premiership at that crucial time, when no one else was willing to come forward, not only had no personal benefit for Sepahdar, but also put him in great danger. At that time Iran was bankrupt, dependent on British funding, and reeling from years of famine and epidemics. World War I had just ended, and although Iran had declared neutrality throughout the war, it was shattered by invasions by the British and Russians in their ever-present quest for control of the country.

Very little is known about Sepahdar following his semi-retirement from politics after the fall of his cabinet in 1921. Known to be a kind and honest man, and a generous philanthropist, on the one hand, he has also been branded as ineffective and politically naïve on the other.

This preface includes my personal anecdotes and information about Sepahdar's personal life. The rest of the book is a historical account focused primarily on his career, including his business dealings, some of which were questionable. He was a patriot but also a pragmatic businessman. Still, after all his business deals and unconventional choices, Sepahdar ultimately used his wealth for the benefit of Iran's 1905 constitutional revolution and the independence of his beloved country.

Some historians have even questioned his command of the Persian language, which seems bizarre, given that during his long political career, he was appointed by two different shahs (Mozaffar al-Din Shah and Ahmad Shah) to serve in multiple cabinets in a

---

1. He was known by his various titles, all variations on "Commander," including Biglarbegi, Salar Afkham, Salar A'zam, and Sardar Mansur, before 1914, and, Sepahdar A'zam (Great Commander) and Sepahdar Rashti, after 1914.

variety of posts. Specifically, he served as Minister of Post and Telegraph, Minister of Justice, Minister of the Interior, and Minister of War, including serving twice as prime minister under Ahmad Shah. Because Sepahdar was from the province of Gilan and spoke Persian with a Gilaki accent, this may have given rise to the rumors, spread by political enemies, about his command of Persian, and such rumors may have been taken at face value by some historians. Whatever the reason for these mischaracterizations, this book refutes them with documents from the British Foreign Service, as well as letters and newly discovered royal decrees by the Qajar shahs.

In addition to the accounts in these documents, I provide family vignettes about my grandfather and his family. My sources are my own father, Mohsen Akbar, Sepahdar's youngest son; my grandmother, Bemani Khanum, Sepahdar's third wife; and some of my grandfather's contemporaries. I am neither a political scholar nor a historian—my stories are those recounted by family members from whose collective memories I have drawn the rich personal anecdotes presented here.

My grandmother was seventeen years old when my grandfather, who was fifty years old at the time, took her as his third wife in 1905. His first marriage had been ordered by the family elders, to keep the vast family fortunes within the clan. His first wife died shortly after the marriage and while his second marriage was not mandated, it also was arranged by the family. Approximately twenty years into his marriage to his second wife, Sepahdar took a third wife whom he was able to choose on his own. She was much younger than him, and strikingly beautiful. This union produced a single child, Mohsen, born in 1906, who was to become my father. Both my grandfather and my grandmother were from Rasht in Gilan province, but soon after their son was born, the entire family moved to Tehran, where my grandfather owned a stately residence in the city and a large summer house in the foothills of the Alborz Mountains in Shemiran. Over the years, my grandparents would spend time in both Tehran and Rasht.

Khanum Joon,[2] as we used to call my grandmother, was an astute and inquisitive young woman, aware of all the comings and goings in the large mansion in the city. She knew, for instance, that the gatekeeper at the front gate of the large garden worked as a spy for the Russians and secretly reported the identity of everyone who entered the premises. The butler, on the other hand, was a spy for the British legation. Khanum Joon also knew what side each maid was working for, and so on, throughout the entire staff. At that time, my grandfather served as minister in various government cabinets and as his positions became more important, the number of spies in the household also increased.

II

Khanum Joon had her own little "spies" whom she tasked with keeping an eye on the actual spies. It was a game of cat and mouse that went round and round. According to my grandmother, the level of intrigue within the walls of the house was stifling, with everyone prying into each other's business. Thus, the Russian spies knew about the British spies and vice versa.

My grandfather was on friendly terms with both the British and the Russians. He had been awarded the Knight Commander of St. Michael and St. George (KCMG) in 1903 by King Edward VII of England (see Chapter 1). The Russians, on the other hand, also recognized his strong influence and power in the Caspian Sea region, where they were the occupiers. My grandfather, well aware of the bizarre but not unusual hive of spying activity at his residence, was willing to keep both sides at peace until the night when the stakes were too high.

---

2. *Khanum Joon*, literally "dear lady" in Persian, is an honorific for referring to a mother or grandmother.

My grandmother told me how, one very cold winter night during his term as prime minister, Agha,[3] as she used to call my grandfather, put on his winter coat and hat, and went out of the back door of the house into the garden. It was just before midnight. My grandmother's curiosity, piqued by Agha's departure at such a late hour, compelled her to investigate further. Rushing to the bedroom window on the second floor, she looked out into the dark yard. Agha was walking briskly toward the stables where the carriages and the horses were kept. There was a door at the end of the garden by which the stable keeper would sometimes enter the mansion in the morning. No one else ever used that door since it did not open onto a main street. Through the bare winter trees, she saw a large horse approaching, led by an exceptionally tall soldier on foot. On seeing Agha, the soldier stopped and tied his horse to a nearby tree before he and Agha started pacing together, deep in conversation. It was long after midnight by the time the meeting broke up, Agha returning to the house and the tall soldier leaving, with his horse, through the garden door. A few days later, according to my grandmother, Agha retired from his post as prime minister.

Khanum Joon told me, my brother, and sister this story years after my grandfather passed away. She would describe, in her pleasant Gilaki accent, how her courageous Agha was able to meet the tall, mysterious soldier, evading the eyes of all the treacherous spies in the house. As Khanum Joon recounted this story, she would embellish it with dramatic details, such as an imitation of howling wolves or stray dogs, or a description of dark clouds partially covering the bright moon at midnight, and I always thought it was just a *ghesseh*, or fairy tale, to entertain us.

Many decades later, however, my father told me that his father, Sepahdar, had held secret meetings on two separate occasions with Reza Khan, the leader of the Cossacks in Iran,[4] back in 1921.

---

3. *Agha*, meaning "gentleman" or "sir" in Persian, was used as an honorific for father or grandfather, and in this case for husband.

4. Formed in 1879, the Persian Cossack Brigade closely resembled the cavalry unit of the Imperial Russian Army.

According to him, both meetings took place in the middle of the night in the back garden of my grandfather's mansion. Reza Khan and Sepahdar used the back door to ensure they would not be observed by the staff. I then realized that the tall, mysterious soldier my grandmother described in her story must have been none other than Reza Khan, the future Shah.

My father never specified who initiated these meetings, but he shared important facts that my grandfather had told him and that answered many lingering questions about the 1921 coup, helping to explain important events in Iranian history. Specifically, Reza Khan insisted that Seyyed Zia al-Din Tabataba'i, Reza Khan's political partner at the time, should be kept in the dark about these secret meetings, while Sepahdar reminded Reza Khan of what everyone already knew, that the country was ravaged by war, famine, and occupation by foreign powers and that strong leadership was urgently needed. Knowing that Reza Khan was planning to occupy Tehran in an attempted coup d'état, my grandfather, who was prime minister at the time, assured Reza Khan that when the latter entered the capital with the Cossack Brigade, of which he was the commander, my grandfather would not send armed forces to oppose him. My grandfather also told Reza Khan that he would resign from the premiership immediately after the coup d'état. Reza Khan advised my grandfather to take refuge in the British embassy, where he would be safe until the dust had settled. Most importantly, at their first meeting, Reza Khan confided in my grandfather his displeasure with the dominant British forces in Iran. These secret meetings had significant and consequential impact on the history of Iran.

When Reza Khan and his troops entered Tehran, my grandfather kept his promise by refusing to deploy the 10,000-strong forces at his disposal.

By all accounts, the coup d'état of 1921 occurred without a drop of blood being shed. This was a rare occurrence in a region of the world where, throughout history, a change of regime, including most recently the Islamic Revolution of 1979, has always been accompanied by immense loss of life.

For his part, Reza Shah Pahlavi never forgot how my grandfather had assisted him. After taking the throne, Reza Shah granted Sepahdar an audience every Monday morning at ten o'clock. The meetings, which were usually held in private and lasted from a few minutes to half an hour, are mentioned in the Iranian magazine *Khandaniha* in an issue from 1976.[5]

My father often talked about these Monday morning audiences, recounting with amazement how Reza Shah would always receive my grandfather in a kind and respectful manner. Reza Shah was more than stern. He was an absolute ruler with an infamously ruthless temper, and strong opinions about his subjects. It was remarkable for me to learn from my father about Reza Shah's unusual respect for Sepahdar. Their collaboration was never revealed because of my grandfather's wishes. After all, he was the prime minister under Ahmad Shah and did not want to appear disloyal. But in his heart, his true loyalty was to his country and not to a particular individual. This can be seen, for example, in his dealings with the British. Before the coup d'état, the British had sought to ratify the 1919 Anglo-Persian Agreement. Regarding it as a one-sided arrangement that would mainly benefit the British, Prime Minister Sepahdar stalled and exhausted his British friends by refusing to give in to their demands, and he was always proud that he had refused to implement the agreement during his premiership.

III

There are many other intriguing stories about my grandfather's life in public office. One episode that comes to mind occurred during the years leading up to the Great Famine of 1917–19. My grandmother often talked about the incredible suffering endured by Iranians during this period. Being the spouse of a wealthy government minister at that time, she led a pampered life and was not affected as much,

5. *Khandaniha*, 32: 24.

and was shielded from the worst of it but she would hear harrowing stories from her staff about the devastating effects of the famine, of children dying in their mothers' arms and dead bodies left lying on city streets. Meanwhile, the Russians and the British were hoarding grain for their troops and very little was left for the population, and Ahmad Shah ordered his own court granaries to be filled, with no consideration for the populace.

Khanum Joon told us children that, to help the hungry people, my grandfather opened all the bakeries in Tehran. I loved hearing this story about her Agha bravely coming to the rescue. We pictured him on a white charger, galloping from one bakery to another in the city, imagining how, as if by magic, flatbreads would pop out of the hot ovens and he would feed everyone. My grandmother's eyes would sparkle when she recounted this particular story, a beautiful memory of my grandfather that lurked, undisturbed, in the deepest recesses of my mind until a few years ago when, quite by chance, I was reading an account of the Great Famine and came across this paragraph:

> Bakers have refrained from opening their shops and resume[ing] baking. The poor and the weak are under great pressure. Under the circumstances, the government had tried to reassure the people. The *Ra'ad* of September 18, 1916 (No. 243), reports that the Minister of Interior in the new cabinet of Vosuq al-Dowleh, Sepahdar Rashti, and Qavam el-Dowleh, the Minister of Public Welfare, had met with the leaders of the bakers' guild to discuss the scarcity and high price of bread. The bakers had agreed to maintain a price of 30 shahis per maund until the government wheat supplies reached Tehran, after which they promised to lower the price of bread.[6]

---

6. Mohammad Gholi Majd, *The Great Famine & Genocide in Iran, 1917–1919*, 2nd edition (Lanham, MD: University Press of America, 2013), p. 36.

So, it was not a fairy tale my doting grandmother told in her charming Gilaki accent. How could I have ever questioned the veracity of her stories about her beloved hero?

Sadly, the famine still persisted for a long time after this episode, but for a short period, because of my grandfather's intervention, the bakers opened their shops and bread was distributed once again.

Khanum Joon gave other examples of Agha's acts of kindness and benevolence. She would describe, for instance, how he built a large hospital in Rasht and arranged for thirty patients of lesser means to be treated at the hospital at his expense every month. She also mentioned two schools that he built in Rasht, modeled on modern Western institutions.

IV

Although he was not a revolutionary, Sepahdar was involved in the nonviolent arm of the Constitutional Revolution of 1905–11, and supported the cause financially. His support for the constitution extended to the point of going himself to Mohammad Ali Shah to express the people's disapproval of the sovereign, after which he was swiftly placed under arrest and banished to Savadkuh, a faraway region of Iran for several months. Another of my grandmother's stories was about the night when Taj al-Moluk Khanum Om al-Khakan, the mother of the Shah, saved Agha's life. Mohammad Ali Shah had ordered Sepahdar's assassination and the Queen Mother secretly sent a messenger to warn Sepahdar, enabling him to cleverly escape the assassins. Chapter 2 includes a detailed account of this story.

V

Khanum Joon's treasure chest of stories included one episode so extraordinary that it seemed like a real fairy tale. According to her,

Sepahsalar Tonekaboni, 1912

when my father was little, hundreds of brave troops were encamped for months in my grandfather's big garden in Rasht, where they were fed three meals a day until they were ready to march and fight despots in Tehran. She recounted how the entire household staff, from the head cook all the way down to the gardener were kept very busy during this time.

Despite its aura of make-believe, this was another one of my grandmother's stories that was borne out by facts. In 1909, during the Constitutional Revolution, Mohammad Vali Khan Tonekaboni, a military commander known by the title of Sepahdar Aʿzam Tonekaboni,[7] led a group of soldiers from Mazanderan through Rasht, on their way to Tehran, in order to conquer the capital.

Although my grandfather had been exiled to Savadkuh by the Shah at that time, he still insisted that Sepahdar Tonekaboni and his five hundred troops camp on his Rasht property for a few months and be treated with the utmost hospitality until Sepahdar Tonekaboni was ready to move them forward. This was one of the many ways in which my grandfather aided the constitutionalists.

Feeding that many troops for a substantial period of time and looking after their well-being was a gigantic task. According to Khanum Joon and historical observers, everyone was surprised by this magnanimous deed. The great Sepahsalar Tonekaboni never forgot this act of kindness towards his troops in a time of need. After his resounding victory in the Triumph of Tehran,[8] Sepahdar Tonekaboni was promoted by the new Shah to the highest rank of Sepahsalar (Greatest Commander), while his title of Sepahdar was subsequently transferred to my grandfather, Fathollah Khan, without whom the Triumph of Tehran would not have been possible.

Wanting to reciprocate Fathollah Khan's generosity, and as a gesture of unity, now-Sepahsalar Tonekaboni consented to the marriage of his only daughter, Taj al-Moluk, to my uncle Ali Amir Mansur, my grandfather's eldest son. Since Taj al-Moluk was only nine years old at the time, her name was written into a family Qur'an to be sealed as a contract between the two families, nominating her as the future wife of Amir Mansur.

---

7. As an aside, in Iran at that time, statesmen usually were referred to solely by their title ("Sepahdar," for example) and not by their actual names. This can be confusing, making it difficult to differentiate between Sepahdar Aʿzam Tonekaboni and my grandfather, Fathollah Khan (Sepahdar A'zam Rashti), who succeeded him. Both Sepahdars were appointed prime minister of Iran during the Qajar dynasty and both hailed from the Caspian Sea region.

8. The Constitutionalists entered Tehran on 13 July 1909, which led to Mohammad Ali Shah seeking refuge at the Russian Legation.

Taj al-Moluk Khalatbari Akbar, daughter of Sepahsalar Tonekaboni, and daughter-in-law of Sepahdar, Rasht, 1919.

This political union between the offspring of two great statesmen had a profound effect on Sepahdar's family. Taj al-Moluk was still only thirteen years old when she finally wed her husband. A petite and shy young girl, she blossomed into a stalwart pillar of her community, took on her husband's title Mansur al-Saltaneh, and ultimately became the beloved matriarch of the Akbar family. Friday lunch gatherings at her home were a tradition for as long as I can remember. An enormous life-size portrait of Sepahsalar Tonekaboni, her father, in full formal regalia, rested against the wall of the large veranda of the house. It was as though he was standing there proudly overseeing the weekly family get-togethers.

This old, Qajar-style house in Shemiran had a beautiful Persian garden with tall, majestic plantain trees and a small pond with water lilies. I still can hear our laughter as we played hide and seek as children behind the jasmine bushes, while the adults partook in backgammon, drank tea, and exchanged pleasantries on the large veranda with its soaring columns. Even though the house was destroyed a long time ago, the trees were cut down, and the people I loved have all passed, my childhood memories still remain, sealed in my mind and brought to life every so often by a certain fragrance or a distinctive sound.

My aunt, Khanum Mansur al-Saltaneh, was a role model for my own mother, Fahimé Yamin Esfandiary Akbar who was twenty years younger. The two sisters-in-law had great affection for each other, and indeed the whole family revered the dignity and strength displayed by the matriarch during her long and challenging life. As the years went by, the Akbars, like many families, faced internal divisions and external crises. But like the great soaring columns of the veranda of her home, Khanum Mansur al-Saltaneh provided unwavering support, the unifying force that kept Sepahdar's family together.

VI

My grandmother told many stories about Agha hosting a beautiful European princess in Gilan, on her journey to visit the Shah in Tehran. Princess Martha Bibesco of Romania stayed for nine days in Rasht in May 1903 and writes about Fathollah Khan's opulent hospitality in a memoir, *Les Huit Paradis*, published in 1908 (see Chapter 1):

> The fame of his spring wallflowers drew us today to the garden of the Lord Sardar Mansur [Fathollah Khan]. All the flowerbeds are rectangular and lead to the gazebo and thus we can walk by them slowly. We sat down for a siesta in the shade of the veranda and for a generous breakfast, blessing Sardar Mansur for giving us the freedom of his garden in the morning without appearing himself, according to the polite rules of Persian etiquette.

Sepahdar cultivated other connections with Europe. He sent his youngest son, Mohsen (my father), to boarding school in Berlin and later to university in France. Sepahdar traveled to Europe several times. On all these occasions, he would spend a few weeks at the fashionable seaside resort of Deauville in northern France. While he was staying there, Mohsen would take the train to visit his father. It was during one of these visits to Deauville that a distinguished young man approached my grandfather and spoke to him in perfect Persian. He was none other than Aga Khan III, Soltan Mohammad Shah Hosayni, the religious leader of the Ismaili sect of Islam. Although my grandfather was twenty years older than his new acquaintance, they became lifelong friends. Over the years, whenever my grandfather traveled to Europe, they always would meet in Deauville, where his young friend liked to attend the horse races, and my father remembered being introduced to him on one occasion.

Even when my grandfather became too old to travel to Europe, he maintained his friendship with Aga Khan by corresponding with him. My father said that the letters he received from the remarkable Aga Khan always began with a poem by a Persian poet. Born in India and educated in England, Aga Khan was nonetheless fluent in the language of his Iranian ancestors and clearly valued the magnificent poetry of the land of his forefathers. When my grandfather passed away in 1937, my father received a telegram from Aga Khan, expressing his sorrow about the demise of his old friend.

In his later years, Sepahdar befriended many contemporary Iranian poets, most of whom wrote passionately about their quest for freedom and establishing a constitution. At least two of these renowned poets, Malek-o Shoara Bahar and Iraj Mirza, wrote about Sepahdar in their verse. Much younger than my grandfather, they were highly involved in the Constitutional Revolution and appreciated Sepahdar's friendship as well as his financial support of the movement.

As an example of his support, after having just been released from exile for opposing the Qajar Shah in 1909, my grandfather instructed his Greek assistant Khariavous to pay a large sum to the striking bazaar workers and resistance fighters in Rasht. Without his support, they would not have been able to join the constitutional movement in opposition to Mohammad Ali Shah and survive financially. Malak al-Shoara Bahar wrote about this support in a touching poem about the dark days of the constitutional crisis. Although he wrote it a few years after the crisis had passed, the poem dwells on the time when the resistance was at its highest. One verse refers to Sepahdar, praising him for his strength and fortitude and for making Gilan, his home province, the envy of all those supporting the cause. Parvaneh Bahar, the daughter of the poet and a good friend and mentor of mine, informed me that the poem was written in appreciation of my grandfather, Sepahdar Rashti, bankrolling the movement.

The second poet, Iraj Mirza, wrote a delightful poem about a Friday night gathering of poets, musicians, singers, and politicians, my grandfather among them. All of them were good friends of the poet. The verses bring to life each of the characters and their personalities. Like a time capsule, it records all the details of a particular evening: the music they heard, the food they ate, and the pleasantries they exchanged.

I had not known about these poems and, to my delight, was introduced to them recently by close friends. It is worth noting that when my grandfather was appointed prime minister in 1920, his cabinet consisted mainly of staunch constitutionalists, like these poets. This surprised the British to such an extent that, in his address to the House of Lords on November 16, 1920, the British foreign secretary, Lord Curzon, heaped praise on the new government in Persia for its modern democratic ideas (see Chapter 6). But such praise was disingenuous: based on previous and subsequent events, Curzon had no wish for a truly democratic Iran.

At the end of the nineteenth century, Arnold Henry Savage Landor, an English author, anthropologist, and painter, traveled to Iran and wrote about his explorations in *Across Coveted Lands*, published in 1902. The book includes a description of my grandfather, who held the title of Salar Afkham at the time:

> The most important political personage living in Resht is His Excellency Salar Afkham, called Mirza Fathollah Khan, one of the richest men in Persia, who has a yearly income of some twenty thousand pounds sterling. He owns a huge house and a great deal of land round Resht, and is much respected for his talent and kindly manner. He was formerly Minister of the Customs and Posts of all Persia and his chest is ablaze with Russian, Turkish and Persian decorations of the highest class, bestowed upon him by the various Sovereigns in recognition of his good work.[9]

In later correspondence, Landor wrote that he found Sepahdar to be intelligent, shrewd, and kind.[10]

Towards the end of his long life, as he became frail and infirm, my grandfather employed a French nurse, Mademoiselle Blondelle, to help care for him. She accompanied him back to Iran after a stay at the Thermal Spa in Vichy, France. Upon arriving in Iran, the middle-aged French nurse took charge of the household and bossed everyone around. My grandmother was not pleased by the presence of this newly arrived quasi "tyrant," and her tales about Mademoiselle Blondelle were somewhat different in character from the pleasant stories to which we were accustomed.

---

9. A. Henry Savage Landor, *Across Coveted Lands* (London: Macmillan & Co., 1902), ch. 4, p. 40.

10. "AKBAR FATḤALLĀH," *Encyclopædia Iranica*, available online at http://www.iranicaonline.org/articles/akbar-sepahdar-e-azam-fathallah-khan-prime-minister-of-iran-from-aban-1299-s

Shaul Bakhash, Clarence Robinson Professor Emeritus of History at George Mason University in Virginia, writes about his own father's dealings with my grandfather in 1937 in his as yet unpublished memoir:

> My father also bought and sold land. Among his property purchases was the house of a prominent landowner and statesman, Fathollah Khan Sepahdar Akbar. Sepahdar was a major landowner in the Rasht area, in the north. He had held a number of cabinet posts as minister of post and telegraph, of justice, and of war, and he had served, briefly, as prime minister. Wealthy in terms of land and villages, Sepahdar had nevertheless fallen on hard times financially in terms of cash, and the sale of his grand house in Tehran was one of the results. The house, on Jaleh Street, with its additional buildings sat on a huge parcel of land that stretched across the equivalent of several city blocks. Like all traditional houses, the main house consisted of a *biruni*, or the outer quarters, where Sepahdar conducted business and received guests, and an *andaruni*, or the inner, private quarters reserved for the wife and children and for family life. In a second and separate large garden linked to the extensive grounds of the main garden, stood a second house where Sepahdar's son lived with his wife and children. There were, in addition, two sizeable bathhouses on the property attached to the two buildings, with hot and cold-water pools, and servants' quarters for the gardener and large household staff. The property was altogether a grand affair, and the sale of such a home by a member of the old, landed aristocracy to a member of the new merchant class caused a stir in elite circles.

Shaul Bakhash goes on to say:

> My father went to see Sepahdar at the house to finalize the deal. In the course of their conversation, Sepahdar said to him: "Mr. Bakhash, I have a lot of expenses in this house, what can I do?" My father told me that in the brief time he

Sepahdar in retirement years, France, 1930.

> was there, he saw maybe a dozen servants, bringing tea and *shirini* [sweets], going up and down the stairs. My father told Sepahdar that the first thing he must do [was] reduce the number of servants in the house. Sepahdar replied that he couldn't do that. They all [came] from the *deh* [the villages] and he [couldn't] just let them go. My father, also remarking on how extensively Sepahdar must have entertained, said that in the *anbar* [the basement] of the house there were a large number of storage closets, where sacks of rice were kept for cooking for Sepahdar's guests.

My grandfather died of cancer in that big house on Jaleh Street on March 25, 1937, before the Bakhash family moved in. Although at times he was financially drained by continuously supporting the constitutional revolution, as well as the charitable deeds in his later years, Sepahdar remained one of the largest land owners in Iran. At the time of his death at the age of 82, he left hundreds of hectares of undeveloped land and over 20 villages in Gilan to his four children and his two wives.

Upon hearing of his death, Reza Shah granted an audience to his three sons, my father included, to express his condolences. A photo from that day shows my father and his brothers dressed in black mourning suits, hats in hand, waiting for the arrival of the Shah. This was Reza Shah's final goodbye to my grandfather. The meeting was described in the Iranian magazine *Khandaniha* in an issue from 1976.[11]

After my grandfather passed away, he was interred in a family mausoleum, consisting of three large rooms and built a few years earlier in the famous Ibn Babawayh Cemetery near Tehran. On special occasions, our parents would take my brother, sister, and me to visit the cemetery. The back room housed Sepahdar's tomb which was encased in white marble and covered with silk carpets from Kashan. Placed on his tombstone were crystal Baccarat candelabras and

---

11. *Khandaniha,* 32:25

Sepahdar's three sons awaiting an audience with Reza Shah after their father's passing. *Left to right,* Gohlam Hossein Akbar (titled Biglarbeigi-e-Rasht), Ali Akbar (titled Amir Mansur) and Mohsen Khan Akbar, Tehran, 1937.

vases in Sèvres porcelain. Heavy velvet curtains adorned the dark, somber room, illuminated only by candlelight. The front room served more as a salon, with French-style furniture. It was always brightly lit and visitors would socialize there. The third room, meanwhile, constituted the mausoleum keeper's living quarters.

Whenever we visited, the old guardian would always serve us tea and dates as he informed my father of all the dignitaries who had paid their respects over the previous months. The caretaker died a few years before the Islamic Revolution of 1979. With his passing, the place was no longer the same. Little did I know at the time that the resting place of my grandfather, a man who was instrumental in the peaceful transition of power in 1921, would later be violently destroyed!

In 1979, during the first few months of the newly established Islamic Republic, the government ordered the demolition of all mausoleums. My grandfather's resting place was annihilated with bulldozers. The family had heard of the intentions of the regime and gathered early on to remove some of the antique items and the silk carpets. These items were distributed among family members. In my living room today, under a black grand piano, rests a threadbare silk Kashan carpet that had formerly adorned my grandfather's final home for many years. Aside from the precious family memories, this carpet is my only connection to him and to my family's past. Everything we possessed, including the vast lands inherited from my grandfather, was otherwise destroyed or confiscated by the new regime.

VII

Like most individuals, Sepahdar was not without his peccadilloes and, in examining his life in greater depth, one can find faults in his political performance and profiteering. However, after reviewing all the source material, one may conclude that throughout his life Sepahdar acted purely out of loyalty to his beloved country. For example, his nonviolent acts of resistance to Mohammad Ali Shah, including vast financial support for the nascent constitutional movement, were instrumental in overthrowing the despotic Qajar Shah.

At times, opponents falsely accused Sepahdar of being a foreign agent, with some saying he was a Russian citizen, and others accusing him of being aligned with the British. In reality, research shows that Sepahdar was a patriot who used his relationship with both occupying states in order to keep them at bay.

Finally, his 1921 collaboration with Reza Shah Pahlavi in ending the corrupt and corroding Qajar dynasty was at the time the most beneficial political solution for Iran, as Reza Shah catapulted the country into a modern state in only sixteen years. Sadly, though, the longed-for constitution, which Sepahdar and his generation fought so bravely to implement, perished just as quickly. Alas, the unceasing call for freedom and democracy in Iran continues to this very day.

Goli Akbar Kashani

The Akbar Family Tree

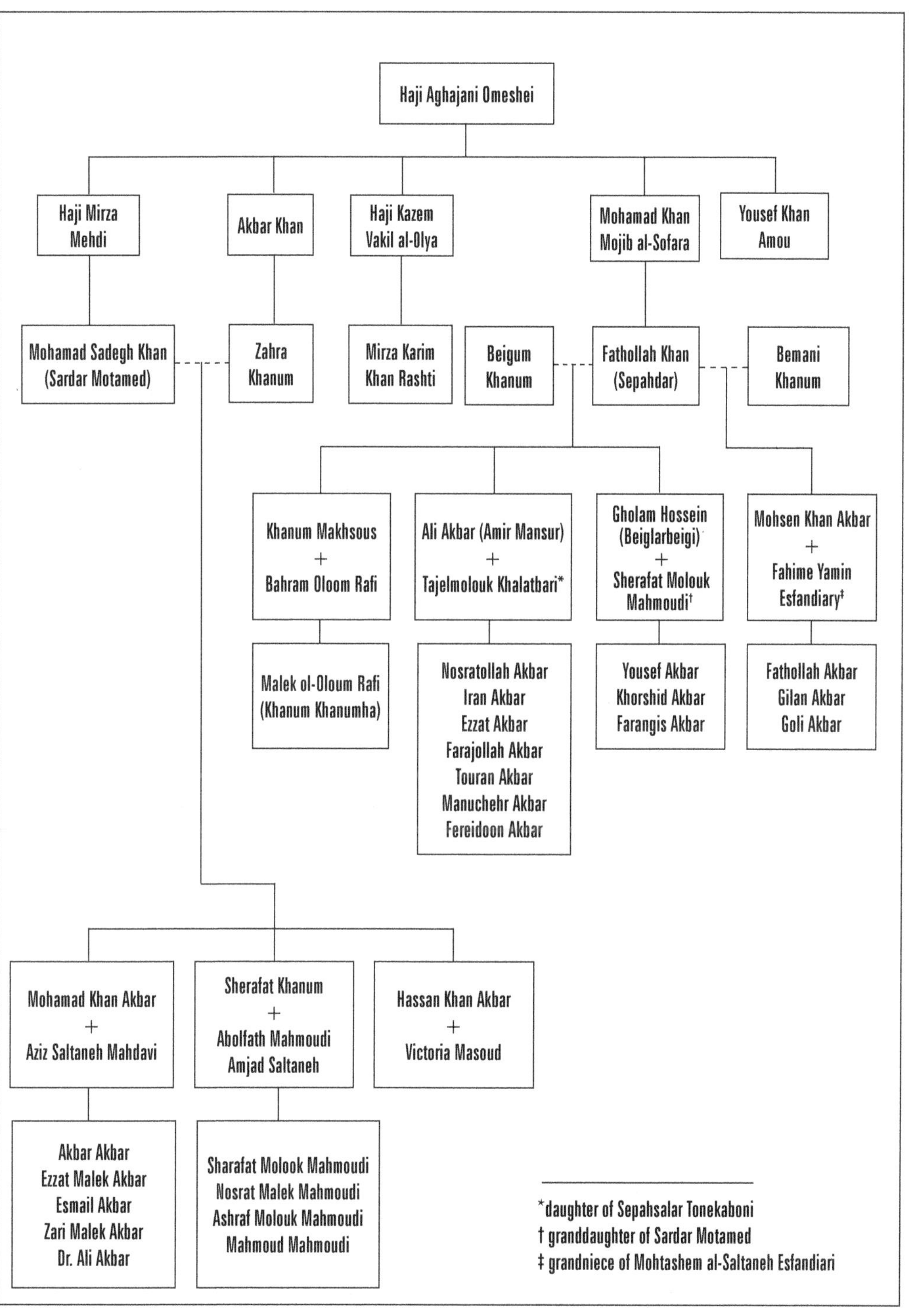

Haji Aghajani Omeshei
Haji Mirza Mehdi
Akbar Khan
Haji Kazem Vakil al-Olya
Mohamad Khan Mojib al-Sofara
Yousef Khan Amou
Mohamad Sadegh Khan (Sardar Motamed)
Zahra Khanum
Mirza Karim Khan Rashti
Beigum Khanum
Fathollah Khan (Sepahdar)
Bemani Khanum
Khanum Makhsous + Bahram Oloom Rafi
Ali Akbar (Amir Mansur) + Tajelmolouk Khalatbari*
Gholam Hossein (Beiglarbeigi) + Sherafat Molouk Mahmoudi†
Mohsen Khan Akbar + Fahime Yamin Esfandiary‡
Malek ol-Oloum Rafi (Khanum Khanumha)
Nosratollah Akbar
Iran Akbar
Ezzat Akbar
Farajollah Akbar
Touran Akbar
Manuchehr Akbar
Fereidoon Akbar
Yousef Akbar
Khorshid Akbar
Farangis Akbar
Fathollah Akbar
Gilan Akbar
Goli Akbar
Mohamad Khan Akbar + Aziz Saltaneh Mahdavi
Sherafat Khanum + Abolfath Mahmoudi Amjad Saltaneh
Hassan Khan Akbar + Victoria Masoud
Akbar Akbar
Ezzat Malek Akbar
Esmail Akbar
Zari Malek Akbar
Dr. Ali Akbar
Sharafat Molook Mahmoudi
Nosrat Malek Mahmoudi
Ashraf Molouk Mahmoudi
Mahmoud Mahmoudi
*daughter of Sepahsalar Tonekaboni
† granddaughter of Sardar Motamed
‡ grandniece of Mohtashem al-Saltaneh Esfandiari

A NOTE ON THE TEXT AND ACKNOWLEDGMENTS

In compiling this book, my aim was to use multiple sources to present a balanced and comprehensive account of my grandfather's life. Much of this book is based on *Fathollah Khan Akbar: Sepahdar Aʿzam Rashti*, a Persian-language biography I discovered in 2017, by Iranian historian Houman Yousefdehi, PhD. In addition, I have included extensive documentation, research, and analysis by Farhad Soleymannejad, an independent scholar based in Iran who used primary sources from British, Russian, French, and Iranian archives. *Sepahdar: Fathollah Khan Akbar, A Biography* is the result of this compilation.

I am fortunate to have Mage Publishers as the publisher of this book. I am especially thankful for Najmieh Batmanglij's invaluable assistance and expert guidance throughout this project. I would like to acknowledge Mr. Soleymannejad and express my gratitude for his further research, additions, and notes. My thanks are also due to Kianoosh Amiri for translating Dr. Yousefdehi's book from the original Persian into English.

I am deeply grateful to: Shaul Bakhash, Sayeh Eghtesadinia, Masumeh Javadinasab, Nini Tavallali, Setareh Ghajar, Nezam Manuchehri, Laleh Akbar, Michael Vali Akbar, Ebrahim Moraveji, and Foroud Amirani for their contributions. I also wish to honor the memory of Manuchehr Akbar, who safeguarded and provided all the family documents which were consulted in the compiling of this book.

I am greatly indebted to my two daughters: Leila Kashani, for her professional editing skills, guidance, and encouragement; and Mariam Kashani, who firmly supports me in everything I do.

Finally, my brother, Fathollah Akbar, who carries our grandfather's name, and my sister, Gilan Tocco Corn, and I are immensely grateful to Dr. Yousefdehi for his unbiased and objective research about Sepahdar, a complex individual who served five monarchs and played a central role in one of the darkest periods of Iran's history.

Goli Akbar Kashani

CHAPTER 1

EARLY YEARS

Throughout his long life, Fathollah Khan Akbar was known by a series of honorary titles: from Biglarbeigi,[1] Salar Afkham, and Sardar Mansur, to Sepahdar Aʿzam.[2] The son of Haji Mirza Mohammad-Ali Khan (Haji Khan) Omshaei, also known as Mujib al-Sofara, he was a member of the famous Akbar family, better known historically as "Al-e Omsheh" (from Omsheh).

Omsheh is a settlement in the rural Sangar district of the town of Rasht (the capital of the Iranian province of Gilan, on the shores of the Caspian Sea).

For centuries, Rasht has been a major center for trade with the Caucasus and Russia. Because of its proximity to the Caspian Sea, Rasht was also a key transportation hub which connected Iran to

1. Biglarbeigi was a high rank for men in the western Islamic world in the late Middle Ages and early modern period, from the Anatolian Seljuks and the Ilkhanids to the Safavid and Ottoman empires.

2. Sepahdār-e Aʿzam, literally meaning "Top Military Commander," was a high distinction awarded during the Qajar rule. In addition to Sepahdar, "Salār" and "Sardār" were also common titles, all carrying the sense of "military commander."

Russia and the rest of Europe. For this reason, Rasht was known for centuries as the "Gateway to Europe."

Rasht has been mentioned in historical documents as far back as AD 682. It has been overrun by the armies of Peter the Great of Russia, and later Russian rulers, as well as those of British colonialism. Because of all this foreign exposure through trade and occupation, the people of Rasht have always been open to new concepts and ideas while also safeguarding their own rich culture and traditions. In fact, the residents of Rasht were among the first Iranian citizens to play a major role in the Constitutional Revolution of Iran of 1905–11.

In addition to being recognized for their receptiveness to new political and cultural ideas, the people of Rasht are known to be especially welcoming and hospitable. The lush vegetation of the province and abundance of provisions have contributed to the generosity of its people. In more recent years, UNESCO designated Rasht as the "2015 Creative City of Gastronomy."

Rasht is also the first city in Iran to have established a public library in modern times, as well as one of the first cities to allow young girls to attend public high schools, over a hundred years ago.

Fathollah Khan grew up in this region of Iran, where the progressive atmosphere shaped freedom-seeking individuals, and where, for decades, democratic governing principles constituted the dominant discourse. His paternal grandfather, Haji Aghajani Omshaei, a landowner from a well-off Gilani aristocratic family, was also originally from the settlement of Omsheh.[3] He had five sons, the most famous of whom was Ali Akbar Khan Biglarbeigi, Fathollah Khan's uncle, who played a major role in young Fathollah's life. Fathollah Khan's father was both a well-known landowner and an officer of the Ministry of Foreign Affairs. His large family comprised nine sons and three daughters.

Fathollah Khan was born in 1855 during the reign of Naser al-Din Shah Qajar, who ruled Iran from 1848 to 1896. After finishing

---

3. *Bamdad*, 1371^{SH}, vol. 1: 145. See also: Chaqueri, 1384^{SH}: 317.

his education at home, as was customary in provincial aristocratic families at the time, Fathollah Khan, along with his cousin Sadegh Khan, was employed as a deputy by his wealthy and influential uncle Ali Akbar Khan Biglarbeigi, who was the governor of Anzali (an important port city on the Caspian Sea) and administrator of Iran's northern customs.[4]

Uncle Akbar Khan, Business Magnate

Fathollah Khan's uncle was one of the wealthiest people of the Naseri era (the reign of Naser al-Din Shah) in Iran and became increasingly involved in the administration of the Gilan province. He was first put in charge of road transport in Sangar. From 1861 to 1862, when the Gilan government decided to widen and develop the road from Rasht to Manjil, Akbar Khan was named as the manager of the Sangar–Kahdom road-building project. His successful completion of the project won him praise from the establishment.

After the road was built, he rented it from the local authorities, paying rent to the state government of Gilan in return for maintaining the route while he, in turn, received tolls from vehicles using the road and for the transport of freight and animals, an enterprise that earned Akbar Khan large profits. Then, in 1864, he was appointed as the government tax collector for Gilan.

An able businessman, Akbar Khan continued to make more profits in various ways, finally renting the Gilan customs from the government in 1878. Four years later, when Iran's state customs came under the authority of Mirza Ali Asghar Khan Amin al-Soltan, Akbar Khan rented the Mazandaran, Khorasan, and Kermanshah customs as well.

His outstanding success as a businessman earned Akbar Khan the honorary title of "Biglarbeigi of Gilan." Furthermore, he was named governor of Anzali, Ghaziyan, and Gaskar, as well as deputy

---

4. *Bamdad*, 1371[SH], vol. 1: 145.

governor of Lasht-e Nesha, one of the settlements around Gilan. In 1888, when the government decided to sell off government lands in Khalesjat, Gilan, Akbar Khan, whose fortune now outmatched anyone else's in Iran, managed to purchase vast parcels of land, thereby becoming the proprietor of numerous villages.

Marriage to Akbar Khan's Widow

Since the administration of customs was an arduous and time-consuming business, and Akbar Khan had no sons to assist him, he appointed his two nephews, Sadegh and Fathollah Khan, to head the documents and registration offices and also arranged for his two daughters to marry these young men. From1885 to 1889 there was an epidemic of typhoid fever in Iran, especially in the northern parts of the country. Fathollah Khan's fiancée died from typhoid before the wedding could take place, and shortly afterwards, in 1888, her father, Akbar Khan, also succumbed to the disease. Akbar Khan's widow, Khanzadeh Khanum, and their surviving daughter, Zahra Khanum, who by now had been married off to her cousin Sadegh Khan thus inherited Akbar Khan's legendary wealth. At this point, at the age of thirty-three, to keep his uncle Akbar Khan's wealth in the family and manage his vast financial empire, Fathollah Khan quickly married his uncle's widow, Khanzadeh Khanum, at the behest of the Omsheh clan.

When Khanzadeh Khanum also died of typhoid fever shortly after the marriage, Fathollah Khan inherited her vast wealth. The Omsheh clan expected him to once more marry within the family and arranged for him to wed Begum Khanum, daughter of Haj Mirza Aghasi, a respected figure in Gilan and a close relative of Fathollah Khan. The couple had a daughter and two sons.[5]

---

5. These details were provided in oral histories from Fahime and Mohsen Akbar (son of Sepahdar-e A'zam).

Akbar Khan Biglarbeigi

It is said that Fathollah Khan's marriage to Akbar Khan's widow was recommended by Mirza Karim Khan Rashti, one of Fathollah Khan's cousins, regarded as the mastermind of the family. He later became a leader of the constitutional movement in Gilan and an important player during the Pahlavi era.[6]

At the beginning of Reza Shah's reign, he was a favorite of the Shah, but later fell out of favor and was exiled to Yazd for many years. After the events of August and September 1941—namely, the occupation of Iran by the Allies and the exile of Reza Shah from Iran—Mirza Karim Khan returned to Tehran and was involved in politics behind the scenes until his death. Thirty years earlier, according to the historian Iraj Afshar, based on the memoirs of the social democrat Seyyed Hasan Taghizadeh, Mirza Karim Khan was the mastermind in the uprising of Gilan against the tyranny of Mohammad Ali Shah and specifically in the formation of the Sattar Committee.[7]

Mirza Mohammad Ali, also known as Haj Sayyah Mahallati, a well-known human rights activist and, like Mirza Karim Khan, a constitutionalist who pursued political reform in Iran (he was the first Iranian to obtain American citizenship in 1875), recalled meeting Fathollah Khan in Anzali during his travels to Gilan in 1879, nine years before the death of Akbar Khan, when the young man was working for him. Mirza Mohammad received a very favorable impression of Fathollah Khan in Anzali, which he recorded in his memoirs: "This handsome youth was very respectful and kind to

---

6. Manuscript account by the late Anoushirvan Naeimi Akbar, son of Hasan Khan Amid al-Soltan and nephew of Mirza Karim Khan Rashti.

7. The Sattar Committee (named in honor of a prominent political hero, Sattar Khan), was a clandestine and revolutionary group in support of a democratic Iran. Afshar (ed.), 1359[SH]: 6. In the same source (pp. 7–25), several letters exchanged between Mirza Karim Khan Rashti and Taghizadeh, as well as excerpts from accounts by contemporaries, including Edward Browne, one of the foremost Iran scholars of his time have been published, which show the key role of Mirza Karim Khan in the Constitutional Revolution.

me. He was in charge of customs then. He also had basic knowledge of French."[8]

In his later years, at the age of fifty, while married to Begum Khanum, Fathollah Khan married Bemani Khanum Behzad as a second wife in accordance with Islamic laws. She was the daughter of Mirza Reza Ziya Issazadeh, who was a prominent precious-stone trader in Tbilisi, Georgia. Bemani Khanum was not related to Fathollah Khan. They had one son.

Gaining Prominence

Having inherited enormous wealth from his uncle, in addition to the Gilan and Mazandaran customs administrations, Fathollah Khan became the Biglarbeigi of Gilan in 1889 and acquired the Anzali governorship as well. In 1890, accompanied by Mirza Mohsen Khan Moshir al-Dowleh, the Iranian ambassador to Constantinople at the time, Fathollah Khan travelled to Europe,[9] where he took the opportunity to brush up the rudimentary French that Mirza Mohammad Ali had commented upon.

It was upon his return from this trip that Fathollah Khan Biglarbeigi and Mirza Mohammad Ali met again, this time in Uzunda, Azerbaijan, an encounter that Mirza Mohammad also recorded in his memoirs:

> I walked into the guesthouse. Mirza Fathollah Khan Biglarbeigi of Rasht had arrived the same day. He had inherited his Uncle Akbar Khan Biglarbeigi's position and title after his death. He was also named director of Khorasan and Mazandaran road and transport office. He was very kind to me. I said: "I can't do anything in return for your kindness, but I have two key quotes, from two world-renowned figures for you. One is from Midhat Pasha [a prominent

8. Mahallati, 1359^{SH}: 211.

9. Churchill, 1391^{SH}: 207.

Naser al-Din Shah Qajar

Ottoman statesman], who said: 'I am not sure whether it is Kismet or the consequence of bloody wars conducted by our predecessors, that, amongst us Moslems, any patriotic and brave man is idle, quite the reverse of Christians.' The other quote is from Bismarck [the prominent German statesman and diplomat], whom I met and when I spoke with hope about Iran and Iranians, he said: 'I have met with the Shah of Iran and Iranian people. These people have no esteem for themselves, and they resort to any self-humiliation to flatter the Shah. It is useless to pin hope on them.'"[10]

It seems that Mirza Mohammad Ali was trying to give life lessons to young Fathollah Khan. These quotes may have been a call to action for him to not be idle, and to stand up for democracy and Iran's independence in his later life. At the time, this conversation seemed superficial but years later, the two quotes from Mirza Mohammad Ali might have sparked the passion and courage in Fatollah Khan to speak up and confront the Shah during the constitutional uprising.

During these early years, Fathollah Khan dealt efficiently with local affairs. As an example, in late spring 1892, the rivers in Gilan were starting to run dry owing to silted-up river mouths and fear was spreading in the province among residents and landowners. Fathollah Khan, along with his own workers, went to the river mouths in order to clear them, thereby releasing abundant water. Within four to five days, Gilan farmlands were irrigated again.[11]

In recognition of this and other achievements, Fathollah Khan was awarded the titles of Jenab (Excellency) and Amir Tuman (Major General), a royal sash, and the Special Order of Merit by Naser al-Din Shah in 1893. The following year, the Shah awarded him the Imperial Portrait Medal encrusted with diamonds.[12]

In May 1896, Fathollah Khan was appointed to receive and host Midhat Pasha, the ambassador extraordinary of the Ottoman government, during his visit to Tehran to attend the fiftieth anniversary of Naser al-Din Shah's ascension to the throne, which coincided with the assassination of Naser al-Din Shah by Mirza Reza Kermani.[13]

---

10. Mahallati, 1359^{SH}: 316–17.

11. *Iran Soltani* (daily newspaper), Dhu-Hijjah 12, 1309^{AH}, quoted in: Nozad, 1398^{SH}, vol. 1: 357.

12. *Iran Soltani*, Rabi' al-Thani 23, 1310^{AH}, Dhu Hijjah 14, 1310^{AH}, and Dhu Hijjah 15, 1311^{AH}, quoted in: Nozad, 1398^{SH}, vol. 1: 358, 368, 462.

13. *Iran Soltani*, Dhu Hijjah 1, 1313^{AH}, quoted in: Nozad, 1398^{SH}, vol. 1: 378.

In the Mozaffari Era

Under the reign of Mozaffar al-Din Shah Qajar, who ruled from 1896 to 1907, Fathollah Khan remained among the wealthy elite of Gilan, as well as serving as the administrator of the Gilan and Mazandaran customs. Due to his outstanding service, he continued to enjoy the favor of the Shah, being awarded, in 1896 and 1897, the regalia of a royal termeh redingote, adorned with a rosette, and epaulettes.[14] In August 15, 1897, upon being put forward by the then grand vizier, Mirza Ali Khan Amin al-Dowleh,[15] Fathollah Khan was placed in charge of most of the customs offices across the country and Mozaffar al-Din Shah issued the following decree:

> Since the administration of the customs of the Guarded Domains of Iran is one of the most critical tasks of the government, an experienced and suitably qualified individual with a sharp mind, who has proven his ability over the years, is required to take on this responsibility. Therefore, with the agreement of Grand Vizier Amin al-Dowleh, who oversees the Guarded Domains' customs, His Excellency Fathollah Khan Biglarbeigi of Gilan is named for three years starting from September, to administer the customs offices attached hereto.[16]

The customs offices mentioned in the Shah's decree were in the cities on the Caspian Sea coast, as well as Khorasan, Estarabad, Qazvin, Khamseh, Kashan, Hamedan, Kermanshahan, Nahavand, Kordestan, Tehran, Garous, Tonekabon, Boroujerd, Golpayegan, and Mohammareh (Khuzestan today), among others.

Commenting on the event in his account of the period, Gholam-Hossein Khan Afzal al-Molk, a political figure of the time, voices the common perception of Fathollah Khan: "I have frequently heard

---

14. *Iran Soltani*, Ramadan 8, 1314[AH] and Rabi' al-Awwl 26, 1315[AH], quoted in: Nozad, 1398[SH], vol. 1, 382, 387. See also: Afzal-ul-Molk, 1361[SH]: 191.

15. Amin al-Dowleh literally means "Confidant of the Government."

16. Manuscript of the Shah's decree, Mr. Manouchehr Akbar's personal archive.

from most people that this man [Fathollah Khan Biglarbeigi] is among the most generous men of the world. He hosts people in his home round the clock. His generosity and kind manners are exemplary."[17]

In June 1898, the Shah dismissed Mirza Ali Khan Amin al-Dowleh as the grand vizier and his son Mirza Mohsen Khan Moein al-Molk (the next Amin al-Dowleh), who was also the Shah's son-in-law from their posts. Consequently, Fathollah Khan was promoted to Minister of Customs. Mozaffar al-Din Shah issued the following decree:

> Given that Mirza Fathollah Khan Biglarbeigi is among the competent servants of the government, and he has proven his competence and efficacy during his administration of customs, I do hereby appoint him as the minister of customs.[18]

Fathollah Khan Biglarbeigi was part of Mozaffar al-Din Shah's entourage during the Shah's first visit to Europe in 1900, a trip that lasted seven months. A year later, when the titles Salar and Sardar became more prevalent, the Shah awarded Fathollah Khan the title of "Salar Afkham" and transferred the title of "Biglarbeigi" to Fathollah Khan's elder son, Mohammad Ali Khan.[19]

Awarded Two British Orders of Chivalry

In 1902, Fathollah Khan, who now held the title Salar Afkham, received Britain's special envoy to Iran, Hugh Richard Dawnay, 8th

---

17. Afzal al-Molk, 1361SH: 191.

18. Afzal al-Molk, 1361SH: 275.

19. Iran Soltani, Safar 1 and 14, 1319AH, quoted in: Nozad, 1398SH, vol. 1: 422–3. It is stated in some sources that Fathollah Khan Biglarbeigi received the title of "Sālār Aʿzam" after that of "Sālār Afkham," which is not correct according to other sources which state that he received the title of "Sardar Mansur" after that of "Salar Afkham." Apparently, this mistake derives from the *Chehre Nama* daily newspaper, published in Alexandria and Cairo in Egypt, in its Jamada al-Awwl 1, 1323AH issue, where his title is mistakenly given as "Salar-e Aʿzam." See: Nozad, 1398SH, vol. 3: 35.

Mozaffar al-Din Shah Qajar's first visit to Europe (1900). Fathollah Khan Sardar Mansur (*front row, far right*), Mozaffar al-Din Shah Qajar (*in the middle with cane*).

Viscount Downe, and his delegation in Rasht.[20] Downe carried a letter from King Edward VII, as well as the insignia of the Most Noble Order of the Garter to present to the Shah. This order of chivalry had been given to Naser al-Din Shah many years before, but when Mozaffar al-Din Shah visited London in 1900, King Edward VII refused to award it to him. This caused a diplomatic row. Eventually, the King awarded the Order to Mozaffar al-Din Shah in December 1902.[21] At the same time, Fathollah Khan was awarded the Knight Commander of St. Michael and St. George (KCMG) for hosting Viscount Downe, which he did in a most stately manner.[22]

---

20. Fortescue, 1379[SH]: 59; Churchill, 1391[SH]: 170, 207.

21. For more information, see: Sheikh al-Islami, 1359[SH]: 55–64.

22. Chakeri, 1386[SH]: 543. This source simply states that the order was awarded without saying when it was awarded. But Ghanei and Elmi (1391[SH]) indicate that Fathollah Khan received the award in 1903 for entertaining the British delegation.

Hosting the Shah

Fathollah Khan Salar Afkham, who was still better known by his former title "Biglarbeigi," hosted Mozaffar al-Din Shah during his second voyage to Europe, which was planned to go through Gilan. Along with the then governor of Gilan, Mohammad Vali Khan Tonekaboni Nasr al-Saltaneh, and other local officials, Fathollah Khan welcomed the Shah and his retinue in Rostamabad (an area near Rasht on the road from Tehran) and gave him a wonderful reception at his estate, in Sangar. In his diary for April 21, 1903, Mozaffar al-Din Shah recalled the visit:

Knight Commander of St. Michael and St. George (KCMG)

> Today, we [went] to Sangar . . . This Sangar is a property of [Fathollah Khan] Biglarbeigi. A beautiful triumphal arch had been built. The walls were all adorned with flags. A poem was inscribed on the arch, which I quote here: "May Allah help Mozaffar al-Din Shah remain on the throne with honor." We continued on our way toward the place of residence of Fathollah Khan. His Excellency Atabak A'zam [Ali Asghar Khan Amin al-Soltan] was there. Nasr al-Saltaneh [Mohammad Vali Khan Tonekaboni] was also in attendance. We went upstairs to the second floor. Across from us was the residence of Atabak A'zam. Shops are built on both sides of the street. Today is Monday Market here, where people from nearby villages come once a week for shopping. All of these belong to [Fathollah Khan] Biglarbeigi. He has prepared

Above: Sepahdar wearing the KCMG medals standing next to Sardar Homayoun, 1902. *Opposite, top:* Sepahdar (*center left*) and Sepahsalar (*center right*), Rasht Governor's Office, 1903. *Opposite, lower:* Mozaffar al-Din Shah and Amin al-Soltan, the grand vizier, in the yard of the Rasht governor's office.

fruits and sweets for us. We were informed the shops are rented out for 3,000 to 4,000 tomans.[23]

Two days later, the Shah visited several gardens in Rasht, including the Salar Afkham Garden, or Salarieh Garden owned by Fathollah Khan (and named after his title, Salar Afkham), who accompanied the Shah as far as Astara.[24]

---

23. Mozaffar al-Din Shah Qajar, 1362[SH]: 12. Tomans are a superunit of the official currency of Iran, the rial (10 rials is equal to 1 toman). Although the rial is the official currency, Iranians used (and still use) the toman in everyday life.

24. Mozaffar al-Din Shah Qajar, 1362[SH]: 18, 27.

Princess Bibesco (Marthe Lucie Lahovary)

A Guest from Europe

A little later, on May 8, 1903, a Romanian-French writer and scholar, Marthe Lucie Lahovary, known as "Princess Bibesco," the wife of Prince George-Valentin Bibesco of Romania, arrived in Gilan. She stayed in Rasht for nine days before departing for Tehran. During her visit, Princess Bibesco was hosted by Prince Azod al-Soltan (then governor of Gilan), and Fathollah Khan Salar Afkham. Princess Bibesco wrote about her stay in Iran, including a lavish dinner party held by Fathollah Khan, in her 1908 memoir *Les Huit Paradis*:

> The dinner party organized by Salar Afkham, the governor of Anzali, was in the European-style and highly generous. After the dinner, we waited for an Iranian-style entertainment. Musicians sat at the end of a long hall. Dancers danced to

the music. Among the singers, there was one whose voice shouted down others' and who sang with closed eyes.[25]

Taken for a Ransom

In March 1904, Grand Vizier Abdol-Majid Mirza Ayn al-Dowleh, as part of a financial review to balance the budget and increase revenue, summoned the wealthy Fathollah Khan Salar Afkham to Tehran, known to have been a close associate and confidant of Ayn al-Dowleh's rival, the dismissed grand vizier, Ali Khan Amin al-Soltan. Upon his arrival, Fathollah Khan was promptly put under house arrest at the home of Mostafa Qoli Khan Qajar Davallu Hajeb al-Dowleh, the chamberlain of Mozaffar al-Din Shah's court. It was only with the intervention of the British Minister in Tehran, Sir Arthur Henry Hardinge, that Fathollah Khan was able to secure his release by paying an exorbitant sum in ransom to the government.[26] According to Hardinge:

> My Gilani friend [Fathollah Khan Salar Afkham] protested that upon his arrival in Tehran, he was immediately taken to Hajib al-Dowleh's residence. During the first few days, he was housed in a quite acceptable room, but one day, abruptly, and without any reason, he was moved to a soiled and repulsive chamber. Hajib al-Dowleh's guards indirectly told this respected Gilani gentleman that the most sensible way for him to be able to return to his properties on the Caspian Sea coast was to present a precious gift to the new Grand Vizier of the country.
>
> During a meeting with Ayn al-Dowleh on this issue, I tried my best to inform the Grand Vizier that any violent and cruel treatment of this respected Gilani gentleman who was decorated with two Orders from the British government, would trigger a negative response in London.

---

25. Bibesco, 1373^{SH}: 14.

26. Chaqueri 1386^{SH}: 543.

Mostafa Qoli Khan Hajeb al-Dowleh and Sir Arthur Henry Hardinge.

> Ayn al-Dowleh, who found himself in a difficult position, changed his method and behavior, and as a result, we managed to find a mutually satisfactory solution.
>
> The aggrieved Gilani who wanted to rid himself of Hajib al-Dowleh's "hospitality" presented a gift to His Excellency (Prince Ayn al-Dowleh) and was released. Before returning to Gilan, he came to me to offer his gratitude for my efforts to secure his release. During our chat, he said sarcastically that he had been held in the worst and most expensive room at Hajib al-Dowleh's residence.[27]

What happened to Fathollah Khan during this episode illustrates how increasingly corrupt and dictatorial the Iranian government had become by this time. In the absence of an independent jury, those in power could abuse their fellow citizens—even a figure as senior and well respected as Fathollah Khan—with impunity, without fear of prosecution or punishment. With no recourse to

27. Quoted in: Sheikh al-Islami, 1392[SH]: 498–9.

justice available within their own country, it becomes clear why Sepahdar and other politicians turned to foreign governments for support in such situations.

Sardar Mansur Title

That same year, a Belgian official, Joseph Naus, was appointed as the chief administrator of Iran's customs. As a result, Fathollah Khan lost control of the management of the customs offices of northern Iran. Furthermore, the administration of customs and the tariffs saw fundamental changes, which caused discontent among the Iranian business community.

In 1905, Mozaffar al-Din Shah embarked on yet another of his extravagant travels to Europe, the third in five years, stopping in Gilan en route, as before, where Fathollah Khan received the Shah and his delegation. In Anzali, he arranged a magnificent dinner party,[28] offering the Shah a gift of 12,000 tomans. The grand vizier, Abdol-Majid Mirza Ayn al-Dowleh, stayed at Fathollah Khan's home during the Shah's stay in Rasht, his previous kidnapping of his host apparently forgotten.[29]

Content with the services rendered by Fathollah Khan, the Shah awarded him the title of "Sardar Mansur" (Victorious Commander) after his departure. To that end, the Shah sent the following decree to the grand vizier:[30]

---

28. Iran Soltani, Rabi' al-Awwl 29 and Rabi' al-Thani 23, 1323[AH], quoted in: Nozad, 1398[SH], vol. 1: 285; *Chehre Nama,* Rabi' al-Thani 15, 1323[AH], quoted in: Nozad, 1398[SH], vol. 3: 26.

29. *Chehre Nama*, Rabi' al-Thani 15, 1323[AH], quoted in: Nozad, 1398[SH], vol. 3: 28–30.

30. *Iran Soltani*, Jumadi al-Awwl 25, 1323[AH], quoted in: Nozad, 1398[SH], vol. 1: 495; *Adab* daily newspaper, Jumadi al-Thani 23, 1323[AH], quoted in: Nozad, 1398[SH], vol. 2: 174.

> His Excellency [the] Grand Vizier,
> Given the good services and sacrifices of Salar Afkham,
> I bestow the title of Sardar Mansur upon the aforesaid.
> Please follow up on the issuance of the decree.[31]

After returning to Iran, Mozaffar al-Din Shah wrote in his diary of September 15, 1905:

> Azod al-Soltan the governor of Gilan is ready for service, and the country's officials, including Fathollah Khan Salar Afkham Biglarbeigi, whom I anointed with the title of Sardar Mansur, and Amid al-Saltaneh Sardar Amjad and others, are arranging the reception.[32]

Upon the Shah's return to Gilan from Europe and until he reached Manjil, Sardar Mansur was in his retinue, tending to him and his courtiers.

Despite the huge ransom he was forced to pay the government after his house arrest, and the loss of the northern customs revenue, Sardar Mansur still lived a regal life, owing to his personal wealth and significant earnings from other customs offices as well as from the governorship of Anzali and Shaft (south of Rasht). He was one of the richest people in Iran at that time. He owned large mansions and beautiful houses in the village of Ghaziyan in Anzali, as well as in Rasht and Tehran,[33] which were mainly reserved as accommodations for high-ranking guests, as well as the vast Salarieh Garden in Rasht.[34] Fathollah Khan's generosity when hosting guests—whether foreign dignitaries, courtiers, government officials, or regular Iranian travelers—all helped win him fame and popularity.

---

31. Manuscript of the Shah's decree, Mr. Manouchehr Akbar's personal archive.

32. Mozaffar al-Din Shah Qajar, 1362[SH]: 211–14; Iran Soltani, Rajab 23, 1323[AH], quoted in: Nozad, 1398[SH], vol 1: 500–501.

33. *Habl al-Matin* (daily newspaper of Tehran), Shawwal 24, 1325[AH].

34. Rabino, 1368[SH]: 349. It later became known as Alirish Garden during the first Pahlavi period. See: Nikoyeh, 1387[SH]: 108.

Rasht governor's office, 1906.
From right to left: Mohammad Ali Khan Mafakher al-Molk, Amir Khan Amin Divan Lahiji, Ali Khan Sarhang, Sadegh Khan Mohtasham al-Molk (Sardar Motamed), Abolfazl Mirza Azod al-Soltan (governor of Gilan), Fathollah Khan Sardar Mansur, probably Moaddab al-Dowleh Nafisi (the governor's retainer), Mirza Nourollah Khan Vazir, Abdol-Hossein Khan Modir al-Molk (Sardar Homayoun), Sartip Khan, Mohammad Ali Khan Moein al-Saltaneh.

One of his most celebrated deeds was to build the Rasht Hospital in 1905. He allocated 4,000 tomans annually to the hospital and ensured that it would receive such funding in the years to come. As mentioned earlier, he also ordered that a number of patients of lesser means be treated regularly in the hospital, at his cost.[35]

Gilan Interim Governorship

In February 1906, after Abolfazl Mirza Azod al-Soltan (the son of the Shah and the then governor of Gilan) was summoned to Tehran

---

35. *Iran Soltani*, Sha'ban 28, 1323[AH], quoted in: Nozad, 1398[SH], vol. 1: 503–4; *Chehre Nama*, Dhu Qadah 1, 1323[AH], quoted in: Nozad, 1398[SH], vol. 3: 46.

for consultation, Fathollah Khan Sardar Mansur was temporarily named as interim governor until Mirza Saleh Khan Vazir Akram took office on August 14, 1906.[36]

After the new governor was appointed, Sardar Mansur returned to his home in Anzali and organized yet another extravagant celebration, this time to mark the fifty-third birthday of Mozaffar al-Din Shah.[37] Fathollah Khan may have felt compelled to entertain the Shah so lavishly, in order perhaps to stay in favor with him and hopefully avoid incidents similar to the one to which he had been subjected at the hands of the grand vizier. Gestures such as these eventually would help pave a path for Fathollah Khan's future political career on a national scale.

---

36. *Iran Soltani*, Rabi' al-Thani 21, 1324[AH], quoted in: Nozad, 1398[SH], vol. 1: 522.

37. *Iran Soltani*, Rajab 23, 1324[AH], quoted in: Nozad, 1398[SH], vol. 1: 524–6.

CHAPTER 2

THE CONSTITUTIONAL REVOLUTION

The establishment of a constitutional regime in Iran, with its own parliament, was the chief objective of the revolution of 1905–11. Like any other major movement of its kind, the Constitutional Revolution in Iran encompassed a broad spectrum of ideas and objectives, reflecting diverse intellectual trends, social backgrounds, and political demands. At the time, even the text of the proposed constitution did not have universal support (it was the first of its kind in the Islamic world and predating that of the Young Turk Revolution of 1908). Yet, in spite of ideological differences among its participants, the Revolution remains an epoch-making episode in the modern history of Iran because of its political achievements and its enduring social and cultural legacy. As a modern revolution, it was aimed at dislodging the old order by means of popular action and by advocacy of the tenets of liberalism, secularism, and nationalism. For the first time in the course of modern Iranian history, the revolutionaries sought to replace arbitrary power with law, representative government, and social justice, and to resist the encroachment of imperial powers with conscious nationalism, popular activism, and economic independence. Constitutionalists also tried to curb the power of the conservative religious establishment through a modern education

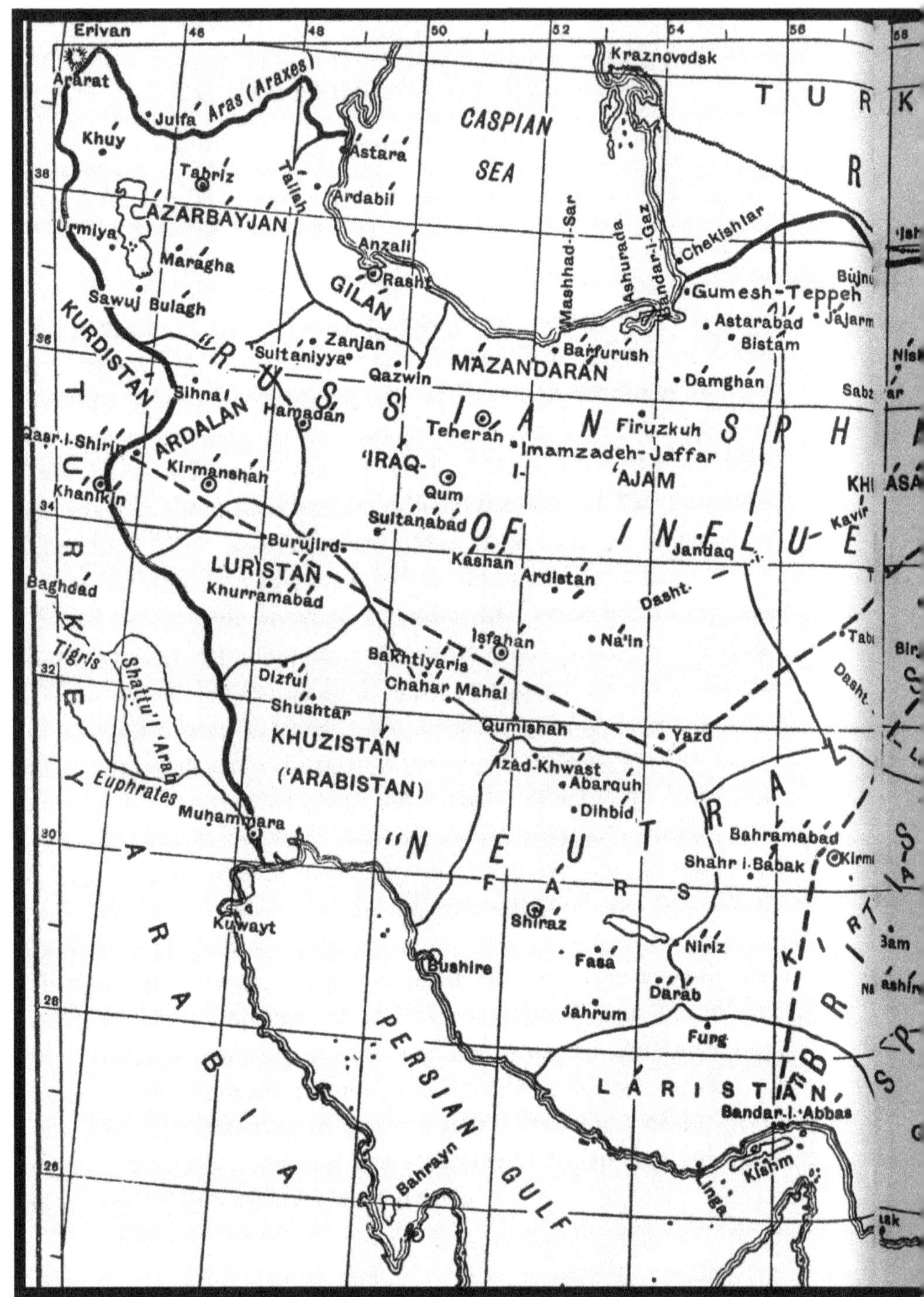

Erivan
Ararat
Kraznovodsk
Julfa
Aras (Araxes)
CASPIAN SEA
TURK
Khuy
Astara
Tabriz
Tallish
Ardabil
AZARBAYJAN
Urmiya
Maragha
Anzali
Rasht
GILAN
Mashhad-i-Sar
Ashurada
Bandar-i-Gaz
Chekishlar
Gumesh-Teppeh
Astarabad
Jajarm
Bistam
Sawuj Bulagh
KURDISTAN
Zanjan
Sultaniyya
Qazwin
MAZANDARAN
Barfurush
Damghan
Sihna
ARDALAN
Hamadan
Teheran
Imamzadeh-Jaffar
Firuzkuh
Qasr-i-Shirin
Kirmanshah
'IRAQ-I-'AJAM
Khanikin
Qum
Sultanabad
RUSSIAN SPHERE OF INFLUENCE
Burujird
Kashan
Jandaq
LURISTAN
Khurramabad
Ardistan
Baghdad
Dasht
TURKEY
Isfahan
Na'in
Tigris
Shattu'l 'Arab
Bakhtiyaris
Dizful
Chahar Mahal
Shushtar
Qumishah
Yazd
KHUZISTAN
('ARABISTAN)
Izad-Khwast
Abarquh
Euphrates
Dihbid
Muhammara
"NEUTRAL"
Bahramabad
Shahr i Babak
ARABIA
FARS
Kuwayt
Shiraz
Niriz
Fasa
Bushire
Darab
Jahrum
PERSIAN GULF
Furg
BRITISH
LARISTAN
Bandar-i-Abbas
Kishm
Linga
Bahrayn

Map showing the three "spheres" of influence in Iran (Russian, British, and Neutral) defined in the Anglo-Russian Agreement of August 31, 1907. (From *The Strangling of Persia* by Morgan Shuster, first published in 1912).

system and reform of the judiciary. By centralizing the state, they sought to curb the power of the tribal and urban dignitaries. The greater sense of nationhood that emerged out of the revolution has remained fundamental to modern Iranian identity.[1]

As Iranians rose up in favor of constitutionalism, the residents of Gilan also gradually became more aware of such concepts as the rule of law and human and labor rights. There were calls for justice from the lower social class in protest at injustice inflicted upon them by rulers and landowners. In Gilan, one of those at the receiving end of such protests was Fathollah Khan Sardar Mansur.

It is undeniable that, as will be shown in this and the following chapters, both during the years he lived in Gilan and after the establishment of the constitutional government, when he moved to Tehran and served in several cabinet posts, Sardar Mansur was no less culpable than other local rulers and statesmen in his profiteering and abuse of power. When he was in charge of customs for northern Iran, for example, he levied as much customs duty as he wished. He imposed taxes on ferrymen and even leased government-owned land under his control.

Another example of his exploitative business practices was his arrangement with the Russian-Armenian merchant Stepan Martinovic Lianozov, who had acquired fishing rights in Anzali waters. Lianozov obtained from the Iranian government the license for catching fish that were regarded as *haram* (forbidden under Islamic law) while Anzali fishermen only were allowed to catch fish that were regarded as *halal* (permitted under Islamic law). However, Lianozov managed to convince the government to give him the *halal* fish license as well. Sardar Mansur then acquired the *halal* fish license from Lianozov under a lease agreement for 22,000 tomans per month and subleased it to the Anzali fishermen for 80,000 tomans per month, thereby earning 58,000 tomans per month in revenue. Under his contract with the fishermen, they had to hand over sander fish

1. *Encyclopaedia Iranica* Online, © Trustees of Columbia University in the City of New York. Consulted online on January 21, 2023.

(*Sander lucioperca*), which had been declared *haram* for unspecified reasons, to the Fishery Authority. The fishermen were obliged to deliver their sander catch to the Fishery Authority free of charge, while Sardar Mansur charged the Fishery Authority for the sander and earned a significant sum as a result. Before the Constitutional Revolution and the delegation of administration of customs to the Belgians, Sardar Mansur earned more than 100,000 tomans a year from the fishing license.[2] Given his profits, Sardar Mansur was at first naturally opposed to constitutionalism and the changes it would bring. He had a reciprocal relationship with Haj Molla Mohammad Khomami, an influential cleric in Gilan who led the opposition to the constitutional movement. However, a constitutional decree issued by Mozaffar al-Din Shah on August 5, 1906, prevented anyone from being openly hostile toward constitutionalism. Sardar Mansur, while still not supporting constitutionalism at the time, no longer expressed any opposition to it.

The Protest by Anzali Fishermen

On November 2, 1906, almost three months after the constitutional decree had been issued by the Shah, Sardar Mansur was summoned by the government to Tehran to take on the Post and Telegraph Office under a lease agreement. This was because Belgian administrator Joseph Naus, who had been in charge of customs as well as the post and telegraph since 1904, had been forced by the newly established Majles (the National Consultative Assembly) to leave Iran due to incompetence.

Apparently, during Naus's time in charge Tehran's telegraph wires were defective, and this naturally raised expectations that the problem would be addressed by Sardar Mansur as the new custodian of the Post and Telegraph Office. It appears that he failed to meet them. One available report states that as a result of Sardar Mansur's failure to resolve the issue, the Russian and British embassies took

2. Fakhraei, 1371^{SH}: 37–8.

immediate action to fix the telegraph wires and complained about Sardar Mansur's negligence.[3]

On November 21, 1906, while Sardar Mansur was working in Tehran in his new post, Anzali fishermen staged a sit-in in the city's Telegraph Office, protesting about the administration of the Fishery Authority by Lianozov. In a telegraphed letter of complaint, they reported to the then grand vizier that Sardar Mansur bought the fishermen's catch at a low price. The deputy governor of Gilan, Amid Homayoun, arrested some of the fishermen in response to their protest. They demanded that the central government prevent Sardar Mansur's "aggression" and force him to buy their fish at a fair price.[4] Meanwhile, another report describes in detail how Sardar Mansur "forced" fishermen to sell fish at a low price.[5]

Apparently, earlier, when Mozaffar al-Din Shah passed through Gilan on his third trip to Europe, the Anzali fishermen had presented their protest to government officials accompanying the Shah, and as a result, Ayn al-Dowleh, the grand vizier raised the price of fish by 25 qrans.[6] The report also mentions that the fishermen had revolted against Sardar Mansur.[7]

The sit-in continued until November 30, when a fisherman was killed in a confrontation with government officers. Mirza Saleh Khan Vazir Akram, the then governor of Gilan, went to Anzali in the company of the influential cleric and landowner Haj Molla Mohammad Mehdi Shariatmadar, in a bid to quash the unrest. But their talks with the protesters backfired and the protesters closed the markets. Akram and Shariatmadar had to return to Rasht after two weeks, on December 15. Sardar Mansur, who had learned about the events via telegram and feared the disclosure of his business

---

3. DCIFM, no. CH1324-K23-P1-4.5.

4. DCIFM, no. CH1324-K23-P7-138.

5. DCIFM, no. GH1324-K23-P7-83.

6. The qran was a currency of Iran between 1825 and 1932. Subdivided into 20 shahi, or 1,000 dinars, it was worth one-tenth of a toman.

7. DCIFM, no. GH1329-K49-P2-43.

dealings with Lianozov, resorted to asking Haj Molla Mohammad Khomami to send 25,000 tomans in cash to the fishermen so that they would stop protesting and take the issue to the National Consultative Assembly instead. After paying the protesters an extra 500 tomans in damages, the sit-in finally ended.[8]

However, the negotiations held in the Majles confirmed that the price paid by Lianozov for leasing rights from the Fishery Authority was a meager sum, and if the concession was terminated by the government, some businessmen would be prepared to pay as much as three times the sum paid by Lianozov, together with damages for the termination of the contract. This issue was put forward by Agha Mirza Seyyed Mohammad Tabataba'i, one of the two leading senior clergy among the constitutionalists, along with Seyyed Abdollah Behbahani, in the seventh session of the first Majles on Sunday, December 2, 1906. Regarding the Anzali fishermen's complaint, Tabataba'i stated:

> The contract with Lianazov was signed by government officials two years ago, and specified that Lianazov will pay the fishermen five tomans per thousand. Also, to compensate the fishermen, two tomans have been added to the five tomans per thousand. For now, it is impossible to oppose the contract.

However, Tabataba'i then went on to say:

> forcing fishermen to sell fish at a specific price, [and] against their will, is against their rights and the law and this contract forced them to do so—no one can force someone to sell something, or sell someone else's property, or give the privilege of buying and selling someone else's property. According to pure sharia law, everyone can do, in their property, according to their will, and the rights of the property belongs to the owner of the property.

---

8. *Habl al-Matin* daily newspaper of Calcutta, Dhu Hijjah 6, 1324[AH]; see also: Rabino, 1368[SH]: 63–4.

Another constitutionalist representative, Hasan Ali Khan, said:

> because it is stated in the concession letter that, in case of violation of the contract by any of the parties, the government and the company, they must pay fifty thousand tomans to the other party, it is clear that the termination of the contract is possible.

The *Habl al-Matin* daily newspaper ran an economic analysis at the time, noting in summary that the penalty inflicted by termination of the Lianozov Concession could easily be paid. According to the newspaper, Caspian white fish (*kutum*) caught in the rivers leading to the Anzali lagoon could be leased to fishermen for between 60,000 and 70,000 tomans a month to cover the payment of the penalty. Then a new lessor would pay four or five times the Lianozov Concession, which amounted to 90,000 tomans for fish caught from Astara to Atrak from west to east along the shores of the Caspian in Iran. Iranian merchants could even set up a company to benefit from the big profits of the fishery business. According to *Habl al-Matin*, Lianozov paid 50,000 tomans for the fish trade, including customs and import–export fees, whereas the Russian government was receiving several million manats[9] for fishing in Salyan Port in Azerbaijan.[10] The Lianozov Concession was finally canceled on June 1, 1918, a few months after the Bolshevik Revolution in Russia, when Samsam al-Saltaneh Bakhtiari was the prime minister of Iran.[11]

In December the same year, residents of Shaft cabled Tehran, demanding that Sardar Mansur be dismissed as their governor.

On April 24, 1907, the daily newspaper of the Tabriz State Association raised another issue connected to the perceived abuse of power by Sardar Mansur, albeit by proxy:

---

9. The currency in many parts of the Caucasus at that time.

10. *Habl al-Matin* (Calcutta), Dhu Hijjah 6, 1324^{AH}.

11. Rabino, 1368^{SH}: 58. For the details of this concession, see: Hasani, 2013.

> Chomethqal is a village occupied by Abbas Khan Amid Homayoun, the former deputy governor [of Anzali], where income from fishing in winter is approximately eighty thousand tomans. When Amid Homayoun was deposed, Hasan Khan Amid al-Soltan, the new ruler of Anzali, took possession of the village at the suggestion of [his cousin] Sardar Mansur. However, Amid Homayoun is trying not to let go of his holdings. It is said that last year Amid Homayoun paid a thousand tomans and obtained an order to rent the village from Tehran. But the story of rent must be a lie, because why should a serf be able to pocket the income of a river and a village, which is ten thousand tomans?! The income must enter the treasury of the state and the nation, as the Bayt al-Mal [treasury] income of Muslims.

Amid Homayoun, who was actually one of Sardar Mansur's appointees, indulged in oppression and mistreatment of the people to such an extent that, before his dismissal, his rice warehouses were set on fire by people fed up with him. The Russian consulate in Anzali pressured the government to find the arsonists.[12]

Support for Constitutionalism and Membership in the Society of Humanity[13]

During his stay in the capital, Fathollah Khan Sardar Mansur was exposed to progressive societies and associations, as well as constitutionalist ideas and ideals. Given his astuteness, he learned very quickly that the constitutionalists were making headway and that the country would soon see fundamental changes in its political structure.

During the Constitutional Revolution, there were many influential people who were instinctively against the rule of law being established

12. See the report of the Russian embassy dated March 1908 in: Bashiri, 1368^{SH}, vol. 1: 82–3.

13. Jāme'-e Ādamīyat was the Persian name for the Society of Humanity.

in Iran. However, they submitted to the rising tide of constitutionalism either because they were pragmatic or opportunistic. Such people both had meetings with autocrats and were friends with constitutionalists. Fathollah Khan Sardar Mansur was one such person.

At the time, he joined the pseudo-Masonic Society of Humanity, which had been established in 1905 by Abbas Qoli Khan Qazvini, a follower of Mirza Malkam Khan Nazim al-Dowleh. Prince Abolfazl Mirza Azod al-Soltan and Prince Nosratollah Mirza Amir Aʿzam were also members of the society, which had nearly 350 members. Consisting mostly of liberal-minded and educated intellectuals, members were theoretically working in favor of constitutionalism, but they were mainly reform-minded and moderate rather than revolutionary,[14] opposed to the more progressive demands of radical constitutionalists, including the abolishment of feudalism. Sardar Mansur established a branch of the Society of Humanity in Gilan. Members included Dr. Esma'il Khan Amin al-Molk Marzban, Mohammad Hossein Khan Salar Asʿad Taleshi, and Mirza Mohammad Khan Moin Homayoun Rashti, as well as Sardar Mansur's cousins Mirza Sadegh Khan Sardar Motamed and Abdol-Hossein Khan Moez al-Soltan, who probably joined through him.[15] During the same period, in 1907, Mirza Isa Khan Soroush, Sardar Mansur's secretary, started publishing an eponymous newspaper in Rasht called *Soroush*, which was funded by Sardar Mansur.[16]

---

14. For further information, see: Hoseini, 1378^{SH}: 64–7.

15. See: Raeen, 1357^{SH}, vol. 2: 641, 682, 686, 689.

16. After the conquest of Tehran by the constitutionalists in 1909, Mirza Isa Khan Soroush moved to the capital and wrote as a political analyst for *Soroush* newspaper under the editor-in-chief Azdal al-Islam Lahiji. After a while, he returned to Rasht, but in 1911, at the request of the Russians, he was exiled for five years. After that, in 1916, when Sepahdar Rashti became the Minister of Interior in the cabinet of Vosouq al-Dowleh, he was employed in this ministry. After the appointment of Sepahdar Rashti as the prime minister in 1920, Mirza Isa Khan became his head of office and adviser and prepared all his speeches and letters. During the Pahlavi period, Mirza Isa Khan held various positions in the Ministry of Interior Affairs, such as the governorship of Tehran (1942) and of Mazandaran (1949). He was then appointed as the first senator of Gilan and died in 1952 at the age of seventy-six. See: Yousefdehi, 1392^{SH}: 144–54.

Collaboration with Members of Parliament

After the first National Consultative Assembly took office and representatives agreed on November 28, 1906, to establish Bank Melli (National Bank), Fathollah Khan Sardar Mansur was among the first wealthy individuals to announce his partnership with the new bank.

On January 3, 1907, four months after his constitutional decree had been issued, Mozaffar al-Din Shah Qajar passed away and was succeeded by his son Mohammad Ali Shah. The beginning of the new Shah's reign was beset by many crises. Owing to the expense of financing his father's third trip to Europe and money owed to the Bank of England, the treasury coffers were empty and chaos and insecurity overwhelmed the entire country. To make matters worse, the northwestern borders of Iran in Azerbaijan had become the target of Ottoman military aggression, and Kurdish leader Esma'il Khan Simitgou, known as Simko Shikak, and his band of soldiers also were looting and pillaging in Azerbaijan, Gilan, and Kurdistan. Meanwhile, Abolfath Mirza Salar al-Dowleh, the Shah's brother, wishing to claim the throne, had set off with a huge army in the west of the country and had advanced to Nahavand (a city in present-day Hamadan province).

Back in Tehran, in the newly established Majles, the minority faction of social democrats, led by Seyyed Hasan Taghizadeh, challenged the government for its incompetence in resolving the country's problems and questioned the authority of the new Shah. Some progressive associations and radical newspapers were fanning the flames of the Shah's suspicion of the newly established constitutional system through harsh statements, insults and aspersions against him.[17] It was in the midst of these problems that the Shah turned to Mirza Ali Asghar Khan Amin al-Soltan Atabak Aʿzam, meaning "Guardian Tutor," who had been unofficially exiled from

---

17. Regarding the misbehavior of the associations at that time, see: Ettehadie, 1381[SH]: ch. 5.

the country four years before but whom the Shah believed was the only person able to take control in the crisis.

Quite apart from Mohammad Ali Shah's confidence in Amin al-Soltan's abilities, a further reason for recalling him from Europe was his belief that Amin al-Soltan could lay the groundwork for the dissolution of the newly established Majles, to which the Shah did not intend to adapt. But he was mistaken in this regard. Amin al-Soltan was now a different person from the one of the Naseri and Mozaffari eras. In the past, to satisfy the rulers and cover their expenses for trips to Europe, he was willing to mortgage the government's few sources of income, including customs and fisheries, to foreign banks in exchange for a loan. Indeed, Amin al-Soltan's four-year sojourn in Europe and his visits to foreign countries, observing their progressive ways, had brought about a fundamental change in his political outlook. As a result, he now knew even better than the radical constitutionalists and representatives of the Majles that rescuing the country from the abyss demanded change and transformation in its governance, which required the constitutionality of the government and the retention of the National Consultative Assembly. Thus, Amin al-Soltan, contrary to Mohammad Ali Shah's expectations, not only did not stand in the way of the Majles, but he tried to establish good relations even with the extremist minority of the Majles, especially Taghizadeh. This was clearly a very different individual from the one the Shah had imagined, an impression further increased by Amin al-Soltan's efforts to normalize relations between the government and the Majles.

At the same time, the radical representatives of the Majles, led by Taghizadeh, were not willing to compromise with Amin al-Soltan. In fact, Amin al-Soltan's political record was so shameful and dark that it was difficult for them to accept his change of heart toward the Majles. Under pressure from the Shah and the court, on one hand, and the minority representatives of the Majles, on the other, Amin al-Soltan clearly had his enemies, and on August 31, 1907, he was shot dead in front of the Majles building. Controversy still surrounds his assassination and the possible perpetrators, with passionate discussions and debates persisting even among contemporary Iranian historians.

Historian Fereydun Adamiyat regards the radical minority faction of the Majles led by Taghizadeh to be responsible for the assassination, while scholar Javad Sheikh al-Islami disagrees, emphasizing that the court and Mohammad Ali Shah himself must have been responsible, owing to Amin al-Soltan's alignment with the Majles and out of dissatisfaction and even fear of his policies.[18]

Regardless of who may have been responsible for the assassination, this incident increased support for the constitution, causing various individuals, some from the government and some from the court, and including Sardar Mansur, to pledge their allegiance to the Majles. Identifying themselves as the "Association of Sardars," they warned the Shah against opposing constitutionalism for they could see that the constitutionalists had no intention of backing down from their demands and that the establishment of a constitutional government was inevitable.[19] According to a diplomat at the Russian imperial embassy in Tehran, "the success of the constitutionalists was so clear and obvious that people such as Zell al-Soltan and the pillars of the autocratic government, such as Sardar Amjad (Khan Talesh), Sardar Mansur, etc., also joined the group of defenders of the parliament."[20] On September 27, 1907, to express their support, the Association of Sardars submitted a bill to the Majles:

> Given that the lower social class contributes largely to the progress of constitutionalism and encouraging the promising is heartwarming, we hereby declare our readiness to stand with this sacred code up to the end. Now that we are presenting this motion, we swear by God that it is exactly what we have in mind, and we intend to assure you that we will spare no effort in favor of the progress of this sacred code.

---

18. For further discussion about Amin al-Soltan and the change in his political outlook after his four-year sojourn in Europe, as well as the underlying causes behind his assassination and the possible perpetrators, see: Sheikh al-Islami, 1366^SH^; Adamiyat, 1379^SH^. See also: Soleymannejad, 1401^SH^.

19. Bashiri, 1368^SH^, vol. 1: 83.

20. Bashiri, 1368^SH^, vol. 1: 82–3.

> [The signatories:] Asef al-Dowleh, Sepahdar Tonekaboni, Ala al-Dowleh, Jalal al-Dowleh, Moein al-Dowleh, Vizier Makhsous, Vazir Nezam, Sardar Mofkham, Sardar Mansur [Fathollah Khan], Sardar Firouz, Amir Nezam, Baha al-Molk, Adjoudan-bashi, Amir Seif al-Din, Amid al-Saltaneh, Zia al-Molk, Bahador al-Dowleh, Amir A'zam, Qavam al-Molk, Sardar Makhsous, Nasr al-Dowleh, Shoja al-Saltaneh.

Their petition to Mohammad Ali Shah, along with his response, was read out in the same session of the National Consultative Assembly. In their petition, they began by heaping praise on "His Majesty," saying that the country owed its survival to the monarch, before going on to state their desire to sit with the members of the Majles because they felt that the very fundamentals of constitutionalism were being threatened and that they felt compelled to express their views on this matter. While they would not disobey any order from the Shah, they intended to stand firm with the members of the Majles.

In reply, the Shah wrote:

> The Constitutional Majles was bestowed upon the nation by the late King of Kings [Mozaffar al-Din Shah] and then, for our part, we endorsed constitutionalism, and we have since been in full agreement with it. We see the Majles as the cause of bliss, prosperity and progress of the government and the nation. This Majles belongs to the nation, and you should follow this belief. Now that you are ready to serve the government and the nation, it is a great honor and we will show our maximum cooperation, God willing, and you should be always ready to serve the government and nation. And as you requested, you should meet with the ministers and lawmakers and discuss how to resolve problems.[21]

---

21. In his meeting in Tehran with the political representative of Russia and the chargé d'affaires of the British embassy, Mohammad Ali Shah also had promised to respect the integrity and immunity of the constitution, which had been granted by his father, Mozaffar al-Din Shah, and which had been approved by himself. See: Bashiri, 1368^{SH}, vol. 1: 83.

Sardar Mansur was among the sixty-three politicians who attended the Majles meeting on September 28, 1907, to sign an oath of full obedience to the constitutional government and to work for its protection. The text of the oath, which was read out by Agha Seyyed Abdollah Behbahani, was as follows:

> While we believe that Almighty God is closely watching us, we hereby swear wholeheartedly in front of God and on the holy Qur'an that we remain committed to the establishment of the Constitution in Iran, and we believe that the independence and prosperity and progress of this nation and dispensation of justice in this country are tied to the establishment of the Constitution. We feel religiously and patriotically compelled to work for the implementation of the articles of the Constitution. And since removal of injustice and promotion of security and equality are a requirement in Islam and a pillar of the Constitution, we swear by God to make efforts in that direction. May I face divine vengeance if I do otherwise.[22]

However, and despite his supportive response to the petition by the Association of Sardars, Mohammad Ali Shah had no intention of following the legislators' decisions and refused to promulgate pieces of the legislation. He even covertly took certain steps to portray the constitutional government as inefficient, trying to turn the population against it.

Unrest Continues in Gilan

By signing the petitions addressed to the Shah and the Majles, as well as participating in the oath read out by Seyyed Abdollah, it is clear that Sardar Mansur was making every effort to align himself with the constitutionalists of Tehran.

---

22. *Sobh-e Sadegh* daily newspaper, Sha'ban 24, 1325[AH].

In addition, after the decision was made in November 1906 at the first Majles to create Bank Melli, he was among the wealthy dignitaries who announced their participation in the establishment of the bank. Among the documents belonging to Taghizadeh, there is a text by an unknown author giving a list of people who might provide financial assistance to the new national bank, along with the amount of money promised by each individual. Sardar Mansur is one of the first names on the list, together with his pledge of 100,000 tomans in financial support.[23]

Sardar Mansur's efforts to prove his loyalty to the Majles and the constitution did not seem to convince everyone, however, especially with the constitutionalists of Gilan trying to portray him as an authoritarian and one of the causes of autocracy and public dissatisfaction. Tehran's *Habl al-Matin* daily newspaper, for example, in its edition of January 28, 1908, published a letter from Agha Mohammad Ali Maghazei, an Azeri constitutionalist based in Rasht, in which he accused Sardar Mansur of hypocrisy and injustice:

> This week, Sardar Mansur was quoted as having stopped levying taxes on vassals and having ordered his agents not to levy any more taxes. He has also claimed to have always supported justice and that he has never encroached upon anyone's rights . . . However, I feel compelled not to remain silent and to speak out. First and foremost, such taxes are not paid at the behest of a particular person. Sardar Mansur is not authorized to decide for others. He is also lying about justice. I am one of his neighbors. Two farmers who were my tenants owed debt to the government. They went to Sardar Mansur and his agents for a loan but nobody cared.[24]

In response, the *Neda-ye Vatan* newspaper, in its edition of February 4, 1908, published a letter from Mohammad Vakil al-Tojjar, a popular and patriotic representative of Rasht in the Majles, in

23. Afshar (ed.), 1359^{SH}: 396.

24. Quoted in: Nozad, 1398^{SH}, vol. 3: 213–14.

support of Sardar Mansur. In his letter, Vakil al-Tojjar said that he had been the one to request stopping the levy of taxes on vassals and that Sardar Mansur had complied with this. He also called on other landowners in Gilan to follow in Sardar Mansur's footsteps in this regard, adding:

> The truth is that these taxes are not so important for the overlords, but not having to pay them is vital for the vassals. Not levying taxes on the vassals is the best service that can be rendered to humanity and constitutionalism. The fact is that some biased people are trying to underestimate this issue and portray it as insignificant.[25]

Sometime later, Sardar Mansur himself sent a response to *Habl al-Matin*, which was published in its March 11, 1908, issue and in which he explained that he had never encroached upon anyone's rights and that the tax relief plan was a positive measure:

> I received a copy of the ledger containing payments made by vassals to the landlords, which had been registered by the Rasht National Association. I reviewed the ledger and, based on what I had seen, I wrote off taxes levied on my own vassals. I am ready to offer proof that I have written off upwards of fifteen thousand tomans a year, which has nothing to do with official accounts . . . Therefore, it has been only for my own property, and those who claim otherwise are doing so just out of bias and enmity.[26]

Not long after Mirza Ali Khan Zahir al-Dowleh, also known as Safa Ali Shah, had been appointed governor of Gilan in February 1908, Tehran's *Habl al-Matin* once again ran a report explaining the issues in Gilan. The columnist had called on Zahir al-Dowleh to expel the agents and representatives of Sardar Mansur and Sardar Amjad

---

25. Quoted in: Nozad, 1398^{SH}, vol. 3: 442–7.

26. Quoted in: Nozad, 1398^{SH}, vol. 3: 230–31.

(another wealthy supporter of constitutionalism) from Anzali and Tavalesh and replace them with qualified individuals.[27] Residents of Anzali also wrote a detailed letter to Zahir al-Dowleh, highlighting problems in their own city, including the issue of the Fishery Authority and Sardar Mansur:

> Anzali is Iran's northern gate, and its residents have no farmland and business but fishing. Even though our country's powerful leaders consider themselves overlords of the poor, they have resorted to every trick to deny the people of Anzali this minimum income. They have resorted to greed and pitting one against the other to achieve their goals. We request that an investigation be launched into the Fishery Authority (Shilat). Sardar Mansur is acting as he did four years ago when in the midst of dictatorship and chaos he had his claws in the rights of residents here . . . It is hereby noted that, under the Lianozov Concession, catching *halal* fish belonged to Anzali residents. On what basis does Lianozov earn an extra forty thousand tomans in revenue other than by paying 2 percent in kickbacks to win the local authorities' agreement? How is Sardar Mansur authorized to funnel this sum entirely into his own treasury? Please take into consideration our requests.[28]

Confronting the Shah

On February 28, 1908, an attempt was made on the life of Mohammad Ali Shah by Haydar Khan Amo-Oghli, an extreme constitutionalist. Following this incident, leaflets defaming the Shah were published in Tehran and Tabriz and it became clear to everyone that no reconciliation was possible between the Shah and the Majles.[29] The Shah decided to subvert constitutionalism by taking back control with the assistance of Cossack forces and Russian officeholders. On May 14,

---

27. Zahir al-Dowleh, 1367[SH]: 215–16.

28. Zahir al-Dowleh, 1367[SH]: 318–19.

29. For the details of the events leading to the failed assassination of Mohammad Ali Shah and an analysis of it, see: Adamiyat, 1379[SH].

1908, Nezam al-Saltaneh Mafi stepped down as prime minister, to be replaced by Mirza Ahmad Khan Moshir al-Saltaneh, an authoritarian politician. Disturbed by these arbitrary acts of the Shah, and the threat they posed to the Qajar dynasty, a deputation of Qajar princes and dignitaries, including Sardar Mansur, Jalal al-Dowleh, Ala al-Dowleh, Nosratollah Mirza Amir A'zam, and Moein al-Dowleh, went to the Qajar tribal chief, Ali Reza Khan Azod al-Molk, demanding that he take action to bring the Shah back into line.

Later, about ten thousand constitutionalists who were suspicious of the Shah also went to see Azod al-Molk and, in the presence of Moshir al-Saltaneh, demanded that some authoritarian figures, including Amir Bahador Jang and the Russian Shapshal Khan, be expelled from the court. Azod al-Molk and Moshir al-Saltaneh informed the Shah of the constitutionalists' request. After resisting at first, the Shah finally backed down and ordered the individuals in question to be expelled.[30]

Yet Mohammad Ali Shah remained determined to bring down the constitution. To that end, at dawn on June 4, 1908, he led a large number of troops, including Cossack cavalry, imperial guards, and some Iranian and Russian officials, to his residence at Bagh-e Shah, outside of the capital, and stationed his forces there. He also transferred weapons, cannons, and other military hardware to the site and ordered telegraph cables to be cut.

Meanwhile, princes and constitutionalist leaders had gathered at Sardar Mansur's residence in Tehran.[31] On June 6, 1908, the Shah dismissed Sardar Mansur (Minister of Post and Telegraph at the time) and Mirza Saleh Khan Vazir Akram (both constitutionalists), and replaced them with two authoritarian politicians, Mokhber al-Dowleh and Hajeb al-Dowleh.

The following day, Sardar Mansur and a number of constitutionalists—Soltan Hossein Mirza Jalal al-Dowleh (son of Zell al-Soltan),

---

30. Kasravi, 1369^SH^: 562–64; Malekzadeh, 1382^SH^, vol. 3: 653–5; Dolatabadi, 3161^SH^, vol. 2: 244–53.

31. Dolatabadi, 1361^SH^, vol. 2: 255.

Mohammad Ali Shah Qajar

Mirza Ahmad Khan Ala al-Dowleh, Mirza Mehdi Khan Qaem Maqam Kashani, and Shokrollah Khan Motamed Khaghan—along with Azod al-Molk (the Qajar tribal chief), went to Bagh-e Shah to encourage the Shah to make good on his pledges and end his enmity toward constitutionalism.

After Sardar Mansur and the rest of the constitutionalists bravely confronted the Shah and put forward their demands, the monarch appeared to accept their proposals and treated them kindly, but as soon as they left his residence in Bagh-e Shah, a group of Cossack forces encircled them and arrested Sardar Mansur, along with Jalal al-Dowleh and Ala al-Dowleh.[32] In his report to the Russian foreign ministry regarding the arrest, Nicholas Hartwig, the Russian ambassador to Tehran, attributed it to the conspiracy of the Shah's opponents to remove him and appoint Zell al-Soltan as the regent, and also identified Sardar Mansur, Jalal al-Dowleh, and Ala al-Dowleh as the "main conspirators."[33] A secret telegram from Charles Marling, the British Minister in Tehran to Sir Edward Grey, the British foreign secretary, described what had happened:

> On the morning of Saturday, June 6 [1908], a compromise was apparently reached between the Shah and the constitutionalists, but the next morning, it was reported to His Highness the Shah that the [progressive] associations had telegraphed Zell al-Soltan in Shiraz, asking him to come [to Tehran] and accept the regency. On the same day in the evening, the eldest son of Zell al-Soltan, [Jalal al-Dowleh], Sardar Mansur, Ala al-Dowleh, and Azod al-Molk, the Qajar tribal chief, who had participated in the revolution last week, were arrested by the Shah.[34]

According to Marling in another report, Mohammad Ali Shah considered Sardar Mansur as the "main driver of the plot" against him.[35] No one can say whether such a plot was actually being planned, but what is known is that Sardur Mansur was one of the main financial supporters of the uprising against the Qajar Shah.

---

32. Zahir al-Dowleh, 1367^{SH}: 328–9; Mahallati, 1359^{SH}: 594; Dolatabadi, 1361^{SH}: vol. 2: 261; Bashiri, 1368^{SH}: vol. 1: 205

33. Bashiri, 1367^{SH}, vol. 1: 201, 219.

34. Bashiri (ed.), 1363^{SH}, vol. 1: 185.

35. Bashiri (ed.), 1363^{SH}, vol. 1: 215.

Two days afterwards, on June 8, 1908, the prisoners were sent in shackles and in a humiliating manner to Kalat in Khorasan province through Sorkheh Hesar.[36] However, to prevent any riots, courtiers spread rumors that they were headed instead to Europe via Mazandaran.[37] According to another report by Hartwig, "the news of the arrest of the three people had a great impact on the nationalists. They did not expect such a decisive action by the Shah . . . The news of this event spread quickly in the city and caused great excitement and disturbances among the associations."[38]

On the same day, the Shah issued a handwritten text titled "The Salvation of the Nation," falsely claiming that he had only intended to arrest some corrupt figures and instigators of riots as well as a group of courtiers who had "conspired to take power from him for the benefit of Zell al-Soltan."[39] The National Consultative Assembly was completely secure and in control,[40] and "the constitutional government will be maintained in the country."[41]

Two days later, the Constitutionalist Commission responded to Mohammad Ali Shah's falsehoods with the following:

> One odd thing which makes us ashamed before the Europeans and every reasonable mind is the claim that "the Iranian government is a constitutional government . . . and Members of the Majles are able to exercise their legal duties in full

---

36. In the documents of the Russian foreign ministry, it is stated that three people who had been arrested were sent to Kalat, and only Ala al-Dowleh was authorized to return to his property in Khorasan. See: Bashiri, 1368^{SH}, vol. 1: 205.

37. Bashiri, 1367^{SH}, vol. 1: 333–4; Rabino, 1368^{SH}: 41; Eskandari, 1361^{SH}: 227.

38. Bashiri, 1367^{SH}, vol. 1: 219, 333.

39. Bashiri, 1367^{SH}, vol. 1: 219.

40. Dolatabadi, 1361^{SH}, vol. 2: 263–4. In his report, Hartwig makes the claim, which we know to be extravagant—that the Shah's handwritten note "met with the sympathy of the people, who were tired of the arbitrariness of the revolutionaries. Those who tried to tear down copies of the statement, which was pasted on doors and walls, were repeatedly beaten by the crowd." Bashiri, 1367^{SH}, vol. 1: 219–20.

41. Bashiri, 1367^{SH}, vol. 1: 333.

> security." The Shah may not be aware that when there is constitutional monarchy and a National Consultative Assembly in charge, the Constitution does not allow any seizure and imprisonment . . . Just three days ago, Ala al-Dowleh along with Jalal al-Dowleh and Sardar Mansur were arrested. The Telegraph Office's director was dismissed overnight two days ago. The governor of Tehran and the chief of police have been discharged over the past two days without any prior notice. Therefore, His Majesty's claim of constitutionalism is false.[42]

Upon hearing about Sardar Mansur's imprisonment, Marling on June 18, 1908, sent a note to Iran's foreign ministry intervening on his behalf:

> His Excellency the Minister,
>
> As I have heard, Sardar Mansur has been feeling unwell for some time. He has fallen ill in Firouzkouh. Your Excellency knows full well that since the aforesaid has been awarded Britain's highest order of chivalry, his circumstances matter a great deal to me and that is why I am sending Your Excellency this note. Is it possible that His Majesty could authorize Sardar Mansur to travel to Europe? Your Excellency is well aware that I have no intention of meddling with the domestic political affairs of the Persian government, and I am always willing to follow instructions set forth by my own government. Nonetheless, I am sure that His Majesty would allow Sardar Mansur to travel to Europe for medical treatment. Such a favour from His Majesty is sure to be rewarded. I hope that Your Excellency would inform His Majesty of my request. Please accept the assurances of my highest consideration.
>
> C. M. Marling[43]

42. Dolatabadi, 1361^{SH}, vol. 2: 264–9.

43. DCIFM, no. GH1326-K3.1-P2-16.2.

However, Marling's request fell on deaf ears and instead, the crisis deepened. Eventually, on June 23, 1908, on the orders of Mohammad Ali Shah, Cossack forces under the command of the Russian Colonel Liakhov bombed the Majles, killing many people and imprisoning the survivors, and constitutionalism was temporarily brought to an end. After the bombing of the Majles, a large number of constitutionalists went into hiding, seeking refuge in foreign embassies, or fled the country.

According to some sources, Sardar Mansur was transferred from Kalat to Mashhad on July 20, while his fellow inmates, Jalal al-Dowleh and Ala al-Dowleh, were exiled.[44] But according to Amir Mansur, the son of Sardar Mansur, they were all sent to Savadkuh, where they were locked up by Esma'il Khan Amir Moayyed Savadkuhi.[45] A letter sent by Malakeh Iran, the daughter of Naser al-Din Shah and the wife of Zahir al-Dowleh, who was a constitutionalist herself, to her husband in Rasht on September 13, 1908, confirms this: "Jalal al-Dowleh and Ala al-Dowleh as well as Sardar Mansur are in Savadkuh. Because Jalal al-Dowleh and Sardar Mansur are both very sick, they cannot be moved."[46]

A letter, filed at Iran's National Documents Center, confirms Sardar Mansur's five-month detention in Savadkuh:

> A description of the whereabouts of Sardar Mansur has been documented. I often meet with Haji Seyyed Mahmud and we exchange views about everything. But nothing has been said of this issue and there is no sign of him having talked with Haj Sheikh Fazlollah.[47] I don't know at all if anything has been done. However, His Majesty is by no means ready to set Sardar Mansur free. If His Majesty was seeking money, he would not have sent the two to exile. They were both ready

---

44. Malekzadeh, 1382^{SH}, vol. 3: 656–9; Agheli, 1380^{SH}, vol. 1: 56; Bashiri, 1367^{SH}, vol. 1: 251.

45. Rabino, 1368^{SH}: 241.

46. Zahir al-Dowleh, 1367^{SH}: 344.

47. Most likely Sheikh Fazlollah Nouri.

> to pay cash, but Sardar Mansur's detention is only to torture him. Seyyed Yahya Khan is trying his best. Everyone knows him. However, he has reached no conclusion yet. I will raise the issue with His Excellency the Grand Vizier [Moshir al-Saltaneh], although it may be difficult to find him. Moshir al-Saltaneh does not even recognize his friends now. He is too busy. As soon as he comes out, thousands flock to him . . . Haji Khomami's cabled message and Haji Sheikh Fazlollah's actions have not reached Najaf yet and nobody has heard about them. However, it is rumored that His Majesty ordered that Sardar Mansur's properties be seized. Mirza Gholam Hossein has said he has heard about the order for the seizure of the said properties.[48]

Revolution in Rasht

After the bombing of the National Consultative Assembly, a group of constitutionalists, including six cousins of Sardar Mansur (Mirza Karim Khan Rashti among them) and a group of their revolutionary friends set up the secret "Sattar Committee" for the purpose of arranging an armed uprising in Rasht against Mohammad Ali Shah's dictatorial rule. Leading the committee was Mirza Karim Khan Rashti, and according to an article, "Rasht and Freedom," that appeared in the *Nasim-e Shomal* daily newspaper on February 15, 1909, the Committee comprised thirteen members in total.

Due to the heavy police crackdown in Gilan and the activities of secret agents within the Russian and British consulates in Rasht, the Sattar Committee decided to source operatives and ammunitions it needed from outside the area. To that end, Mirza Karim Khan Rashti travelled to the Caucasus, where he developed ties with the leaders and members of the Russian Social Democratic Labor Party to gain their support for the committee's plans. The Sattar Committee purchased large quantities of arms and ammunition and smuggled them secretly into Rasht, along with a number of Georgian and

48. National Documents Center of Iran, no. 296-9154; see also: Akbar, 1395^{SH}: 133.

Sardar Mansur's cousins who took part in the Rasht uprising, *from right to left:* Ahmad Ali Khan, Hasan Khan Amid al-Soltan, Abdol-Hossein Khan Sardar Mohyee, Abou Torab Khan, Mojib al-Saltaneh, Abbas Khan.

Armenian mercenaries who had been trained for armed and guerrilla operations. Taghizadeh comments upon the clandestine activities in his memoirs: "[while] Sardar Mansur was captured and imprisoned by Mohammad Ali Shah . . . they [Fathollah Khan's cousins] were secretly helping [the constitutionalists] in all kinds of ways. They had gradually collected weapons and hid those who came from the Caucasus in the basements of their houses."[49]

After making all the necessary arrangements, the Sattar Committee settled on February 8, 1909, as the date for revolutionary action to occupy Rasht and made their move on that day. Agha Bala Khan Sardar Afkham, the authoritarian governor of Rasht, was murdered in the Modiriyeh Garden and, after heavy fighting, the Rasht governor's office was occupied by the combatants. By the

49. Taghizadeh, 1391^{SH}: 111.

end of the day, all key locations in Rasht had been taken over by the constitutionalists.

Sardar Mansur's Residence as the Base for the Constitutionalists

The day after the Rasht Revolution, Mohammad Vali Khan Sepahdar A'zam Tonekaboni (later known as Sepahsalar) led a group of fighters from Tonekabon to Rasht to take command of the revolutionary combatants. He headed straight to Sardar Mansur's residence, where he and his five hundred troops lodged for two months and enjoyed the hospitality of Sardar Mansur's wife, Begum Khanum, in her husband's absence, as he was still imprisoned in Savadkuh. Throughout their stay at the house, they were supplied with breakfast, lunch, dinner, and refreshments, the hospitality of Begum Khanum far exceeding the expectations of guests and observers alike.[50]

The notes and cabled messages from that period indicate that the guests at the house consisted not only of Sepahdar Tonekaboni and the fighters in his company, but also the members of various government departments that had to vacate Tehran following the bombing of the Majles, including the Gilan Provincial Association, the Department of Finance, and the Extraordinary Commission.[51]

Years later the same house was occupied in 1915 by the Jangali (Jungle) Movement[52] partisans who accommodated their own guests.[53] After the arrival of the Bolsheviks and the establishment of the Persian Socialist Soviet Republic in Rasht in 1920, Sardar Mansur's house was repurposed as their urban control center.[54]

---

50. Rabino, 1368^{SH}: 214.

51. Rabino, 1368^{SH}: 248–50.

52. The Jangali Movement in Gilan was a rebellion against the monarchist rule of the central government. The Movement lasted from 1915 to 1921.

53. Gilak, 1371^{SH}: 114–15.

54. Gilak, 1371^{SH}: 298. The house was demolished during the Pahlavi II reign and a commercial center built instead i.e., after being used as an urban control center

Sepahdar's house in Rasht during the 1909 Constitutional Revolution.

Sardar Mansur is Transferred to the Capital

The Gilan Constitutional Corps conquered Qazvin in March 1909 and Sepahdar Tonekaboni and his troops moved there from Sardar Mansur's house. Governing the affairs of Gilan was assigned to Mirza Karim Khan Rashti, taking over from his (and Sardar Mansur's) cousin, Sadegh Khan Sardar Motamed.

During the time when Sepahdar Tonekaboni was stationed in Qazvin and engaged in negotiations with the Shah and the Russian and British embassies, Sardar Mansur was transferred from Savadkuh to Tehran and was kept under observation in the house of Hossein Pasha Khan Amir Bahador Jang, a staunch anti-constitutionalist and the head of the Royal Guard. Haj Sayyah Mahallati gives an account of what then transpired:

---

by the Bolsheviks.

> [Loyalists to the Shah] summoned Fathollah Khan Sardar Mansur from Savadkuh. He was detained instead at the house of Amir Bahador. He was asked to pay bribes, but he refused out of his own patriotism. He finally managed to take refuge at the Russian legation, where Haj Hossein Agha Amin al-Zarb joined him. Sardar Mansur secretly supplied funds to the constitutionalists of Rasht to support them. He did not hesitate to make such sacrifices.[55]

In a letter addressed to Hasan Khan Aʿzam al-Vozara Qodsi, Sardar Mansur gives a detailed account of his time at Amir Bahador Jang's residence and his decision to seek refuge at the Russian legation:

> Five months after I was banished [to Savadkuh], one day my jailer Amir Moayyed [Savadkuhi] came and declared that I had been summoned to Tehran and that I should depart for Tehran the following day. I offered my thanks to God and woke up early in the morning. We departed for Tehran along with a group of Mazandarani horsemen. It was a difficult journey and I fell ill. We arrived in Tehran after one week and I was taken straight to Amir Bahador's house.
>
> Fortunately, a close friend of mine was also there. He was Mirza Saleh Khan Vazir Akram, [the former governor of Gilan] later named Asef al-Dowleh. We were housed in the same room. I was happy to be with him. However, my situation was precarious, and I had yet to meet with Amir Bahador.
>
> One night, Asef al-Dowleh asked me if I knew why I had been summoned to Tehran. I replied that I had no idea. He said: "They know that you are very wealthy, and they intend to steal your money, because the government has run out of funds. The Shah is planning a military

---

55. Mahallati, 1359[SH]: 618.

expedition to Azerbaijan and needs supplies. Be aware that the money you give them will be used to crush the freedom fighters. Do not help them if they approach you." I was happy to have been warned of the developments.

The following night, Amir Bahador's nephew came to me, expressing regret on behalf of his uncle, and said that his uncle would eventually compensate me for the harsh treatment I was enduring. The nephew went on to say that if I provided one hundred thousand tomans in aid to the government, Mohammad Ali Shah would reward me. I immediately replied that it was beyond my power, and I poured cold water on their hands.[56]

At night, I was consulting with Asef al-Dowleh and we decided that I should seek refuge at the Russian legation to escape from this plight. That night, I asked for Amir Bahador's permission to take a bath the following day, on the pretext that I had been deprived of bathing for months. I asked Amir Bahador to order his personal carriage to take me to the public bathhouse. I have to note here that during my stay at Amir Bahador's house, he asked me several times why I didn't go to my own home for a short visit. I told him that as my situation was not clear yet and my family was in distress, I did not want to upset them any further, and therefore I preferred not to go home. In reality, I wanted to deceive him.

When I requested that his carriage take me to the bathhouse, he immediately accepted my request. Then, I kissed Asef al-Dowleh and thanked him for his advice. I went straight home. After getting out of the carriage, I paid gold coins to the coachman and the footmen and told them to pick me up in the afternoon. Then, I briefly met with my family and quickly searched for all of the title deeds of my properties, which I put in a bag to take with me. I then quickly called for a public coach to take me to the Russian legation, which was in the Pamenar district, where I sought refuge.

---

56. A Persian expression meaning "I sent them away empty-handed."

In the afternoon, when the coachman and footmen came to pick me up, they were told that I had already departed on a paid coach. When Amir Bahador learned about the story, he said, "We lost a big catch"! Sa'd al-Dowleh came to try to persuade me to leave the embassy premises, but I refused. I did not leave the embassy until the Shah's officials had signed a written pledge with the embassy to release me.

Several days later, I was summoned by Mohammad Ali Shah. When I was in the Russian embassy, I learned that my cousin Sardar Mohyee and a group of others had launched a revolution in Rasht and killed Agha Bala Khan Sardar Afkham. As soon as I arrived in the palace and was presented to the Shah, he furiously informed me that my cousins had triggered riots in Rasht and killed the governor of Rasht. He then pledged that he would take action and make my life miserable. He ordered me to cable messages to the rioters and advise them to stop their activities or they would face harsh consequences. I replied to the Shah that I would go and cable them messages, but I doubted that they would listen to me.

Nevertheless, I went to the telegraph office. The man in charge there was among those liberal-minded people whom I knew quite well. I told him to first cable a message, saying that what I was about to send was cabled out of necessity and did not reflect my personal opinion. Then, I wrote a message, which was cabled immediately. Sepahdar Tonekaboni and the commanders of the constitutionalists replied that they would not relent unless Constitutionalism was re-established and elections were held. I carried their response to Mohammad Ali Shah and then went home.

Two days after, Banan al-Molk came to me in a great hurry and said: "Go at once to the Russian legation before it is too late. You are facing a big threat tonight." I asked him what the threat was. He said: "Half an hour ago, Akhtar al-Saltaneh, the daughter of the late Yahya Khan Moshir al-Dowleh, came to my wife to say that Mohammad Ali Shah's mother, Om al-Khakan, wanted to see me. She had an urgent message for Sardar Mansur, which should remain secret. She asked me to warn you that your life is in danger. According to the Queen Mother, Mohammad Ali Shah had a private meeting with Mojalal, Sani Hazrat, Mofakher al-Molk, and [Seraya] Shopshal, to discuss the problem of the constitutionalists. They decided to murder you and have plotted to send a group, disguised as thieves, to your home to assassinate you."

"She further said that when you were in charge of Iran's northern customs and she was dependent on the funds from there, you always paid her on time, and you even paid her advance payments whenever she needed them. In response to your kindness, she felt compelled to warn you against this threat to your life. Your planned murder is in response to the murder of Agha Bala Khan Sardar Afkham in Rasht."[57]

Having heard this, I headed once again to the Russian legation and sought refuge there. The following day, I was told that masked intruders had raided my home, only to flee upon learning of my absence. I stayed at the Russian legation for several months until summer arrived. During the hot summer months, the embassy household moved, as usual, to Zargandeh in the mountains, where it was cooler. There I rented Monsieur Ketabchi Khan's Garden in Zargandeh, close to the Russian embassy. During the day, I would stroll to the legation and enjoy the fresh air.

One day, as I approached the embassy's entrance, I saw that a group of Indian cavalrymen were waiting there. In front of the Russian flag flying above the embassy, the British flag was also flying. I was surprised and immediately thought that Mohammad Ali Shah must have sought refuge at the legation. As I approached the entrance, an embassy servant rushed to me and asked me not to come any further, as Mohammad Ali

57. Taj al-Moluk, nicknamed Om al-Khakan, was the mother of Mohammad Ali Shah Qajar and the daughter of Mirza Taghi Khan Amir Kabir and Princess Ezzat al-Dowleh (sister of Naser al-Din Shah). Due to their enmity with Mohammad Ali Shah, the radical constitutionalists insulted her and called her inappropriate names, not knowing of how she had secretly helped Sardar Mansur. She died shortly after this incident in Qasr-e Shirin in November 1909, on her way to Atbat to visit her son.

Russian legation in Tehran in early 1900.

> Shah along with the Queen and the Crown Prince had indeed sought refuge at the embassy and therefore other refugees were not allowed in. I told him that he had given me good news and gave him each and every gold coin I had in my bag.[58]

Sardar Mansur's stay at the Russian embassy had lasted six months and ended when the pro-constitutionalist forces that he bankrolled conquered Tehran.[59]

After the Triumph of Tehran

After Tehran fell to the constitutionalists in 1909, Sardar Mansur was appointed by the Supreme Advisory Council established by the constitutionalists to head a committee tasked with adopting a bill to depose Mohammad Ali Shah and declare the reign of twelve-year-old

58. Akbar, 1395^{SH}: 133–7, 205.

59. Ghanei and Elmi, 1391^{SH}: 193.

Ahmad Shah Qajar as monarch, in his place, with Ali Reza Khan Azod al-Molk as regent. The bill stated:

> As the present circumstances of Iran indicate that establishment of order and security is not possible without changes to the monarchy, and the former king is now detested to the greatest degree and has sought refuge at the Russian legation backed by the Russian and British governments, he has naturally been deposed. Nonetheless, in the absence of the Senate and the National Consultative Assembly, the Supreme Advisory Council held an extraordinary session in the Baharestan building on July 16, 1909, to appoint Crown Prince Soltan Ahmad Mirza as the monarch of Iran with the title of regent awarded to Ashraf Azod al-Molk. After the parliament is established, pursuant to Article 38 of the Constitution, the authority of the regent shall be determined.[60]

The Supreme Advisory Council communicated the bill to the deposed Mohammad Ali Shah and his family at the Russian legation, and appointed an administrative board to run state affairs. The board sent a delegation to the Russian legation to escort the underage king. The child was separated from his parents and respectfully brought to the Golestan Palace.

The regent appointed Mirza Hasan Khan Mostofi al-Mamalek as Court Minister, while Mirza Ebrahim Khan Hakim al-Molk was tasked with overhauling court affairs. In his first action, Hakim al-Molk expelled corrupt courtiers and offensive constitutionalists from the palace. Ahmad Shah's Russian teacher, Captain Smirnov, was also expelled, to the fury of the Russians, who declared that they were prepared to withdraw half of their troops recently deployed to Iran, in return for his reinstatement. Their request was rejected. The Russians then tried to apply pressure via the Russia-led Accounting

---

60. Malekzadeh, 1382^SH^, vol. 6: 1237–1238.

Ahmad Shah Qajar

and Loan Bank of Persia that had given loans to most of the government officials. The bank set a 24-hour time limit to pay back their loans. Among those who had taken out loans with the bank were Sepahdar Tonekaboni (a loan of 800,000 tomans), Sardar Mansur (a loan of 350,000 tomans), and Ali Reza Khan Azod al-Molk. However, the administrative board did not back down, and Smirnov was eventually expelled.[61] Taghizadeh writes in his memoirs about this incident:

> This demand fell on the country's authorities like a thunderbolt. A strange fear and anxiety gripped them. That day, when I entered the Golestan Palace, the seat of the [temporary] Board of Directors, the late Sardar As'ad [Bakhtiari] shouted and told me to come and see what had happened. But Russian threats had no effect, and the Russian teacher was fired.[62]

The Accounting and Loan Bank of Persia did not let the Iranian government officials off the hook, however. As it appears from documents in the Ministry of Foreign Affairs of Iran, during the second cabinet of Sepahdar Tonekaboni (1911), the Russian embassy in Tehran requested the then foreign minister, Ala al-Saltaneh, to obtain an order from the chancellor to pay Sardar Mansur's debt to the Accounting and Loan Bank of Persia based on the income of his property in Gilan.[63] After being instructed by the chancellor, the foreign minister announced to the Russian embassy that an appropriate order had been issued to seize Sardar Mansur's income in Gilan.[64] Finally, sometime after issuing the chancellor's order and as a result of repeated follow-ups by the Russian embassy, Ala al-Saltaneh announced the receipt of 6,000 tomans in cash from Sardar Mansur, noting it had been decided that the rest of his

---

61. Sheikh al-Islami, 1392[SH]: 30.
62. Taghizadeh, 1379[SH]: 106.
63. DCIFM, no. GH1326-K58-P10-3.
64. DCIFM, no. GH1326-K58-P10-1. For the text of the order, see: DCIFM, no. GH1326-K58-P10-5.

debts would be paid from the proceeds of his rice harvest.[65] Sardar Mansur was at the time, it should be added, the Minister of Post and Telegraph and a colleague of Ala al-Saltaneh in the second cabinet of Sepahdar Tonekaboni. This incident shows that the cabinet of constitutionalists was behaving scrupulously, in paying its debts, in contrast to previous corrupt practices.

65. DCIFM, no. GH1326-K58-P10-9.

CHAPTER 3

COOPERATION WITH CONSTITUTIONAL CABINETS

Headless Cabinet

Due to his close ties to Sepahdar Tonekaboni, the commander of Tehran, and having already served as Minister of Post and Telegraph, in a previous administration, Fathollah Khan Sardar Mansur joined the headless (there was no prime minister) constitutionalist-led cabinet established on July 17, 1909, after the Triumph of Tehran and the fall of Mohammad Ali Shah. Regent Ali Reza Khan Azod al-Molk issued the following decree:

> His Excellency Sardar Mansur
>
> Given your expertise, competence and qualifications and your background in administering the Telegraph Center and Post Office, because of your foresight and knowledge, you are qualified to serve as the Minister of Telegraph and Post of the Guarded Domains. You are requested to prove your

> competence and reliability in this new post and be responsible for the administration of these two ministries. July 18, 1909.[1]

The first steps undertaken by the new cabinet included: appointments to government posts; holding an election for the second National Consultative Assembly; the prosecution and execution of notorious authoritarian figures, including Mafakher al-Molk, Ajoudanbashi (adjutant-in-chief), Sani'e Hazrat, Seyyed Hashem, and Sheikh Fazlollah Nouri; recognizing the Crown Prince and making his reign official; and repairing the bombed parliament building.

A notable event during the initial two-and-a-half-month mandate of the new cabinet was the arrest and imprisonment of Mirza Seyyed Hasan Kashani, the manager of the *Habl al-Matin* daily newspaper in Tehran. The sixth issue of the newspaper had run an article strongly criticizing the clergy and the negative consequences of the Arab religious conquest of Iran in 632–54. This article, which was originally written by Seyyed Nour al-Din Kharghani, the son of a constitutionalist cleric, but without mentioning his name, caused fury among ordinary citizens as well as the clergy. Sardar Mansur, as the Minister of Post and Telegraph, had received a telegram from a prominent and high-ranking constitutionalist cleric based in Najaf, Akhound Molla Mohammad Kazem Khorasani, and was asked to raise the issue with a group of ministers and members of the Majles. In his telegram, Akhound Khorasani had taken an uncompromising stand against the publication of such articles and demanded that the perpetrators be punished. Therefore, Seyyed Hasan Kashani was prosecuted, sentenced to two years in prison, and his newspaper banned.[2] Constitutionalists Seyyed Nasrollah Taghvi and Hasan Moshir al-Dowleh Pirnia strongly objected to the sentence and Seyyed Hasan Kashani was released from prison, but the epoch-making *Habl al-Matin* newspaper, which played a significant role

1. Manuscript of decree, Mr. Manouchehr Akbar's personal archive.
2. Malekzadeh, 1382[SH], vol. 6: 1228–92.

in enlightening Iranian society in the pre- and post-constitutional era, remained banned.

In the judgment issued by the Tamiz Court (or court of appeal) overturning the sentence issued by the lower court against Seyyed Hasan Kashani, he was quoted as saying that after the publication of the sixth issue of *Habl al-Matin*, the Minister of Post and Telegraph, Sardar Mansur, deprived him of the ownership license of *Habl al-Matin* and thereby deprived him of the responsibility of publishing the disputed article.[3]

An interesting point about this incident should be noted. After returning from forced exile in the Caucasus for several months following his release from prison, Seyyed Hasan Kashani decided to go to Calcutta to resume the publication of his newspaper. But Seyyed Hasan Taghizadeh dissuaded him from doing this and, with Taghizadeh's advice, instead of going to Calcutta, Seyyed Hasan Kashani secretly entered Rasht to resume the publication of *Habl al-Matin* in Iran. During his time in Rasht, Seyyed Hasan Kashani stayed at Sardar Mansur's house. In this way, Sardar Mansur could be said to be a secret supporter of Kashani in the publication of *Habl al-Matin* in Rasht. Considering that Kashani's forced departure from Iran was due to the reactionary political pressure on him as a result of the publication of *Habl al-Matin* in Tehran, Sardar Mansur's support for him indicates his liberal tendencies at this juncture.

Radical and Moderate Constitutionalists

After constitutional sovereignty was reinstated in Iran, the constitutionalists split into two factions. There were now radical and moderate constitutionalists. The heads of the radical constitutionalists were: Seyyed Hasan Taghizadeh, Hoseinqoli Khan Navab, Mirza Ebrahim Khan Hakim al-Molk, Agha Seyyed Mohammadreza Mosavat, Prince Saleiman Mirza, and Abdol-Hosain Khan Vahid al-Molk Sheibani. The heads of the moderate constitutionalists consisted of: Agha Seyyed

3. Golban, 1384^{SH}: 76.

Abdollah Behbahani, Abolhasan Khan Moazed al-Saltaneh Pirnia, Seyyed Yahya Naser al-Islam Nedamani, Mirza Seyyed Mohammad Sadegh Tabataba'i, and Haj Mirza Ali Mohammad Dolatabadi. The leaders of the Constitutional Revolution and the Triumph of Tehran showed an inclination for one or the other of these factions, with Sardar As'ad Bakhtiari and Ali Mohammad Khan Tarbiat joining the radical faction, while Sepahdar Tonekaboni, Sardar Mansur, Seyyed Abdollah Behbahani, and Abdol-Hosain Khan Moez al-Soltan (Sardar Mohyee) joined the moderate members.[4]

Sepahdar Tonekaboni's Cabinets

In 1909 Sephadar Tonekaboni became prime minister of Iran. Sardar Mansur served as Minister of Post and Telegraph in three of Sepahdar Tonekaboni's cabinets, then in the fourth cabinet, which came into being three weeks after the third one, on May 21, 1910, he was appointed Minister of Justice.

Sepahdar Tonekaboni's cabinets were not always unified. Therefore, it didn't take long for disagreements to arise among its members. In his second cabinet, Sani'e al-Dowleh, Vosuq al-Dowleh, and Moshir al-Dowleh were known as freedom-loving democrats and considered liberal, while Sardar Mansur and Ala al-Saltaneh, due to their past history as well as a suspected affiliation with Russia, were especially hated by the democrats and were eventually forced to resign.[5] The accusation regarding Sardar Mansur's affiliation with Russia was so strong that, as will be explained later, it even led to unfounded accusations of Russian citizenship.

Sardar Mansur's tenure in the Ministry of Post and Telegraph in three successive cabinets was plagued by various issues, which in one case dating to his previous tenure as Minister of Post and Telegraph during the time of Mohammad Ali Shah, strengthened the suspicion of his abuse of power.

---

4. Dolatabadi, 1361[SH], vol. 3: 120–30.

5. Ettehadie, 1381[SH]: 371.

Mohammad Vali Khan Tonekaboni, Sepahdar Tonekaboni.

This particular case concerned a German businessman, Monsieur Haneke, who lived in Shiraz and did business there and whose goods were apparently stolen while in transit. The German embassy complained to the Ministry of Foreign Affairs of Iran and stated that damages should be claimed from Sardar Mansur.[6] As the senior official of the Ministry of Post and Telegraph, he was in fact responsible for paying compensation. Iran's foreign ministry also told the German embassy that it was pursuing compensation from Sardar Mansur and that he would pay it.[7]

At the same time, it was announced to the foreign ministry via the British embassy that Sardar Mansur, as the Minister of Post and Telegraph, had taken out a loan of 50,000 tomans guaranteed by Sepahdar Tonekaboni from the Imperial Bank and that he had not been paying the installments. The British embassy considered the loan to be a debt of the Ministry of Post and Telegraph, and thus the Iranian government was responsible for paying it.[8]

In reply to the British embassy, Iran's Ministry of Interior declared that the loan was personal and had nothing to do with the telegraph office.[9] The foreign ministry conveyed the same message to the British embassy, stating that repayment of the loan should be demanded from Sardar Mansur himself and that the Iranian government was not responsible for it.[10]

In response to the foreign ministry, the British embassy submitted all the documents relating to the loan proving that Sardar Mansur had been given the loan as a legal entity and therefore the Iranian government was responsible for paying it.[11] The foreign minister of Iran, Ala Al-Saltaneh, sent all the documents to the British chancellor.[12] The Telegraph Office also confirmed the receipt of 50,000 tomans by Sardar Mansur from the Imperial Bank and

6. DCIFM, no. GH1326-K38-P8-72.

7. DCIFM, no. GH1326-K38-P8-3.

8. DCIFM, no. GH1326-K33-P17-8.

9. DCIFM, no. GH1326-K33-P17-6.

10. DCIFM, no. GH1326-K33-P17-4.

11. DCIFM, no. GH1326-K33-P17-7.

12. DCIFM, no. GH1326-K33-P17-9.

the commitment to pay seven thousand tomans monthly from the telegraph office's revenues.[13]

This conflict continued for almost a year, until finally, the Iranian foreign ministry announced to the British embassy that the Ministry of Finance had been ordered to pay off the loan in installments.[14]

Despite the fact that a significant number of documents relating to this dispute, including correspondence between the Iranian ministries of Foreign Affairs, Finance and Post and Telegraph, are available, it is not known what the loan had been used for, both now and at the time, and as a result, suspicion regarding personal misuse of the loan by Sardar Mansur remains strong. Among the documents there is a letter from the Ministry of Foreign Affairs to the Ministry of Finance, which states that Mokhber al-Dowleh announced that the received loan was personal and the Telegraph Office had no responsibility for it.[15]

However, given that Mokhber al-Dowleh had replaced Sardar Mansur as the Minister of Post and Telegraph (prior to the bombing of the Majles) and as there was hostility and political confrontation between them, one cannot trust the impartiality of his statement. Since Monsieur Haneke did not file any further complaints against Sardar Mansur, it is possible that the loan in question was used to pay off the German businessman.

Russian Citizenship Rumors

One of the truly disturbing accusations against Sardar Mansur at this time were rumors that he had obtained Russian citizenship, as claimed by the *Esteghlal* daily newspaper. The issue was discussed in the Majles, but it was not taken seriously because of its inaccuracy.

13. DCIFM, no. GH1326-K33-P17-1.

14. DCIFM, no. GH1327-K40-P9-13.

15. DCIFM, no. GH1327-K40-P9-4.

As a result, Iran's Minister of Foreign Affairs sent the following letter, which was published in the October 17, 1910 issue of the *Esteghlal* newspaper:

> From the Minister of Foreign Affairs
> The *Esteghlal* daily newspaper has claimed in one of its issues that Mr. Sardar Mansur has acquired Russian citizenship and that he along with several Cossacks had been sent to Rasht by the Russian legation.
>
> It is hereby noted that, in response to my questioning the Russian minister plenipotentiary has stated that Sardar Mansur has never acquired Russian citizenship, nor has he even requested it. In response to my question about him being escorted by the Russian legation-appointed Cossacks, the minister plenipotentiary said that the legation had never appointed any escorts. It has only been a coincidence between Mr. Sardar Mansur's departure for Rasht and the legation logisticians taking diplomatic papers. Therefore, Sardar Mansur and the legation's logistician had departed together from Tehran.
>
> In order to remove any misunderstanding, you are requested to publish this note so that our dear countrymen would know that Sardar Mansur has never thought of changing his nationality and he has always been a national of the Government of Iran.

The *Esteghlal* newspaper, which had initially spread the rumor about Sardar Mansur, added the following note of apology after the letter:

> We did not write with certainty that Sardar Mansur is a citizen of Russia. What we meant was that he had departed along with the Russian legation's logistician. Now that the Russian

> legation has officially denied [the rumor about] Mr. Sardar Mansur's Russian citizenship, we offer our apologies.[16]

The foreign ministry's letter was also printed in the Majles' journal two days later.[17]

At the same time, as attested by archive documents in Iran's Ministry of Foreign Affairs, there is no doubt that Sardar Mansur had the support of the tsarist Russian state, including its embassy in Tehran and consulates in Rasht and Anzali.[18] Many other dignitaries of that era, including some radical constitutionalists like Seyyed Hasan Taghizadeh, whose patriotism and opposition to the excessive interference and meddling in Iran by Russia and Britain cannot be doubted, also had the support of the British government, and this is clearly evident in the account of the bombing of the first Majles and constitutionalists seeking refuge in the British legation.

During that era, reliance on foreign embassies was common in Iran's political environment. Even when the Constitutional Revolution entered its final stages in the form of a sit-in by the constitutionalists, this occurred at the British legation. But what *Esteghlal* had accused Sardar Mansur of was, in fact, surrendering to a foreign government, which explicitly implied treason and harming the national interest, rather than the usual relations between politicians and foreign embassies at that period.

It is an important distinction because Sardar Mansur's dependence on foreign nations, especially Britain, continued to be remarked upon throughout his political career. Even when he became prime minister,

---

16. Clipping from the *Esteghlal* newspaper, Shawwal 12, 1328[AH], in: DCIFM, no. GH1327-K25-P14-4.

17. Clipping from the Majles' journal, Shawwal 14, 1328[AH], in: DCIFM, no. GH1327-K25-P14-5.

18. For example, according to document no. GH1326-K25-P14-1.1, the Russian embassy had ordered the Russian consulate in Anzali to protect Sardar Mansur's properties and the wellbeing of his relatives and trustees (named as Moez al-Soltan, Mirza Karim Khan, Naser al-Islam, Ebtehaj al-Molk, Saeed al-Molk, Mobasser al-Molk, and Moin al-Mamalek). See also: GH1326-K25-P14-1.

many of the nationalist politicians presented him as the puppet of British policies and his cabinet as one that could pave the way for the implementation of the 1919 Anglo-Persian Agreement, though there is no evidence for this, as will be shown. While Sardar Mansur may have taken advantage of his position at various points during his political career, he was not a traitor to his country. Even when the conflict over the 1919 Anglo-Persian Agreement was at its peak and many of the popular nationalist elite were unwilling to accept the post of prime minister, he selflessly accepted the role and, despite being under British protection, he avoided the implementation of the 1919 Agreement in whatever way he could. Leaving aside the fact that if he was really under the protection of Russia, naturally, the Russian embassy officials should have prevented Mohammad Ali Shah from arresting him in the days leading up to the bombing of the Majles, which we know that they did not, and Sardar Mansur was humiliatingly arrested and exiled. Whatever his relations with Russia, according to Taghizadeh, they were not comparable to those of Sepahdar Tonekaboni. While the latter was commander of the constitutionalists at the time of the Triumph of Tehran, "he was very dependent upon the Russians and leaned towards them."[19]

Chaos

On July 21, 1910, two months after setting up his fourth cabinet, Sepahdar Tonekaboni stepped down as prime minster owing to differences with the Bakhtiari tribe. Three days later, Mirza Hasan Khan Mostofi al-Mamalek became prime minister, but he stepped down the following year, on March 9, 1911, upon the death of the regent, Ali Reza Khan Azod al-Molk, and the subsequent regency of Abol Qasem Khan Naser al-Molk. On March 10, 1911, Sepahdar Tonekaboni was again appointed as prime minister. He nominated a new cabinet on May 24, 1911, before a reshuffle on July 19, 1911. Sardar Mansur held no posts in these new cabinets.

---

19. Taghizadeh, 1391[SH]: 122.

These events coincided with the deposed Mohammad Ali Shah and his brother Malek Mansur Mirza Shoa al-Saltaneh attempting to regain the throne with the help of Bakhtiari tribesmen. In addition, their brother, Abol Fath Mirza Salar al-Dowleh was trying to help the former shah through his own efforts in western Iran. After only two months in office, Sepahdar Tonekaboni was dismissed and Najafgholi Khan Samsam al-Saltaneh Bakhtiari became prime minister, in the hope that his good standing with the Bakhtiari tribe could help thwart the power grab by the deposed Shah. Most of the focus of the new cabinet, until it ended in January 1912, was devoted to countering the attacks of the deposed Shah and his allies.[20]

Quite apart from the internal chaos caused by Mohammad Ali Shah's attempt to regain the throne, the country's financial situation was chaotic and disorderly in its own right, and the government also had a budget deficit, which was a chronic problem and not just during this period.

To address this issue, both the government and the Majles sought to hire financial advisers and obtain loans from governments other than Russia and Britain, who naturally resisted such efforts. After much debate and consultations, the government, with the approval of the Majles, decided to employ the American lawyer and financial adviser William Morgan Shuster and place him at the head of the country's financial affairs. Thus, Shuster came to Iran with his family and a small group of colleagues, though, from the very beginning, he faced opposition from both the Russian and British governments.[21]

Among Britain's objections were its opposition to the employment of the Englishman Major Stokes by Shuster. Owing to their mutual interests in Iran, the British government had in fact agreed with the tsarist Russian government to evoke the Anglo-Russian Convention of 1907, based on which the employment of Stokes was considered to be a violation of its terms and British relations with Russia.

---

20. See Floor, 2018.

21. See Shuster, 1912.

Russian opposition to Shuster came to a head after Shuster announced the confiscation of the properties of Shoa al-Saltaneh, the brother of the deposed Mohammad Ali Shah who was at the time fighting government troops to regain the throne. In response, the Russian government sent troops to Iran and issued an ultimatum to the Iranian government that if Shuster was not expelled from Iran, and if the government hired any foreign advisers without first obtaining Russia's consent, Tehran would be occupied by Russian forces.

The condition of the Russian government to obtain their approval before hiring any foreign consultant was accepted by the Iranian government and the foreign minister, Mirza Hasan Khan Vosuq al-Dowleh, drafted a bill to be presented to the Majles. Politician Mehdi Gholi Khan Mokhber al-Saltaneh Hedayat writes about this bill in his memoirs:

> The problem lies in the second article, which denies the right to request a foreign adviser, except with the approval of the [Russian and British] ambassadors. In this article, there was more discussion and it was decided that the government will take into account the hiring of advisers so that it did not contradict the friendly relations with the governments [of Russia and England].[22]

Russia's ultimatum to Iran, and this decision by the Iranian government, caused a fierce confrontation between the Majles and the government. While the government accepted the ultimatum without hesitation, the Majles, led by the democratic minority, was strongly opposed to it. Finally, as Russia's threats intensified, the regent, Naser al-Molk, ordered the dissolution of the second Majles. He had very bad relations with the democrats and said, according to Taghizadeh, "that all sedition in the world comes from the Bakhtiari and democrats."[23]

---

22. Hedayat, 1363^{SH}: 241.

23. Taghizadeh, 1390^{SH}: 149. Shuster himself gave a full description of the events in his book *The Strangling of Persia*, 1912.

Sepahdar standing third from left in middle row at diplomatic reception, Tehran, 1916.

Third National Consultative Assembly

After a three-year interregnum following the tsarist Russian invasion, Ahmad Shah Qajar attained his maturity and officially became the monarch. His coronation was held on July 22, 1914. However, only six days after his coronation, World War I began, and despite the Iran government's declaration of neutrality, the warring parties began encroaching upon Iranian territory. Southern, western, and northern Iran were invaded by British, Ottoman, German, and Russian forces. The third National Consultative Assembly was inaugurated under such conditions on December 5, 1914, by Ahmad Shah in the presence of sixty-eight representatives. Fathollah Khan Sardar Mansur was one of the six representatives from Gilan.

Minister in Successive Cabinets

After Mostofi al-Mamalek's cabinet collapsed on March 12, 1915, owing to the onset of World War I, Mirza Hasan Khan Moshir al-Dowleh was assigned the task of forming a cabinet, but his cabinet also had collapsed by May. Then Abdol-Majid Mirza Ayn al-Dowleh,

Abdol-Majid Mirza Ayn al-Dowleh

the dictatorship-era grand vizier, was appointed as prime minister. On May 5, 1915, Ayn al-Dowleh nominated his cabinet to the Shah and appointed Fathollah Khan Sardar Mansur as Minister of Justice.

Sardar Mansur gave up his Majles seat to join the cabinet, but this cabinet was also short-lived and collapsed after two months. During this two-month period, Iran was the scene of a political tug-of-war between Russia and Britain on one side, and Germany and the Ottomans on the other. The Ottomans were active in western

Abdol-Hosain Mirza Farmanfarma

and northwestern Iran, while Russian troops were advancing on Tehran from Gilan.

Because of the advancing foreign forces, Ayn al-Dowleh was set aside, only to be succeeded in July 1915 by Mirza Hasan Khan Mostofi al-Mamalek, who had been prime minister before. In the face of Russian and British troops advancing into Iran, national resistance emerged across the country. With the consent and encouragement of Mostofi al-Mamalek and other freedom fighters in Tehran, Mirza

Kouchek Khan Rashti established the armed Jangali Movement in Gilan in order to counter Russian troops.

Sardar Mansur in October 1915, was elected representative of Anzali, Ghaziyan, Chahar Farizeh, Toulom, and the surrounding areas in Gilan.

Encouraged by the prime minister, a large number of representatives of the third National Consultative Assembly, including three from Gilan, migrated to Qom and Isfahan to be able to govern far away from the advancing foreign troops. Mostofi al-Mamalek stepped down five months later and was replaced on December 23, 1915, by Abdol-Hosain Mirza Farmanfarma, whose cabinet included Fathollah Khan Sardar Mansur as Minister of Post and Telegraph.

However, Farmanfarma proved unable to run state affairs and stepped down on March 1, 1916, after forty days in office. Meantime, under pressure from Russian troops, National Defense Committee forces withdrew from Kashan, Kermanshah, and Ghasr-e Shirin. To bolster defenses in Fars province in the south, the British government established the South Persia Rifles (SPR), an Iranian military force recruited by and under the command of the British.

Receiving the Title Sepahdar A'zam

On March 4, 1916, Mohammad Vali Khan Tonekaboni was appointed prime minister once again, and promoted from "Sepahdar A'zam" (Great Commander) to "Sepahsalar A'zam" (Commander-in-Chief). Meanwhile, Fathollah Khan Sardar Mansur was awarded the title "Sepahdar A'zam" by the Shah. But in order to distinguish him from his predecessor, Sepahdar Tonekaboni, he was referred to as "Sepahdar Rashti."

On March 6, 1916, Sepahsalar Tonekaboni nominated his cabinet in which, once again, Fathollah Khan, now Sepahdar Rashti, was appointed Minister of Post and Telegram.

This era is known as one of the most fraught periods in the history of Iran. SPR forces, headed by Brigadier-General Percy Molesworth Sykes, commenced their military operations in the south, while

Russian forces, under the command of General Baratov, occupied large swathes of land in northern, western, and central Iran. Owing to the chaotic conditions, the government could not collect taxes to be spent on national development. Two weeks after forming his cabinet, the prime minister, Sepahsalar Tonekaboni, met with General Baratov and reviewed the Russian troops. In April 1916, under financial pressure, as well as pressure from the Russian and British governments, Sepahsalar Tonekaboni was forced to accept the occupiers' control of Iran's finances and military in return for an injection of 200,000 tomans per month. He also agreed to the establishment of an 11,000-strong military force under British command, as well as increasing the number of Russia-led Cossack troops.

At the same time, conflict between the Russians and the Iranian nationalists, who had formed a government in exile under the aegis of the Ottoman and German governments in western Iran, continued to grow in the Hamedan province. Finally, with the advance of Ottoman troops on Qazvin, Sepahsalar Tonekaboni was deposed as prime minister on August 12, 1916.

CHAPTER 4

VOSUQ AL-DOWLEH'S FIRST CABINET

Amid chaotic conditions, Ahmad Shah Qajar appointed Mirza Hasan Khan Vosuq al-Dowleh as prime minister. He nominated his cabinet on August 29, 1916, and chose Fathollah Khan Sepahdar A'zam Rashti, now known simply as Sepahdar, for the key portfolio of Minister of Interior Affairs. This cabinet dealt with many challenges, including a raging bread crisis, which Sepahdar played a major role in resolving.

The first action by Vosuq al-Dowleh was to try to end the British and Russian control of Iran's financial and military sectors. However, Iran remained a battlefield between Russian and British troops on one side, and Ottoman and German forces on the other.

Confronting the Jangali Movement

Vosuq al-Dowleh also moved to quell the Jangali Movement that posed a challenge to the central government. He first dispatched renowned liberal fighter Haj Agha Shirazi to Gilan to convince Mirza Kouchak Khan of the need to cooperate, but the latter rejected the prime minister's advances, accusing Vosuq al-Dowleh of being submissive to foreign governments. The fact is that Vosuq al-Dowleh's policy was a typical one of keeping close to the Russian and British governments in order to coordinate the operations of their respective governments in Iran with the central government. Vosuq al-Dowleh also tried to suppress the Jangali Movement with the help of Russian military forces. When in November 1916, Mohammad Ali Khan Mafakher al-Molk, the head of police and interim governor of Gilan deployed 300 troops to Fuman and Kasma, at the order of the Russian consulate, to fight the Jangali combatants, he was captured and murdered by them. That struck a heavy blow to the central government and further strengthened Vosuq al-Dowleh's resolve to suppress the Jangali Movement.

In February of the following year, a battalion comprising 100 soldiers from Tehran and 30 Taleshi[1] Cossacks went to fight the Jangali troops in Masal and Shanderman, but they were again defeated and had to withdraw. Yet the government remained determined to quash the Jangalis. Sepahdar, as the Minister of Interior Affairs, hoped that Russian troops would assist Iran in countering the Jangali Movement, as he expressed in a letter, dated March 6, 1917, to Haj Mafakher al-Dowleh Nabavi, the governor of Gilan:

> First, I would like to enquire about your health. Then, I have to confide in you. You must have heard about the commendable advance of Imperial Government troops on Iranian fronts, the withdrawal of Ottoman troops and the recapture of Hamedan and other cities occupied by the Ottomans. Also, the British troops' advance on Mesopotamia and the fall of Kout al-Amarah and Aziziya and the high possibility of the imminent fall of Baghdad to British troops.
>
> Therefore, with such encouraging developments, it would be unwise not to make arrangements to prevent the mischief and pillage in Gilan by a group of Jangali fighters, and not to quell them. I am surprised that despite the seriousness of the Russian consul about this issue, the affair has dragged on. If

1. A tribal group in a region of the same name in Gilan renowned for its fearless soldiers.

Mirza Kouchak Khan Jangali

300–400 Imperial Government troops may be deployed along with the Taleshis, I am certain that this plot will be terminated.

I think that we should not lose this opportunity but take this message to the [Russian] consul asking him to take immediate action and then inform me of the results.

> Truth be told, in my opinion it would be wrong to attack from the side of Khalkhal and its surroundings, because they are not familiar with the Gilan Jangalis. I fear that the Jangalis would make advances just as they did successfully during the late Mafakher al-Molk's engagement. In any case, please hold talks with His Excellency the [Russian] consul. It is likely that General Baratov will return this week. I am certain that, he too, will definitely share my view.
>
> Minister of Interior Affairs, Fathollah[2]

But Russian troops were not forthcoming and the efforts of Vosuq al-Dowleh and Sepahdar to suppress the Jangali Movement were unsuccessful.

Holding the Fourth Legislative Assembly

One of the urgent tasks of Vosuq al-Dowleh's first cabinet, for which Sepahdar was directly responsible, was to hold the election for the fourth term of the National Consultative Assembly. Following a decree issued on May 9, 1917, by Ahmad Shah to form a Majles, Sepahdar announced:

> Considering the decree issued by His Highness and the Prime Minister's desire to speed up the holding of the [National Consultative Assembly] election, it is announced to the public to proceed with the utmost haste and accuracy in the matter of the election to enjoy their national rights within the scope of the Election Law dated November 4, 1911. The monitoring association will be formed in Tehran on May 20, 1917, and in the states and provinces fifteen days after receiving the instruction and ballot papers.
>
> May 14, Fathollah, Minister of Interior Affairs[3]

---

2. Fakhraei. 1371[SH]: 162–3; Gilak, 1371[SH]: 42–3; *Jangal*, Sha'ban 26, 1335[AH].
3. Afshar (ed.), 1368[SH]: 51.

In Gilan, however, it appeared that Russian nationals and their troops had taken election measures of their own, which forced Sepahdar to cable the following message to Mafakher al-Dowleh, governor of Gilan, on April 25, 1917:

> To the Gilan Governor's Office
>
> According to reports received, some opportunists are organizing speeches and meetings in an attempt to mislead the public and have managed to incite local residents. These instigators pursue their own agenda, and they are doing this under the guise of populism. It had been announced in a cabled message from the Prime Minister that as long as the government has made no decision regarding elections and the inauguration of the National Consultative Assembly, such provocative measures, which are at odds with national order and interests should be strongly avoided. However, it is surprising that Your Excellency has remained passive in the face of these corrupt rioters. I must hereby reiterate that the government is consulting with esteemed politicians in the capital, who are trustees of the entire nation, and will make a decision which would be in the best interests of the country. Any decision would be communicated afterwards. Until the government finalizes its decision, do not hesitate to arrest, and transfer to Tehran, anyone holding such meetings in order to deliver provocative speeches. Any person violating this order should be arrested immediately and transferred to Tehran to face a harsh punishment. You are responsible in person for non-execution of the provisions set forth in this order.
>
> Fathollah, Minister of Interior Affairs[4]

Finally, two weeks later, Sepahdar ordered a general election for the fourth National Consultative Assembly to be held, though, due to the ongoing imbroglio, it took four years to hold the election.

---

4. *Jangal* daily newspaper, Tir 5, 1296[SH].

In fact, despite the government's efforts to hold an election, neither Vosuq al-Dowleh's first nor his second cabinet were successful, the main reason being the nationwide turmoil in the final months of the World War I: Jangali militants rioted in the north; the terrorist Punishment Committee (aimed at confronting politicians whom it regarded as traitors) assassinated officials in the capital; and, in the north and south, the virtual occupation of the country by Russian and British forces.

Vosuq al-Dowleh's first cabinet was dissolved on May 29, 1917 less than a year after it was formed. He was succeeded by four other prime ministers within the space of a single year. During this one year, various developments changed the political landscape across the globe. These included the collapse of the tsarist Russian state and the formation of a Bolshevik regime; the signing of the peace treaty between Russia and Germany; and the withdrawal from Iran of the Russian, Ottoman, and German troops. In Gilan, the Jangali Movement took all administrative affairs of the province into their own hands, and in January 1918, they nominated Amir Ashayer Khalkhali as interim governor.

As the global picture changed and Russia experienced upheavals of its own, only British troops remained in Iran, though the British government, because it had changed its international policies at the end of the World War I, as will be explained later on, wanted to remove its forces over time. Nonetheless, the British needed to send specialist personnel and equipment to oil wells in the northwestern Iranian Caucasus. To this end, in June 1918, British forces captured Gilan and pushed the Jangali militants back to Fuman. The British considered that the weakness of Iran's military and the danger posed by the newly established Bolshevik military threatened their interests, the latter being the main reason for Britain's delay in withdrawing its troops from Iran.

At the same time, Ottoman Pan-Turks,[5] hoping to expand their territory and establish an Islamic Turkic empire, penetrated Iran and

---

5. Pan-Turkism is the name given to the idea of uniting all Turkic-speaking

captured parts of Azerbaijan before heading towards the Caucasus. In view of this, Ahmad Shah Qajar reluctantly submitted to pressure from public opinion and dismissed Samsam al-Saltaneh as prime minister and, in response to demands from the clergy and reformists, reinstated Vosuq al-Dowleh as prime minister on July 18, 1918. In fact, following World War I, and with the fall of tsarist Russia, many high-ranking dignitaries and clerics believed that Vosuq al-Dowleh could restore the authority of the central government despite the various crises, both internal and external, besetting the country.[6] They also believed that Vosuq al-Dowleh's good relations with Britain would permit the government to enact the many urgent reform programs that the country needed. In general, with the removal of tsarist Russia from the political equation, the implementation of any reform program in the country was conditional upon establishing a secure and stable central government. Thus, the British played a pivotal role, and the Iranian government needed to accept this. Even the popular nationalist elite acknowledged this. When news spread about the possible resignation of Vosuq al-Dowleh and the name of Moshir al-Dowleh, known for his good relations with the British, was proposed again as a candidate for prime minister, Mohammad Ali Foroughi, who was abroad at the time as a member of the Iranian delegation to the Paris Peace Conference, wrote in his diary: "Moshir al-Dowleh may not accept [the proposed premiership] at all, but if there is a reason for him to accept it, it is to ensure British government assistance."[7]

In the end Moshir al-Dowleh did not become prime minister because Vosuq al-Dowleh did not resign.

---

peoples under the aegis of a greater Turkish state.

6. See, for example: Mostashar al-Dowleh, 1367^{SH}: 231.

7. Foroughi, 1396^{SH}: 414.

Mirza Hasan Khan Vosuq al-Dowleh

Vosuq al-Dowleh's Second Cabinet

Fathollah Khan Sepahdar A'zam, who was Minister of Interior Affairs in the first cabinet of Vosuq al-Dowleh, refused to accept this post in al-Dowleh's second cabinet. Seyyed Mohammad Kamarei,

Sir Percy Cox (*left*) and Sir Charles Marling.

a political commentator of the time, wrote an account of the events in September 1918. His notes indicate that there was a split between Iranian dignitaries in their support for British officials: Vosuq al-Dowleh, Moshar al-Molk, and several others supported Sir Charles Marling (a former British minister), while Sepahdar, Dr. Esma'il Khan Amin al-Molk Marzban, and Sardar Mohyee backed the British diplomats Richard Stokes and Sir Percy Cox (then ambassador). In a bid to encourage both groups to support the British diplomats, Vosuq al-Dowleh urged Sepahdar to serve as interior minister, but as the latter hoped to become prime minister himself, he turned down the position.[8]

One of the first actions taken by the second cabinet of Vosuq al-Dowleh was to prosecute members of the Punishment Committee terrorist group, who, under the slogan of fighting traitorous and collaborationist dignitaries, had assassinated various officials and inspired fear and insecurity in the capital. According to Emad al-Kottab, one

8. Kamarei, 1382[SH], vol. 1: 477–8.

of the leaders of the group, even Vosouq al-Dowleh was on its list of target assassinations.[9]

At the same time, World War I ended with Germany being defeated. Ottoman troops withdrew from Iran for the last time. That gave Vosuq al-Dowleh a chance to address the lack of security across the country. He launched a strong suppression of outlaws and highwaymen who had spread insecurity in central and western Iran.

Vosuq al-Dowleh's next plan was, once again, to attempt to suppress the Jangali Movement in Gilan. He had to compromise with the British in August 1918, ending the central government's control of northern Iran. In February 1919, he sent Seyyed Mohammad Tadayyon Birjandi to Mirza Kouchak Khan, together with influential clerics and residents of Gilan, to seek a negotiated settlement. But the Jangali militants kept accusing the government of being affiliated with Britain, and hence refused to cooperate.

Vosuq al-Dowleh then resorted to trickery and deception to try to sow discord among the movement leaders. He also secretly issued a guarantee of safe conduct for various fighters who had agreed to break away from the Jangali Movement, including Haj Ahmad Kasmaei. The guaranteed safe conduct, which was issued on February 26, 1919, had been mediated by Sepahdar, as indicated in this letter to a relative, Agha Sheikh Mahmud Kasmaei.

> His Excellency Agha Sheikh Mahmud Kasmaei
>
> Two notes from Your Excellency, attesting to non-opposition of Haj Ahmad Kasmaei and his relatives and associates to the government and agreement to government proposals in return for guarantee of safe conduct, were reviewed by Sepahdar A'zam. Given the fact that the government has always favored reforms and sought a peaceful settlement, it considers Your Excellency's

9. Emad al-Kottab, 1384^{SH}, 71; see also: Kamarei, 1382^{SH}, vol. 2: 98.

> remarks, thereby providing guarantee of safe conduct to Haj Ahmad and his brothers, relatives and associates.[10]

Baha al-Din Amlashi, a member of the Islamic Unity Committee, confirms Sepahdar Rashti's involvement in the issuance of the guarantee of safe conduct for Haj Ahmad Kasmaei. According to his memoirs, Haj Sheikh Mirza Ali Bahr al-Oloum, the son-in-law of Sepahdar, negotiated with him through one of Haj Ahmad Kasmaei's relatives (most likely Sheikh Mahmud Kasmaei), swearing on the Qur'an to guarantee his security. He also put his seal on a Qur'an and sent it to Haj Ahmad.[11]

Finally, Vosuq al-Dowleh decided to resort to strong-arm tactics to quash the Jangali Movement altogether. In April 1919, he appointed Abdol-Hosein Khan Sardar Moazzam (later known as Teymourtash—and Reza Shah's first Court Minister) to govern Gilan. He also gave full authority to Colonel Vsevolod Starosselsky, commander of the Iranian Cossack Brigade, to drive the Jangali Movement fighters out of Rasht. Many Jangali fighters were killed and the rest subsequently scattered to the eastern and western forests of Gilan. And the Jangali fighters who had surrendered in return for the guarantee of safe conduct were deceived by the government, including Haj Ahmad Kasmaei, who was arrested in a humiliating way, transferred to Tehran, and imprisoned.

Although Sepahdar was firmly opposed to the Jangali Movement, and had even proposed setting up a bounty for the capture of the Jangali leaders, he nonetheless criticized the government for its deceitful behavior. He was quoted as having told Naser al-Dowleh: "I feel ashamed and disgusted over the killing of Dr. Heshmat, a Jangali leader, imprisonment of Haj Ahmad Kasmaei, and arrest of Mashallah Khan [an infamous outlaw], because the government had promised them security, yet it reneged on its pledge of honor."[12] Not

---

10. Gilak, 1371^{SH}: 192–3.

11. See: Amlashi, 1352^{SH}: 277.

12. Kamarei, 1382^{SH}, vol. 2: 183–4.

content with simply voicing criticism, Sepahdar, along with Seyyed Hasan Modarres, managed to secure the release of Ahmad Kasmaei after he served six months in the Bagh-e Shah Prison,[13] even though Kasmaei was then promptly placed under house arrest.

The "Agreement" Cabinet

The failure to hold the election of the fourth Majles resulted in tensions precipitated by the 1919 Anglo-Persian Agreement. Iranian nationalists considered the agreement as effectively a colonization contract with Britain and its signatory, Vosuq al-Dowleh, and a symbol of Iran's dependence on a foreign country. According to the constitution, as with any other contract with foreign governments, the agreement had to be approved by the Majles. However, since the Majles was not in session, the agreement was also put on hold. Despite the widespread public opposition to it, none of the cabinets that came to power after the conclusion of the agreement—even the Supreme Advisory Council, consisting of high-ranking officials and clerics, which was set up by the order of Ahmad Shah during Sepahdar's first cabinet—could come to a definitive decision to reject it.

On August 7, 1919, Vosuq al-Dowleh reshuffled his cabinet to establish a third one, which was known as the "Agreement" Cabinet. Although he was a rival of Vosuq al-Dowleh and unhappy with the recent developments in Gilan, Sepahdar agreed to join the cabinet as the Minister of War, owing to the dire situation within the country.

At that critical juncture, Vosuq al-Dowleh, who had taken office under tough economic and security conditions on the one hand and who was close to British statesmen on the other, saw that the only way to revive the power of Iran's central government, gain funding for the military, and reform state affairs was to have the support of the British. Years later, in the eleventh session of the sixth National

---

13. Kasmaei, 1383^{SH}: 103.

"Agreement" Cabinet.
Front row from right to left: Mirza Hasan Khan Moshar al-Molk, Mahmud Khan Mohaseb al-Mamalek Ghaffari, Mirza Hasan Khan Vosuq al-Dowleh, Akbar Mirza Sarem al-Dowleh, Fathollah Khan Sepahdar A'zam, Ghassem Khan Sardar Homayoun, Firouz Mirza Nosrat al-Dowleh, Mirza Ahmad Khan Nasir al-Dowleh Badr.

Consultative Assembly (September 21, 1926), he defended his position when challenged about it by Dr. Mohammad Mosaddegh:

> The real genuine emergency demanded that either we surrender the country to events and run away from the battle, or we enter negotiations with the single center that we could rely on at that time [that is, Britain] and make an agreement. God willing, one day you will read about these issues in the works of political scholars. They will write books about it, and then you will judge cases of this kind with a clearer mind.

Of course, as mentioned earlier, this belief was not exclusive to Vosuq al-Dowleh. With the exception of idealistic and nationalist politicians such as Dr. Mosaddegh, other members of the elite, such as Foroughi, with their political pragmatism and awareness of the weakness of the country's economic and military base, also did not oppose having such relations with Western countries. The fact that some aspects of the 1919 Agreement could be objected to, or that the taking of bribes from British officials by Vosuq al-Dowleh was morally condemned, does not disguise the all-round weakness of the Iranian government and the inevitability of having to seek help from the West.

Therefore, with all this in mind, in August 1919, Vosuq al-Dowleh arranged for an agreement to be drawn up between the Iranian and British governments. Under the terms of this agreement, the British government agreed to respect the "independence and integrity of Persia," while pledging to provide it with as much financial aid as needed in return for controlling customs and other sources of revenue of the Iranian government. More interestingly, the agreement specified spending as follows:

- First, the British government promised to "supply, at the cost of the Persian government, the services of whatever expert advisers may, after consultation between the two governments, be considered necessary for several departments of the Persian administration."
- Second, it agreed "to supply, at the cost of the Persian government, such officers and such munitions and equipment of modern type as may be judged necessary by a joint commission of military experts, British and Persian, which shall assemble forthwith for the purpose of estimating the needs of Persia, in respect to the formation of a uniform force which the Persian government proposes to create for the establishment and preservation of order in the country and on its frontiers."
- Third, "the British government, fully recognizing the urgent need which exists for the improvement of communications in Persia, with a view both to the extension of trade and the prevention of famine, [promised] to be prepared to cooperate with the Persian government for the encouragement of

> Anglo-Persian enterprise in this direction, both by means of railway construction and other forms of transport; subject always to the examination of the problems by experts and to agreement between the two governments as to the particular prospects which may be most necessary, practical and profitable."

Financing the implementation of the provisions of the agreement was the responsibility of the Iranian government, and the repayment of the loans granted by the British government was to be determined from customs revenue and other possible revenues of the Iranian government.

In addition, in a letter from Sir Percy Cox, British Minister in Tehran, attached to the text of the agreement, it was stated that if the agreement was signed, the British government would revise the existing treaties between the governments, to compensate the economic losses and damage inflicted on Iran by the hostile governments, and to amend the border lines fairly and with the consent of both sides.[14]

On September 17, 1919, Vosuq al-Dowleh put the Anglo-Persian Agreement to the vote in the cabinet, where ministers duly endorsed the agreement, which would go into force subject to the approval of the National Consultative Assembly.[15]

It only later became known that the British government had paid Vosuq al-Dowleh (prime minister) 200,000 tomans, and Nosrat al-Dowleh (Minister of Foreign Affairs) and Sarem al-Dowleh (Minister of Finance) 100,000 tomans in cash each and granted them political asylum. Although part of these handouts was thought to have been spent on winning over other political figures and journalists in

---

14. For the text of the agreement and quoted letter attached to it, see: Makki, 1361^{SH}, vol. 1: 22–3.

15. Kamarei, 1382^{SH}, vol. 2: 1126 and 1190–91.

the country.[16] The alleged bribery associated with the 1919 Anglo-Persian Agreement was not proven at the time, and it was disclosed only after Sepahdar took over as prime minister.

Disclosing the content of the Anglo-Persian Agreement elicited a wave of opposition among politicians and ordinary people alike, in whose opinion the agreement effectively made Iran a British colony. This view was misguided, however. The British authorities, headed by Lord Curzon, the British foreign secretary and the main drafter of the agreement, did not seek to make Iran a protectorate, let alone colonize it. Through the agreement they sought to curb the influence of communism in Iran by bringing the Iranian government closer to the British government and, in this way, protect their interests in Iran and India. And this is what Lord Curzon himself stated. In the first meeting of the British cabinet in London after the signing of the agreement, as recounted by the historian Ahmad-Ali Sepehr (Movarekh al-Dowleh), Curzon addressed the members of the cabinet:

> We have not received a letter of support from Persia, and Persia has not given us any of its freedoms. We also have not made new and heavy onerous commitments that may cause us trouble in the future. The geographical situation of that country and the importance of our interests there and the future security of the east of the empire make it impossible for us to show ourselves disinterested in events in Persia. Now that we have the responsibility of supporting Mesopotamia and in this way we will form a border with Persia on the west side, we cannot allow an environment of disorder and provocations of enemies and financial disintegration and political turmoil to exist between the borders of India and the borders of the new protectorate [Iraq]. If we leave Persia alone, it is feared that

---

16. Among the people who have been named as bribe-takers are Moin al-Tojjar Boushehri and Haj Emam Jom'e Khoei. See: Kamarei, 1382[SH], vol. 2: 1126 and 1358. Ali-Akbar Dehkhoda also states that the government gave export licenses for food and shoes to Zein al-Abedin Rahnama, Seyyed Mohammad Tadayyon, Malek al-Sho'ara Bahar, Seyyed Zia al-Din Tabataba'i, Ali Dashti, and a businessman named Kasraei, in order to get them to agree to sign the agreement. They then sold the permits in the Tehran bazaars and earned several thousand tomans each. See: Parto, 1377[SH]: 91.

Ahmad-Ali Sepehr (Movarekh al-Dowleh)

the Bolshevik influence will lead to the conquest of the entire country. We have large oil fields in the southwest of Persia, which are exploited by the kingdom's [Britain's] navy.[17]

17. Sepehr, 1374^{SH}: 42.

As well as being a historian, Sepehr was a politician during this period and well into the middle of the Pahlavi era, and during World War I, he also served as the first secretary of the German imperial embassy in Tehran, one of Britain's enemies. As the chairman of the board of directors of the Iranian Fishery Organization in the first cabinet of Dr. Mosaddegh, he also played a major role in the nationalization of Iran's fisheries and in cutting off foreign companies from Iran's fisheries. Therefore, his objectivity as a commentator is difficult to assess in the quote above.

As we have seen, Curzon's purpose in concluding the agreement with Iran was to protect British interests in Iran, India, and Iraq by creating a barrier against Bolshevik influence. As he clearly stated in his report to the British cabinet, he did not seek to make Iran a British protectorate. In fact, if Iran was militarily strong during the Qajar era and could defend the security of its borders, especially from Bolshevik forces, there perhaps would have been no need to implement the 1919 Agreement in the first place.[18]

By contrast, and more importantly, as stated by Sir Denis Wright,[19] the British ambassador to Tehran from 1963 to 1971, the British government after the end of World War I appeared intent upon withdrawing its military forces from Iran as fast as possible for mainly economic reasons and under the pressure from the British public who were opposed to the Anglo-Persian Agreement. This new British policy required that Iran's security should be left to the Iranians themselves, fulfilling the ideal of seeking independence, which was one of the major demands of Iranian nationalists many years ago.

When the Iranian government hired Morgan Shuster in 1911 to take charge of Iranian finances, they thought that an American would be impartial, whereas a British or Russian national would be more likely to be under his government's influence. As we have

---

18. Sepehr, 1374^{SH}: 43.

19. Wright, 1977: ch. 12; see also: Sheikh al-Islami, 1392^{SH}: 179–84.

seen, however, the British and Russian governments were unhappy when Shuster's actions were somewhat successful, and forced him to leave Iran in 1912.

Curzon's proposal in 1918 was that the British government should help Iran create an orderly and well-integrated financial and military organization, which was not possible to achieve at that point without the help of foreign advisers and financing. According to Curzon's proposal, within the terms of the 1919 Agreement, a high-ranking British military officer and a senior British economic manager would be placed at the head of Iran's army and financial system, respectively.[20]

Many Iranian nationalists also sought to save the country by employing foreign advisers. But the fact that they did not want to carry out the urgent fundamental reforms with the cooperation of the British reflects their justifiable skepticism toward the British government, owing to its role in the not-so-distant past, especially the signing of the Anglo-Russian Convention of 1907, which violated Iran's national sovereignty by dividing Iran into northern and southern regions under the influence of Russia and Britain. Contrary to such perceptions, none of the provisions of the 1919 Agreement, viewed objectively, would have violated Iran's national sovereignty. However, there were many people who disagreed, including Seyyed Hasan Modarres, who maintained that:

> By signing this Agreement, the control of our money and troops will be taken from us and will fall into the hands of foreigners. If Iran is supposed to remain independent, then everything of Iran must belong to Iran and be in Iranian hands. But this Agreement made the alien a partner in two things: one in our money and the other in our military force.[21]

---

20. Sheikh al-Islami, 1392^{SH}: 167–178.

21. Sheikh al-Islami (trans. and ed.), 1365^{SH}: 302–3.

A letter from various Iranian dignitaries to the French ambassador to Tehran, while mocking the declaration of the British regarding the guarantee of Iran's independence, made the point that

> The independence that is guaranteed by someone else is not called independence, but it is called instability . . . If he [the British Foreign Minister] considers Persia to be independent, then why has the British government intervened in the affairs [of Persia] as a whole, during the past ten years, sometimes by Russia, sometimes jointly [with Russia], and recently alone?! [In Persia, which] of the prime ministers, which of the cabinet members, which of the governors at all levels [have been chosen without the intervention of the British government?!] Which general and minor work has happened in this country without the permission of the British embassy?! Is this the meaning of independence?![22]

Due to the prevalence of views of this kind, the capital became the scene of daily protests against the 1919 Agreement. Newspapers ran articles criticizing its provisions and the Iranian signatory of the Agreement, Vosuq al-Dowleh, was accused of conspiracy and treason.

In December 1919, Nosrat al-Dowleh, the foreign minister, informed Lord Curzon of Iran's demands regarding changes to Iran's borders, which Curzon did not accept. As a result, Vosuq al-Dowleh sent Curzon a telegram criticizing him for not respecting "the expectations of the Iranian nation," and for being indifferent to the spirit of the agreement. He also asked Curzon to support Iran's territorial demands at the Paris Peace Conference. Vosuq al-Dowleh emphasized to Curzon that the main problem of the Iranian government at the time was how to interpret the spirit of the agreement as well as ensuring its correct and unambiguous implementation by the British government. According to Vosuq al-Dowleh:

> If the main content of the agreement is consistent with Iranian authorities' understanding of it, Iranians can hope that the agreement will bring strength and power to Iran.

---

22. Haghani (ed.), 1379^{SH}: 237.

Front row, from right to left: Colonel Jan Mohammad Khan Amir Alaei, Gholam Ali Khan Aziz al-Soltan, Fathollah Khan Sepahdar A'zam, Crown Prince Mohammad Hasan Mirza Qajar, Hasan Khan Vosuq al-Dowleh, Maghrour Mirza Movassegh al-Dowleh, Akbar Mirza Sarem al-Dowleh, after Ahmad Shah's trip to Europe, *ca.* 1919 (Contemporary History Studies Center)

> But if the British government is reluctant to bear heavy costs for Iran and not even willing to provide effective moral support at the Paris Peace Conference to enable Iran to bring its legitimate claims and rights for approval by members of the Paris Peace Conference, then the spirit of the agreement has unfortunately been interpreted in only a very narrow sense, and such an interpretation on the part of the British authorities is completely contrary to the understanding that Iranian authorities have had of its concept, and which we also have forced upon the Iranian people hoping that they would accept this same understanding.[23]

23. For the full Persian text of Vosuq al-Dowleh's telegram to Lord Curzon, see:

The key point here is that Vosuq al-Dowleh's concern that the British government would not act in accordance with the spirit of the agreement—in the way that he understood it, does not reflect the attitude of a traitorous statesman. However, at the time, no one cared about such details and anti-British sentiment was running strong among Iranian nationalists, so even if these details had been revealed, it is unlikely to have had a calming effect on the antagonism toward the agreement and, by association, Vosuq al-Dowleh, and therefore protests were gaining momentum.

Amid all the political turmoil, Ahmad Shah travelled to Europe. In the absence of the Shah and the National Consultative Assembly, Vosuq al-Dowleh was the top decision-maker in the country. He declared martial law in September and set about banishing, imprisoning, and suppressing opponents. But public demonstrations did not subside and even the U.S. government, which was opposed to the 1919 Agreement, cut its food aid, the equivalent of 200,000 tomans a month, to Iran in protest.

Of course, opposition to the agreement was not limited to domestic opponents; the governments of France, U.S., and Russia and even some British statesmen and diplomats were also against it, as it would give Britain an unfair advantage in the region. The French and American embassies in Tehran communicated with the Iranian opponents to the agreement and encouraged them to intensify their opposition.[24] Even the American ambassador promised a group of Iranian opponents present at the American embassy that if the agreement was canceled, his government would provide any amount of financial aid requested by the Iranian government and would also send financial, military, and economic advisers to Iran.[25] On September 9, 1919, the American embassy in Tehran published a statement by the U.S. Department of State in response to an article in *Ra'ad*

Haghani (ed.), 1379[SH]: 285–90.

24. Kamarei, 1382[SH], vol. 2: 1062; Sepehr, 1374[SH]: 35–7.

25. See: Bahar, 1371[SH], vol. 1: 71.

newspaper (edited by Seyyed Zia al-Din Tabataba'i) criticizing U.S. policies toward Iran. In this statement—the first public statement by the U.S. about the 1919 Agreement—the agreement was blamed for the failure of the Iranian delegation at the Paris Peace Conference.[26] According to Lord Grey, the British ambassador to Washington, the reason for the Americans' opposition to the agreement was that they viewed it "as a conspiracy aimed at the practical annexation of Iran to the British Empire" and the government of Iran as "a creature of the will of the British."[27]

Charles Bonin, the French ambassador to Tehran, opposed the agreement so strongly that Sir Percy Cox asked Lord Curzon to ask the Paris authorities to recall Bonin from Tehran.[28] Prince Nosrat al-Dowleh Firouz, the foreign minister and the architect of the Anglo-Persian Agreement who was in Paris at that time, while expressing concern about France's stubborn resistance to the agreement, commented that the French press was "trying to humiliate the current government of Iran in the eyes of the world and present it as a government that has left the fate of Iran in the hands of Britain, despite the opposition of the nation."[29] The French government's opposition to the agreement was so strong that it was even said that French teachers living in Tehran were inciting their Iranian students to take action against the agreement.[30]

The opposition of the Bolshevik Russian authorities to the agreement was even stronger. They accused the Iranian authorities of selling their country to Britain by signing the agreement.[31] In fact, the Bolsheviks were concerned that Iran would become a British base through the agreement, which naturally threatened their own interests. Dependents and supporters of the overthrown tsarist regime,

---

26. See: Bahar, 1371[SH], vol. 1: 92–3.
27. See: Bahar, 1371[SH], vol. 1: 135.
28. Sheikh al-Islami (trans. and ed.), 1365[SH]: 39–40.
29. Sheikh al-Islami (trans. and ed.), 1365[SH]: 62.
30. Sheikh al-Islami (trans. and ed.), 1365[SH]: 90.
31. Sheikh al-Islami (trans. and ed.), 1365[SH]: 174–5.

including Colonel Starosselsky, the commander of the Cossack forces, were also among the opponents of the agreement.

But the most interesting point is that the first objections to the 1919 Agreement were expressed by the British themselves. In the press, the *Manchester Guardian*, which was oriented to the left of center, stated on August 17, 1919: "If another country had made such an agreement with Iran, it would undoubtedly be called a protectorate and would be considered a kind of guardianship." The liberal *Daily News* wrote sarcastically on September 11, 1919: "As long as this Agreement guarantees Iran's independence as stated in it, Iran's hand will not be open to any action." And the *Liverpool Post* in September 11 described the secrecy of the negotiations to conclude the agreement as unpleasant and suspicious.

When Lord Curzon took the initial draft of the agreement to the British cabinet for approval, he was opposed by Edwin Montague, Secretary of State for India, and Lord Viscount Chelmsford, Viceroy of India.[32] In fact, officials of the British Raj believed that the administration of Iran's affairs should be under their control, because Iran was a neighbor of India. Zoroastrian Parsee Sir Ardeshir Ji Reporter, who worked as an intelligence officer of the British Raj, declared in a report to the Viceroy of India that "the 1919 Agreement has no value and should be annulled and canceled as soon as possible as a victory for Iran."[33]

In view of the dire economic situation in Britain after World War I and the government's budget deficit, the British Treasury, which as a rule would have fulfilled the financial obligations of Britain in the agreement, including the granting of any loans, was not in favor of the agreement.[34]

The aforementioned Lord Grey, British ambassador to Washington, was himself a critic of the agreement. He believed that

---

32. See: Katouzian, 2000, ch. 5.

33. The testament of Ardeshir Reporter archived in the Institute for Iranian Contemporary Historical Studies, Tehran, 47305 to 47325.

34. See: Abadian, 1390^{SH}: 482.

Britain should involve the U.S. in Iran's affairs and that American advisers should be used in Iran. Criticizing Cox's policies in Iran, Grey wrote to Lord Curzon:

> The policy of Cox [British Minister in Tehran] is nothing but the establishment of a protectorate regime in Iran. When Russia regains its power, then England alone will have to defend Iran's independence, and this is a burden that I think is unfair to impose on the British people. The policy we want to implement in Iran will make all the big governments of the world pessimistic towards us.[35]

Among British officials, the most extreme opponents of the agreement were the members of the Eastern Committee of the War Cabinet of the British government, who basically believed that the British government should withdraw its military forces from Iran and leave Iran alone "to go to whatever hell it wants."[36] This duality and opposition among British statesmen is an important factor in understanding the context of the 1921 Seyyed Zia–Reza Khan coup d'état which will be discussed in the following chapters.

Sepahdar Resigns from the Agreement Cabinet

Amid tense public opposition in Iran to the 1919 Agreement, divisions emerged between Vosuq al-Dowleh and Sepahdar about its provisions and implementation. Vosuq al-Dowleh decided to resign and leave for Europe, but the Crown Prince, Mohammad Hasan Mirza, rejected his resignation, and Ahmad Shah, who was abroad, opposed it as well. In his talks with the Shah, Vosuq al-Dowleh said he could not remain in office, due to his disagreements with ministers Sepahdar and Sarem al-Dowleh. Finally, following arrangements between the Crown Prince and the British Minister in Tehran, Sepahdar and

35. Sheikh al-Islami (trans. and ed.), 1365[SH]: 171–2.

36. Great Britain, Imperial War Cabinet, Committee of Imperial Defence, 23/41, no. 20/5, p. 24.

Sarem al-Dowleh resigned on March 6, 1920. Sarem al-Dowleh was named governor of western Iran in order to be kept far from the capital, and Sepahdar was rumored to have been sent into exile in Europe.[37] According to Mohammad Ali Foroughi, writing in his diaries at the time, the reason for the resignation of Sepahdar and Sarem al-Dowleh from the cabinet is not known,[38] but Seyyed Zia al-Din Tabataba'i, the 1921 coup d'état plotter, revealed years later that Sepahdar A'zam Rashti had in fact opposed the 1919 Agreement: "The only thing to say about Sepahdar A'zam is that he was kind-hearted to the highest degree and honest to the point of purity. He was firmly opposed to the 1919 Agreement, pursuant to which the British were authorized to install advisers in government offices and control Iranian military forces."[39]

Brigadier General Shams al-Din Roshdieh, the son of Mirza Hasan Roshdieh Tabrizi, a high-ranking commander of Iran's gendarmerie and a teacher of the Madrasa Nezam (military academy) during the reign of Reza Shah, also commented on the reason for Sepahdar's resignation from the Agreement Cabinet:

> The first person strongly opposing the 130,000 pound sterling [bribe paid by the British government] issue and signing the Agreement was Sepahdar A'zam Rashti. Since no one took his opposition seriously, he stepped down as war minister, at which point Abbas Mirza Salar Lashkar, a son of Farmanfarma, succeeded him.[40]

At the same time, the Azerbaijan Democratic Party, led by Sheikh Mohammad Khiabani, occupied Tabriz in April 1920 and took control of all key offices and buildings. In defiance of the central government, they renamed Azerbaijan "Azadistan" (Freedom State).

---

37. Kamarei, 1382[SH], vol. 2: 1371–85.

38. Foroughi, 1396[SH]: 355.

39. Quoted in: Elahi, 1393[SH]: 31.

40. Roshdieh, 1362[SH]: 191–2.

Front row, from left to right: Khalou Qorban and Khalou Morad. Middle row from left to right: Pelayev, Abukov, Mirza Kouchak Khan, Kazhanov, Gaok. *Back row:* Babayev, Moztarzadeh, Esma'il Khan Jangali, Sadollah Darvish, Seyfollahzadeh, Karbalaei Hossein

To make matters worse, in the following months, Bolshevik troops entered Gilan and joined forces with Mirza Kouchak Khan and the Jangali Movement to drive out the governor and other representatives of the central government. Together they established the Socialist Soviet Republic of Gilan in Rasht. Despite claims by officials of the newly established Bolshevik government, such as Foreign Minister Georgy Chicherin, that they were "friends of Iran's independence" and would return "what Russia had previously taken from Iran by force and aggression" and "order the withdrawal of its forces from Iran,"[41] their actions proved the opposite. In fact, the occupation of

41. Foroughi, 1396[SH]: 398.

Gilan by the Bolshevik forces was typically the first manifestation of the imperialist policies of the communist Soviet Union and of the ComIntern in an independent country.[42] As a result of this aggressive move, a significant proportion of the residents of Gilan fled to Qazvin and Tehran, which caused a huge crisis for the Iranian government and the nation as a whole.[43] In his diaries, Mohammad Ali Foroughi comments on the crisis, quoting a telegram from Mansur al-Molk, a deputy official of the Iranian foreign ministry, in 1919:

> The Bolsheviks are very busy plotting and Chicherin's statements are completely false. They have sent their military forces to both Gilan and Astara. The various newscasts are broadcast from Tabriz. On the one hand, it is said that the residents there are resisting and have even changed the name of Azerbaijan to Azadistan. On the other hand, it is said that they will soon declare a republic. In short, the situation is very bad and whatever I think, there is no hope for the future, and I don't know how things will turn out.[44]

Despite this aggressive policy of the Bolshevik Soviets toward Iran, Ahmad Shah, in a meeting in Nice, France, in 1924 with Ali Asghar Rahimzadeh Safavi, the envoy of Seyyed Hasan Modarres, gave an explanation about the Gilan issue which indicates his and Sepahdar's efforts to achieve some kind of agreement and convergence with the Soviets:

> After the brutal capture of the Caucasus by the Soviets, British agents were expecting us to surrender to them, and many were fearful. I was sure that there would be calm after the storm. Sepahdar [Rashti] can testify that I sent a message through

---

42. The Communist International (ComIntern) was a Soviet-controlled international organization founded in 1917 that advocated for global communism.

43. For further discussion about this, see: Barzegar, 1377^{SH}: 34–41.

44. Foroughi, 1396^{SH}: 415.

> him to Mirza Kouchak Khan to send reliable representatives to the Caucasus to reconcile with the Russians, and to make them understand that the Iranian government was faced with terrible restrictions and that it had to appease the [British] government, whose forces had surrounded the country, until Russian troops arrived at the border. But unfortunately, the militants of the Jangali Movement went on a rampage and changed the nature of the reconciliation with the Russians.[45]

Since Sepahdar Rashti was accused of being an anglophile both at that time and later, these comments by Ahmad Shah, which indicate his and Sepahdar's actions to get closer to the Bolshevik Soviets, provide evidence to the contrary.

Given the strained relationship at the time between Sepahdar and Vosuq al-Dowleh, there was a suspicion that Sepahdar might have been involved in the events in Gilan and the occupation of the city by the Bolsheviks, with the intention of hurting Vosuq al-Dowleh and laying the groundwork for his downfall. It could also be that he was trying to weaken the British involvement by hurting Vosuq al-Dowleh. An entry in Foroughi's diary dated June 11, 1920 captures the nature of some of the speculation:

> Today, a telegram has arrived from Tehran stating that a republic has been established in Rasht, and Mirza Kouchak Khan is its chief commissioner, chancellor, and minister of war. Also, a Red Committee has been established and a telegram has been sent to Tehran regarding the abolition of the monarchy and the establishment of a parliamentary republic. It is known that the Bolsheviks brought Caucasians and corrupt people to Gilan and they want to disrupt the country through them. The situation is completely messed up. Apparently, Sepahdar is also involved.[46]

---

45. Rahimzadeh Safavi, 1362^{SH}: 124.

46. Foroughi, 1396^{SH}: 400.

Ahmad Shah Qajar

In fact, there were a number of unverified and contradictory suspicions of Sepahdar. The research shows that all of the conjecture about Sepahdar's involvement with the Russians are unsubstantiated and that Sepahdar's involvement in Gilan was at the request of Ahmad Shah who wanted to contain both Russian and British powers in Iran. As mentioned in the preface, Sepahdar did align with both the Russians and British but mainly for strategic purposes with the goal of securing Iran's best interests.

Moshir al-Dowleh, New Prime Minister

Upon Ahmad Shah's return from Europe, the Vosuq al-Dowleh cabinet was disbanded due to pressure from public opinion and opposition to the 1919 Agreement. In an attempt to stabilize the situation, Ahmad Shah, on June 28, 1920, appointed Mirza Hasan Khan Moshir al-Dowleh, an aristocrat and politician of some integrity who was considered to have support among the populace, as prime minister.

Moshir al-Dowleh's acceptance of the post was based on two conditions for the British, both of which were approved by Herman Norman, the new British Minister in Tehran who had just replaced Sir Percy Cox. The first condition was that ratification of the 1919 Agreement should be postponed until the Majles was operational, and the second that the monthly British financial aid of 350,000 tomans should continue to be paid to the Iranian government, especially the wages of the Cossacks. The response of Lord Curzon, conveyed via Norman, was that the Majles should start working as soon as possible, and that the agreement should be approved by the Majles within four months at the latest. Otherwise, British financial aid to Iran would be cut off. But Moshir al-Dowleh had no intention of ratifying the agreement, and he thus delayed the opening of the Majles by making various excuses, including having received complaints about fraud in some electoral constituencies, which would require holding new elections in those constituencies.[47] Curzon's four-month deadline expired; the Majles had still not opened and the agreement remained unratified.

Moshir al-Dowleh came to power while the country was in a state of chaos, as a result of which the government had no tax revenues to pay the salaries of civil servants and military staff. The National Consultative Assembly had been shut down and the fourth round of

47. See Moshir al-Dowleh's statement as prime minister in: Makki, 1361^{SH}, vol. 1: 34.

Mirza Hasan Khan Moshir al-Dowleh

legislative elections was in limbo. The only income the government had on a regular basis was the monthly amount paid by the British government, part of which was paid to the Cossacks as salaries. Russian Bolshevik forces were present in large swathes of Gilan, and British forces led by General William Edmund Ironside had been deployed in Qazvin, Zanjan, and as far away as the borders of Rasht. On top of this, Sheikh Mohammad Khiabani and the Azerbaijan Democratic Party had taken over Tabriz and its environs, and as of April 6, 1920, government offices were still under their control. Meanwhile in Rasht, the radicals had established the Socialist Soviet Republic of Gilan.

In a bid to quell the Khiabani riot, Moshir al-Dowleh appointed his finance minister, Haji Mokhber al-Saltaneh Hedayat, who was popular in Azerbaijan, as governor there. After taking office in Tabriz, Mokhber al-Saltaneh sought in vain to negotiate a settlement with the leaders of the uprising. Then, backed by Cossack forces, he finally cracked down on Sheikh Mohammad Khiabani and his allies, and on September 13, 1920, Khiabani was killed during skirmishes.[48]

Shortly afterwards, the Shah and Moshir al-Dowleh resolved to bring an end to the Bolshevik presence in Gilan, which was threatening the country's political system, with a multi-pronged approach. First, the prime minister sent Moshaver al-Mamalek Ansari to Moscow at the head of a delegation with full authority to dissuade the Russian authorities from supporting the Socialist Soviet Republic of Gilan. Then, he sent delegates to Mirza Kouchak Khan, demanding that he dissociate himself from the Bolsheviks. In fact, Mirza Kouchak had already left Rasht in protest of the Bolsheviks' radical and arbitrary acts and settled in Fuman. The Communists had nationalized the property of several top landowners, including Sepahdar and Princess Fakhr al-Dowleh. Subsequently, the government dispatched Cossack forces under the command of Colonel Starosselsky to drive the Bolsheviks out of Gilan. But due to the betrayal by their Russian commanders, led by Colonel Starosselsky,

---

48. Makki, 1361[SH], vol. 1: 40–54.

Colonel Starosselsky

the Cossacks were severely defeated by the Bolsheviks and forced to retreat to Qazvin. In his memoirs, Lieutenant General Ahmad Amir-Ahmadi—a senior Cossack commander, along with Reza Khan Mirpanj (the future Reza Shah)—clearly states, quoting Reza Khan, that the debacle was caused by the betrayal by the Russian Cossack officers, and specifically Colonel Starosselsky, alluding to a secret agreement between Starosselsky and the Bolshevik commanders to allow the Cossack forces to be defeated and thereby remove this obstacle that prevented the Bolsheviks' advancing toward Tehran.[49]

After the defeat and retreat of the Cossacks, whose salaries they paid, the British asked Moshir al-Dowleh to dismiss Starosselsky and other Russian commanders of the Cossack force and replace them with British officers. In a telegram to Lord Curzon, Norman stated that Starosselsky had become an incompetent commander in the eyes of the Iranians due to the defeat of the Cossack forces. Consequently, from Norman's point of view, and that of General Ironside, now would be the best moment to force the Iranian authorities to remove him. Norman emphasized that he and General Ironside believed that there would not be another opportunity to achieve this important goal. To this end, in a meeting with Moshir al-Dowleh in the presence of General Ironside, Norman announced that his government was no longer willing to pay for an army under the command of such a "corrupt and inconsiderate" individual and whom he wished to be

49. For a detailed description of the betrayal by the Russian officers and Colonel Starosselsky, see: Amir-Ahmadi, 1373[SH]: 145–57.

replaced by an English commander.[50] Moshir al-Dowleh resisted this request, however, knowing that it meant implicit acceptance of the 1919 Agreement. Instead, he tried to solve the problem of the Bolsheviks in Gilan diplomatically through negotiations with the Soviet government, which he had already initiated by sending Moshaver al-Mamalek Ansari, as Iran's special envoy, to Moscow. The Bolsheviks' takeover of Rasht once again after the defeat of the Cossack forces had caused the people to flee in fear for their lives. Thousands of people, from landowners and merchants to peasants, fled to the surrounding areas, as well as to Qazvin and Tehran.[51] Gregory Yeghikian, an Iranian-Armenian left-wing activist of that time, who personally witnessed events, described the exodus:

> All vehicles, such as horse-drawn carriages, carts and bicycles, were used to transport people, but the majority of the fugitives left the city on foot. Women and children, old and young, rich and poor, clerics and policemen walked in front of the Cossacks and went to Qazvin.[52]

The displaced Gilanis flooding Qazvin and Tehran added to the government's problems. Ghahreman Mirza Ayn al-Saltaneh, who was in Qazvin at the time, described the great influx of refugees from Rasht:

> Rashtis are arriving every day, about 8,000 people continue to be registered daily. Across Iran, no city was as rich as Rasht. All its people lived in revelry, while being overly generous and kind. Now the city is in ruins and broke. I went to a government office in Qazvin, where a large park was inundated with Rashti refugees.[53]

---

50. For more details, see: Sheikh al-Islami, 1392[SH]: 157–160.

51. See: Makki, 1361[SH], vol. 1: 186; Elahi, 1393[SH]: 155.

52. Yeghikian, 1363[SH]: 252.

53. Salour, 1378[SH], vol. 7: 5732.

In this critical situation, a rumor spread of an imminent attack by the Bolsheviks on Tehran. Finally, on October 25, 1920, under pressure from British authorities to dismiss Starosselsky from the Cossack command, Moshir al-Dawleh was forced to resign.[54]

54. Makki, 1361^{SH}, vol. 1: 67–95; Dolatabadi, 1361^{SH}, vol. 4: 182.

CHAPTER 5

PRIME MINISTER

After the resignation of Moshir al-Dowleh, in a bid to restore Britain's financial aid, which partly covered the expenses of the royal court and the salaries of courtiers, Ahmad Shah had to appoint a prime minister who would be acceptable to the British government, in addition to having a good understanding of domestic conditions and public opinion. He considered Mirza Ahmad Khan Qavam al-Saltaneh, Abdol-Hosein Mirza Farmanfarma, Fathollah Khan Sepahdar A'zam, and Shokrollah Khan Qavam al-Dowleh for the post. Finally, after lengthy deliberations, he chose Sepahdar as prime minister. Mirza Hasan Khan Mostofi al-Mamalek is said to have encouraged Sepahdar to accept the premiership so that the post would not be assigned to someone else,[1] and Seyyed Hasan Modarres was in favor of this too.[2] According to Abdollah Mostofi, a renowned bureaucrat of the Qajar era who was familiar with the political situation and interacted with politicians:

---

1. Kamarei, 1382^{SH}, vol. 2: 1634.

2. In response to those who were opposed to the Sepahdar's premiership, Modarres had said: "What have others done that this one cannot?" See: Mostofi, 1360^{SH}, vol. 3: 156–7.

> Some politicians in Tehran and the leaders of the social democrat minority (without whose consent no prime minister could be chosen) were not opposed to this appointment, because with Sepahdar in power they could achieve their objectives more easily and could even recommend their own friends for official posts, parliamentary seats, or other functions. Perhaps the proponents, particularly Modarres, believed that the prime minister being a native of Gilan would be able to convince insurgents in that province to give up on their rebellion and renounce Communism. Furthermore, Sepahdar would show more interest in ending the rebellion, in a bid to safeguard his own properties there. The qualifications of this candidate were established such that most circles did not have the slightest doubt about his competence.[3]

Of course, accepting recommendations based on how they might affect future appointments or dismissals was not limited to the appointment of Sepahdar and his cabinet. Furthermore, the idea that the social democrats accepted Sepahdar simply for his or their own personal benefit is wrong. Vosuq al-Dowleh also owned property in Gilan, while Sepahdar, serving as his Minister of Interior Affairs and Minister of War, had failed to counter the Jangali Movement. A more plausible reason why the social democrat accepted Sepahdar as prime minister was because they had no other option, and nobody else but Sepahdar was willing to accept the post and take on the administration of the country in its abysmal state.

Abdollah Mostofi, although not particularly fond of Sepahdar, gave this very even-handed account:

> Sepahdar Aʿzam does not need to accumulate wealth and is not involved in bribery, as senior officeholders often are. Furthermore, he is generous and, like other residents of Gilan, his home is open and he is hospitable, down to earth and

---

3. Mostofi, 1360^{SH}, vol. 3: 155.

> straightforward. As for education, he was from the provinces fifty or sixty years ago and did not have much formal learning. Thanks to his travels abroad, he is familiar with European customs. His appearance is always elegant and pleasing and representative of Iranians who have lived in Europe. As a result, he knows foreign leaders and has some familiarity with foreign politics. He has also managed to appear in diplomatic gatherings and he speaks some French. Needless to say, his lifestyle is entirely European, and he socializes within European circles in Tehran. Rarely is Sepahdar A'zam absent at embassy receptions. Of course, he also invites foreign diplomats in return. In the previous cabinets, because of his straightforward demeanor, he has served as minister of interior affairs, minister of war, and minister of post and telegraph. He has gained fame among Gilanis for being a free-thinking and tolerant man. Yet, in Tehran, he was known to be a simple, forthright man, whom courtiers therefore did not welcome.[4]

Most of the qualities attributed to Sepahdar by Abdollah Mostofi are corroborated by other sources. But as Mostofi notes, some criticism of Sepahdar, and false allegations against him, by royals and corrupt politicians in the capital stemmed from the fact that they could not tolerate a wealthy and influential Gilani in power, because that would imply that they themselves must be incompetent and not capable of holding high office.

In the end, despite provincial origins, Sepahdar was chosen as prime minister following Norman's direct recommendation to Ahmad Shah. Norman sent a telegram message below to Lord Curzon on October 26, 1920:

> Although the Shah was not influenced by my words, he noted that he was willing to cooperate with Britain to secure Persia's interests and he voiced readiness to accept my proposal. Of course, he demanded one day to reflect on it . . . The Shah also said the current cabinet would have to step down because of

---

4. Mostofi, 1360^{SH}, vol. 3: 155–6.

> the status quo and he asked me for guidance about appointing a new prime minister. I suggested Sepahdar A'zam, whom he accepted. I have to note that I had already investigated and was assured that Sepahdar was ready to implement my proposed policy. I have another meeting with the Shah tomorrow.[5]

Norman always exaggerated his knowledge of Iranian affairs and his level of influence with the Shah and other dignitaries, and Curzon was aware of this. Later events also indicate that he did not have a full understanding of Iranian politicians either,[6] while the British foreign ministry had a more detailed knowledge of Iran's political situation due to the presence of George Percy Churchill, who had served in Iran for many years during the Naseri and Mozaffari eras and knew Iran's leaders well and some of them intimately.[7] However, we know that Norman did not have a very favorable view of the 1919 Agreement and was in fact against it. For this reason, Seyyed Hasan Taghizadeh describes his appointment as the British Minister in Tehran instead of Cox as "Iran's happiness," because "he with all his power stopped the interventions of the Ministry of Foreign Affairs [i.e. the meddling of Britain in Iran's affairs] and removed Vosuq al-Dowleh."[8]

Premiership Decree

On October 27, 1920, Ahmad Shah issued the following decree for the premiership of Fathollah Khan Sepahdar A'zam Rashti:

---

5. Makki, 1357[SH]: 339.

6. Regarding the differences between Norman and Curzon on issues relating to Iran, see: Sheikh al-Islami, 1392[SH]: 504–8.

7. George Percy Churchill (1877–1973) was Oriental Secretary at the British legation in Tehran from 1903 to 1919. He could read and write Persian, and translated *The Constitution Granted to Persia, 30 December 1906*. In 1906 he wrote *Biographical Notices of Persian Statesmen and Notables*.

8. Herman Cameron Norman (1872–1955) was part of the British delegation at the Paris Peace Conference and served as the British Minister in Tehran from May 1920 to October 1921; Taghizadeh, 1391[SH]: 171.

Fathollah Khan Sepahdar A'zam Rashti during his time as prime minister.

> Given the complete trust we place in His Excellency Sepahdar A'zam's competence and dedication to service, His Excellency is hereby appointed as prime minister."[9]

9. Manuscript of decree, Mr. Manouchehr Akbar's personal archive.

Sepahdar had already served in many governments, including his stint in the anglophile Vosuq al-Dowleh cabinet. Seyyed Yahya Dolatabadi, who knew Sepahdar, gives this frank assessment of Sepahdar's capabilities.

> Sepahdar A'zam Fathollah Khan Gilani is patriotic and a man of good deeds. However, he lacks the statesmanship that's needed these days for running a country with all these interior and exterior obstacles. Furthermore, he is very accommodating toward foreigners. Due to his generosity, Sepahdar has won fame politically among the elite, but since much of his property was pillaged in Gilan, he has lost this ability. And, perhaps, it is this lack of capital that has given him the courage to accept such a heavy responsibility. The new head of government has to yield to British demands, because every decision needs money, which the Imperial Bank can pay only with permission from the British legation.[10]

On the day he was appointed prime minister, Sepahdar went to Norman to discuss the composition of the cabinet. The following day, October 28, 1920, in a telegram marked as extremely urgent, Norman cabled a brief account of their exchanges to Curzon.

> Sepahdar came to me yesterday and explained how he would form his Cabinet. The new cabinet faces a budget deficit of 1.5 million tomans, 1 million tomans of which would be covered by the Anglo-Persian Oil Company's debts to the Imperial Bank of Persia. Sepahdar says the back wages of gendarmerie staff, civil servants and courtiers should be partly paid. The government's current expenses for up to the end of November should be provided to him. Sepahdar also states that the monthly 300,000 toman aid

10. Dolatabadi, 1361^{SH}, vol. 4: 180.

> should be paid for at least one or two months and that the government be provided with stipends for Cossack forces.[11]

In another part of his report, Norman writes:

> Sepahdar tells me that the approach of the previous cabinet [of Moshir al-Dowleh] to the [1919] Agreement has made the task of the current cabinet extremely difficult; so that before the Agreement is endorsed by [the] Majles, he and his colleagues are not able to accept any financial aid from the British government, because that would elicit public fury, especially because the government has now dismissed the Russian officers and plans to replace them with British officers. By doing this, [the cabinet] is implementing the plan that the previous government refused to execute, and hence eventually collapsed.[12]

In fact, Sepahdar was willing to follow in the footsteps of Moshir al-Dowleh, but in his own way. In a bid to allay the financial pressure, he was shrewdly seeking to secure necessary funding from the British government under the 1919 Agreement, in which 6 million tomans had been proposed before deducting Iran's debts, once the agreement had been approved by the National Consultative Assembly, which he knew would never happen. But unlike Norman, Curzon was not deceived. In a telegram of November 5 in response to Norman's, he heaps scorn on the latter for his capitulation to Sepahdar's cabinet:

> None of the recent developments—the departure of Moshir al-Dowleh and the arrival of Sepahdar—has caused any fundamental change to our Iran policy. If you remember, five months ago, i.e., since June, we insisted on the formation of the National Consultative Assembly, so that the Moshir al-Dowleh cabinet would submit the

---

11. Makki, 1357[SH]: 341.

12. Sheikh al-Islami, 1392[SH]: 521.

> Anglo-Persian Agreement for approval within a four-month deadline. On the same date, we made it clear that after the expiry of the deadline, we will no longer pay a penny to the Government of Persia. Relying on your assurances that the election process has begun, unfortunately we see that nothing has happened now. Aside from its reasons, we see that all this has been intentional. The British government will by no means accept the current situation, which would be political deviation. Therefore, we insist that the National Assembly be formed within one month of receipt of this telegram in order to decide about the Agreement by the end of the year [1920]. Should the Government of Persia refuse to accept this condition, or prolong its fulfilment, it would have to accept the consequences of its behaviour which have already been explained in previous months.[13]

Curzon notes in his message that Iran's financial situation was not as critical as described by Sepahdar, because 350,000 pounds sterling had recently been paid by the Anglo-Persian Oil Company (APOC) and that Armitage Smith, the financial adviser to the Iranian government, was trying to assess Iran's liabilities. Furthermore, Sepahdar could take the 2 million pound sterling loan envisaged in the agreement, which the previous cabinet had ignored. But since British officers had replaced Russian officers in the Cossack Division, Britain would pay for the upkeep of the division.

Armitage Smith

But Sepahdar, despite all the problems he faced, did what his predecessor had done and ignored

13. Sheikh al-Islami, 1392^{SH}: 521–2.

the offer of the 2 million pound sterling loan, because it would have meant implementation of the 1919 Agreement, even before it had been approved. That would also have violated the constitution, which would have triggered unrest and chaos across the country.

Colonel Starosselsky Fired

On October 28, 1920, Colonel Starosselsky was received by Ahmad Shah in Tehran and tendered his resignation.[14] However, the following day, October 29, Starosselsky, along with the chargé d'affaires of the tsarist Russian government in Tehran, met with Sepahdar to protest against the seizure of buildings, arms, ammunition, and other property of the Cossack Division that belonged to the Russian Empire.[15] The *Ra'ad* daily newspaper gave the following account of this meeting:

> Colonel Starosselsky has protested about the decision of the government and His Majesty to dismiss Russian officers, saying the Russians' presidency of the Cossack division was a privilege given to the Russian government by Naser al-Din Shah. Given the fact that the Cossacks look after Russian interests in Iran, dismissal of Russian officers violates the Iranian Government's commitments to the former Russian government. [16]

Finally, with the intervention of the British legation and upon the order of Ahmad Shah, the Russian officers were expelled from Iran, and Ali Khan Vali Sardar Homayoun was appointed the same day by Sepahdar to command the Cossack Division. The decree issued for the new commander reads as follows:[17]

---

14. Makki, 1361^{SH}: 96-99; Mostofi, 1360^{SH}, vol. 3: 176–7.

15. Makki, 1357^{SH}: 342.

16. *Ra'ad* daily newspaper, Aban 9, 1299^{SH}, quoted in: Sheikh al-Islami, 1392^{SH}: 513–14.

17. Makki, 1357^{SH}: 342.

Ali Khan Sardar Homayoun

His Excellency Sardar Homayoun

Pursuant to His Majesty's order, Your Excellency has been chosen to command the Cossack Division. The Ministry of War has been ordered to delegate

> authority over the Cossack Division to Your Excellency to start fulfilling the duties assigned thereto.[18]

Prime Minister's Statement

Given Sepahdar's experience of serving in the cabinet of Vosuq al-Dowleh, opponents of the 1919 Agreement worried that it could be implemented under the new prime minister. Fearing this, merchants closed their shops in the Grand Bazaar in Tehran and staged protests. In response, Sepahdar, on October 30, 1920, released a statement, calling for cooperation:

> Political upheavals and economic crises have torn the country apart and caused serious disruption to both commercial and administrative affairs, spread disorder, and presented an alarming image of the nation. Various groups have conspired to cause chaos and pillage in the beautiful areas of northern Iran and have spread lawlessness. Gilan law enforcement forces have failed to fulfill their duty out of negligence and following the opportunistic views of some Russian officers, thereby giving rise to tragic political and social developments, consequences which have caused irreparable damage to the country. The former cabinet stepped down, leaving peasants, craftsmen and farmlands unprotected and abandoned the Constitution, leaving it to its own fate. Under such circumstances, the public task of serving this nation has been assigned to me, chosen by His Majesty from among other candidates. Although, due to illness and the necessity of making foreign trips for medical treatment, I initially declined to assume such a difficult and onerous responsibility, His Majesty refused to accept my request, and finally, following orders from His Majesty, I saw no option but to agree to shoulder this responsibility as it would otherwise have been unfair not to accept it. After trusting in God and His immaculate servants, only my own self-

---

18. Haghani (ed.), 1379^{SH}: 245–6.

> confidence and the assistance of genuine patriots, as well as the population as a whole would be of help to me. . . I hope that I will be able to conquer hearts and minds, to unite the entire nation in order to implement reforms . . . Over recent days, unfounded rumors have been swirling about government decisions. I would like to make it clear that no decision has yet been adopted by the government in terms of internal and external policies. Regarding the Anglo-Persian Agreement, we have been following in the footsteps of the previous cabinet. No action would be undertaken prior to submission to the National Consultative Assembly. After the formation of the Cabinet, the government will officially release its manifesto to present its policies. Following His Majesty's orders, government troops, currently defending the country, have executed some plans, only to prevent concerns. The plans include the dismissal of the Russian commander of the Cossack Division and appointment of an Iranian commander.[19]
>
> Fathollah Sepahdar-e Aʿzam, Prime Minister

Three key points can be taken from this statement:

1. The government needed the assistance and cooperation of politicians and the people to function properly and make progress.
2. Without the approval of the National Consultative Assembly, the government would not implement the 1919 Agreement, which was a clear message to the British government and also aimed at assuring people.
3. While the government dismissed the Russian commanders of the Cossack Division to appease the British government, it appointed Iranian and not British officers in their stead.

19. *Ra'ad*, Safar 19, 1339[AH]; see also: Makki, 1361[SH]: 99–110.

On October 31, 1920, the Grand Bazaar in Tehran was still closed, with some protests being made against foreign interference, the resignation of Moshir al-Dowleh, and the appointment of Sepahdar. A number of protesters were arrested in front of the Friday Mosque and taken to police stations. A group of students of the School of Politics gathered at Sepahsalar School before going to the residence of Seyyed Hasan Modarres, and finally heading toward Nasirieh Street to protest. Law enforcement forces ordered the protesters to disperse at the Telegraph Office but they defied the order. Police officers scuffled with the protesters, beating some of them with their guns, and taking some of them to the police station. A number of officers were also injured after being pelted with stones.[20]

The same day, Qasem Khan Vali, who was in Qazvin, sent a report to the prime minister to inform him of what was under way. He noted in his report that two tsarist Russian officials addressed the Cossacks, inciting them to disobey orders. Vali called for their arrest. He also cabled the following message:

> His Excellency the Prime Minister
>
> The payment of salaries of the Cossacks has been delayed, which is likely to have unfavorable repercussions. It is hereby requested that at least 100,000 tomans be immediately deposited through the Imperial Bank in advance payment to the Cossacks. This has been proposed by General Ironside and its immediate implementation is requested.[21]

The following day, Qasem Khan sent a comprehensive report on the Cossack forces to Sepahdar. The main points were:

1. Starosselsky and all tsarist Russian officers had been expelled and the headquarters handed over to Iranians.

---

20. Kamarei, 1382^{SH}, vol. 2: 1628.

21. Haghani (ed.), 1379^{SH}: 248–50.

2. Sympathy was offered to officers and Cossacks in Aghababa and Youzbashi-chai.
3. The Cossacks were exhausted and depressed, complaining about their unsuitable quarters, shortage of provisions, and the unfriendly atmosphere.
4. It would be better if the Cossacks were paid several thousand tomans for their back wages, and be offered suitable quarters near Qazvin, in order to have the chance to rest for at least one month.
5. Urgent action should be taken for the delivery of food for both animals and soldiers.
6. General Ironside along with General Dixon and Colonel Smith visited the Cossack Division and reviewed the guard of honor. Then they called in Cossack leaders to remind them that despite the fact that the British government had paid for the Cossacks' costs for three years, the British were being subjected to insults and tirades. In the present circumstances, they should cooperate with Sardar Homayoun, the new commander of the Cossack Division.

Of course, General Ironside wanted to remind the Cossack commanders that their real benefactor was the British government and thus encouraging cooperation with Sardar Homayoun was a secondary issue because the British government had insisted that Cossack forces remain under the command of General Ironside.

Meanwhile, the Ardebil regiment, backed by the Jangali Movement, encircled Rasht and managed to recapture it from the Bolsheviks.[22]

---

22. *Ra'ad*, Safar 19, 1339^{AH}.

Seyyed Zia's Cooperation

Sepahdar, who knew very well that the British were unhappy and would refuse to make payments, resorted to using one of their own agents, Seyyed Zia al-Din Tabataba'i. Seyyed Zia, son of Seyyed Ali Agha Yazdi, was a Constitutional-era cleric who had been involved in journalism since the age of fifteen. He first published the *Neda-ye Islam* (Voice of Islam) newspaper in Shiraz. He moved to Tehran in 1909 and within a few years launched several newspapers: *Shargh* (East), which was banned within a year due to its harsh criticism of government officials; *Bargh* (Spark), which was also banned shortly thereafter; and launched *Ra'ad* (Thunder) at which time he was exiled. His return from exile coincided with the outbreak of World War I.

Ra'ad, supported Russia and Britain and also firmly supported the 1919 Anglo-Persian Agreement. Zia developed close ties to Vosuq al-Dowleh and Britain. In 1919, Vosuq al-Dowleh sent him at the head of a delegation to Baku to discuss commercial ties with the newly established Azerbaijan government. Amid public opposition to the 1919 Agreement, Seyyed Zia was named the head of the Steel Committee in Tehran, comprising pro-British politicians and set up under the aegis of Britain's consul in Isfahan. After moving its headquarters to Tehran, the committee held its meetings at Seyyed Zia's home in the Zargandeh district, becoming known, as a result, as the Zargandeh Committee.[23] A well-known member of the committee was Mirza Karim Khan Rashti, Sepahdar's cousin, who undoubtedly shared with Sepahdar information about the committee's activities and its ties with the British legation. Indeed, Seyyed Yahya Dolatabadi believed that the committee was instrumental in the appointment of Sepahdar as prime minister: "The Zargandeh Committee, assisted by the British, promoted Sepahdar-e A'zam Gilani to premiership. The Nationalists who are connected with the Committee hope they would see their friends become ministers."[24]

---

23. Taghvi, 1383^{SH}: 14–16; Makki, 1361^{SH}, vol. 1: 180–89.

24. Dolatababdi, 1361^{SH}, vol. 4: 180.

Sepahdar, relying on Seyyed Zia's intervention, finally managed on November 7, 1920, to obtain 10,000 tomans from Britain to pay the back wages of the Cossacks and distribute wheat and barley among them.[25] The British government's positive response to Seyyed Zia's mediation is believed to have been due to the role envisaged for him in future events. The following day, another group of tsarist Russian officers were expelled from the Cossack Division,[26] which might well have been in return for the British payment.

Aid Committee

As mentioned earlier, many residents of Gilan had fled their homes due to the takeover of Rasht once again by the Bolsheviks. Some of them abandoned their property and came to Qazvin and Tehran. A significant number of these displaced persons had assets in their own province, but, in fleeing Gilan, had been forced to abandon all their property. Therefore, one of the first measures by Sepahdar, himself of Gilani origin, was to set up what was known as the Aid Committee, headed by Prince Hasan Ali Mirza Nosrat al-Saltaneh, Ahmad Shah's uncle, in order to urgently gather aid, mainly from princes, merchants, and wealthy individuals, to be distributed among the displaced Gilanis. Sepahdar, later on, dipped into British government aid in order to further help the displaced Gilanis in their plight, though this elicited objections and criticism from bureaucrats in Tehran.

Dr. Mosaddegh, Governor of Fars

Dr. Mohammad Khan Mosaddegh al-Saltaneh, who had been named governor of Fars province under the government of Moshir al-Dowleh, and established good security in the region, remained in post after Sepahdar took over. But when Mosaddegh appointed Solat al-Dowleh Ghashgha'i as the tribal chief, Sepahdar objected.

---

25. Makki, 1361^SH^, vol. 1: 102; Elahi, 1393^SH^, 156–60.

26. Makki, 1361^SH^, vol. 1: 102–103.

Dr. Mohammad Khan Mosaddegh al-Saltaneh

Addressing the fourteenth National Consultative Assembly many years later, Mosaddegh explained:

> After I was named governor, I brought Solat al-Dowleh to the city of Shiraz and appointed him the head of the Ghashgha'i tribe. Sepahdar Aʿzam objected to my decision, asking me why I had named him the tribal chief without getting permission from the prime minister. I responded that

> there was no law barring me from doing so. Traditionally, the governor of Fars has named the heads of the tribes. I said that I had no vested interest in naming him tribal chief and I did so only in the best interests of the country. What matters for me is the security of Fars and nothing else.[27]

Apparently, Dr. Mosaddegh had interpreted this objection to his appointment of Solat al-Dowleh as reluctance on the part of the new prime minister to renew his term as the governor of Fars, but, in any event, Britain's consul, who was happy with Dr. Mosaddegh's mandate, informed Norman, who in turn sent a letter to the prime minister asking him to retain Mosaddegh:

> Britain Legation, on November 4, 1920
>
> Your Excellency [Sepahdar]
>
> Based on a telegram relayed from Britain's resident consul in Shiraz, Mosaddegh al-Saltaneh is unhappy with the dissolution of the former cabinet and the formation of a new one, fearing that the new cabinet may not be cooperative enough and he may choose to step down. The reports we have been receiving from Britain's consul in Shiraz indicate his satisfactory governorship. At Your Excellency's discretion, it would be worth relaying a message to him, asking him to remain in his post and abandon his resignation.
>
> With best wishes,
>
> Norman

Norman's Key Message

Among classified messages at the British Foreign Office relating to this period, one is particularly significant. It is the message Norman

27. The negotiations of the National Consultative Assembly, period 14, session 4, Esfand 17, 1322[SH] (March 8, 1944).

relayed on November 8, 1920, to Lord Curzon, which shows very clearly that the British government was intensifying pressure on Sepahdar to implement the 1919 Agreement:

> During lengthy talks which I had yesterday with Sepahdar, I tried my best, albeit in vain, to convince him to draw on the two million pounds sterling, set forth in the Agreement, to resolve the government's financial problems and cover current costs for the coming two months as he faces a credit crisis. But Sepahdar opposed this proposal, arguing that it would elicit a harsh reaction from people in addition to being in conflict with a statement he had released at the start of his premiership. He would only promise to consult with his friends and political peers on this issue to see if he can form a new cabinet by relying on my pledge of the possibility of APOC's allocation of a significant sum in coming days as part of its liabilities.
>
> This morning, I received a new message from Sepahdar, saying he would postpone up to November 10, the formation of a cabinet on the strength of my promise. However, if after the deadline expires, no official promise is given, he would tender his resignation to the Shah. In response, I asked him not to act hastily in setting the deadline and I sought to assure him that the financial aid would be secured. Now, if Sepahdar decides finally to step down, we will have to find a prime minister who would dare to draw on the 6 million tomans provided in the Agreement without fearing the opposition of the masses.
>
> A bread crisis is looming. The merchants of the capital's suburban areas traditionally pre-sell their wheat and barley to the government, which it pays for by cash from the Imperial Bank of Persia in Tehran. Then, from the revenues gained by selling wheat and flour to bakers, it pays back its loan to the Bank. However, as long as a responsible government is not in power, the president of the Imperial Bank hesitates about releasing such sums.[28]

---

28. Seikh al-Islami, 1392^{SH}: 524.

Further in this telegram, Norman refers to people's unhappiness, particularly wholesale merchants, with the situation in Gilan, commenting that despite the Bolsheviks' withdrawal from Rasht, the government had not taken any action due to the absence of a cabinet. The passiveness of British troops in their failure to defend Iran against the Bolsheviks was eating away at the people's trust in Britain's good intentions. A fear that was not unfounded, as Norman goes on to explain:

> Upon his arrival in Persia, the commander-in-chief of Norper Force [General Ironside] imagined that he would no longer face restrictions, which were imposed on his predecessor, and that he would be able to overcome the Bolsheviks. Relying on his firm pledge, I promised the Shah and Sepahdar that Britain's military forces would temporarily carry out the task assigned to the Cossack Division. However, I found on October 31 that Britain's ministry of war had banned the advance of forces under General Ironside beyond Manjil, and this decision has placed me and General Ironside in a very difficult situation . . . Although I have so far refused to reveal to Sepahdar that the war ministry blocked the recapture of Rasht, however, such an important issue may not remain hidden for long, and when the truth is revealed, our political and military prestige will have seriously been harmed. Therefore, now that recapturing Rasht is so easy for our military forces, the instruction by the ministry of war is depriving the Norper Force's commander from benefiting from such a unique opportunity.[29]

What Norman was referring to in his telegram is representative of measures by the British government to ramp up pressure on the Iranian government to implement the 1919 Agreement. These measures included:

---

29. Seikh al-Islami, 1392^{SH}: 252.

- Trying to lure Sepahdar into using the loan set forth in the agreement to ease the government's financial burden.
- Preventing APOC's payment of liabilities to the Iranian government.
- Non-payment of the Imperial Bank of Persia's regular aid to the government to resolve the bread crisis.
- Refusal to deploy British troops to purge the Bolsheviks from Gilan.

After corresponding with Winston Churchill, Britain's Minister of War, General Ironside's Gilan issue was resolved by recapturing Rasht in November 1920. However, the other problems facing the Iranian government still remained, and Sepahdar made every effort to solve them. The following is a summary of his actions:

- Rejecting Britain's insistence on using the loan set forth in the 1919 Agreement.
- Threatening to step down as prime minister if APOC refused to pay its liabilities to the Iranian government.
- Delaying and dragging out the formation of the National Consultative Assembly until the talks between the Iranian government and Bolshevik Russia were finalized.
- Obtaining money by any means possible from the British government to meet urgent needs in the country.

CHAPTER 6

SEPAHDAR'S FIRST CABINET

After the royal decree appointing him as prime minister, Sepahdar reviewed options for the formation of his cabinet, and after seventeen days, he finally managed to appoint his ministers. Referring to the delay in the formation of the cabinet, Abdollah Mostofi comments:

> The prime minister could not bring together his future cabinet. Some did not accept responsibility, there were some whom he did not like, and there were also some who did not like him. Of course, those who were planning a coup are also to be blamed for the delay in the formation of the cabinet, because that would have given them more time to put their plan into action.[1]

On November 13, 1920, Sepahdar finally presented his cabinet to the Shah at Farahabad Palace.

Sepahdar's cabinet consisted of:

Minister of Justice: Mirza Soleiman Khan Meykadeh served briefly as the comptroller of the Ministry of War. He joined the

---

1. Mostofi, 1360[SH], vol. 3: 173.

constitutionalists and was arrested following the bombardment of the first Majles and imprisoned in Bagh-e Shah.[2] After the Minor Tyranny period, he was appointed deputy to Finance Minister Vosuq al-Dowleh before becoming governor of Soltanabad and elected to the third Majles to represent Naein. In 1916, he became Deputy Minister of Interior Affairs in Vosuq al-Dowleh's cabinet. He retained the same post in successive cabinets until Sepahdar was appointed as prime minister.[3]

Acting Minister of Foreign Affairs: Mostafa Gholi Kamal Hedayat Fahim al-Dowleh was from the famous Hedayat clan. He studied law and political science in Tehran and Europe. He was employed by the Ministry of Foreign Affairs and held various posts, the last of which was deputy foreign minister.[4]

Minister of Finance: Dr. Esma'il Marzban Rashti Amin al-Molk studied medicine in France. Upon his return to Tehran, he started practicing medicine. He joined the Society of Humanity and became engaged in the constitutionalist movement. Following the bombing of the first Majles, he left for Europe. After the Triumph of Tehran, he returned to Iran and was elected to the second Majles to represent Rasht and to the third to represent Bandar Anzali. He served as Minister of Post and Telegraph in the cabinets of both Ayn al-Dowleh and Vosuq a-Dowleh.[5]

Minister of War: Hosein Gholi Khan Gharegozlou Hamedani Amir Nezam served as minister of finance in the cabinets of Naser al-Molk and Ayn al-Dowleh. He studied in Iran and Europe. After the Constitutional Revolution, he was appointed by Naser al-Molk Nayeb al-Saltaneh as governor of Kermanshah. He was among the

---

2. The period lasting from the bombardment of the Majles on June 23, 1908, by the force of Mohammad Ali Shah to the capture of Tehran by the revolutionary forces on July 13, 1909 is called the "Minor Tyranny."

3. Agheli, 1380^{SH} a, vol. 3: 1587.

4. Agheli, 1380^{SH} a, vol. 3: 1294–5.

5. Yousefdehi, 1392^{SH}: 48–9.

top landowners in the country but lived in Europe for years, and was proficient in both English and French.[6]

Minister of Education: Abdol-Hosein Sheibani Vahid al-Molk, was the governor of Kashan. He studied in Kashan, Tehran, India, and Britain, receiving his law degree in London. Upon returning to Tehran, he joined the Constitutionalists. He was a correspondent for *The Times* of London. Elected to the second Majles, he also was a lecturer at Dar al-Fonun School. He left for Europe to continue his studies before returning to Iran and representing Tabriz in the third Majles. He was one of the representatives who migrated to Kermanshah and Constantinople. He lived for some time in Germany until he was nominated as a minister in Sepahdar's cabinet.[7]

Minister of Commerce, Agriculture, and Public Works: Abbas Farmanfarmaian Salar Lashkar studied in Tehran, Beirut, and trained as an army officer in Britain at the Royal Military College in Sandhurst, Berkshire. Upon his return to Tehran, he was appointed as governor of Hamedan. During the migration to Kermanshah and Constantinople, he was accompanied by his father-in-law, Nezam al-Saltaneh Mafi, in whose cabinet he became Minister of War. He also served as Deputy Minister of Justice.[8]

Minister of Post and Telegraph: Sadegh Khan Akbar Sardar Motamed was Sepahdar's cousin, and the son-in-law of Akbar Khan Biglarbeigi. A popular figure among Gilanis, he served as the acting governor of Gilan for several terms and was officially appointed to that post after the Triumph of Tehran. He also was elected to the third Majles to represent Rasht in later years.[9]

Minister of State: Hasan Ali Kamal Hedayat Nasr al-Molk studied in Iran and France, where he received his law degree and was employed by the Iranian embassy in Paris. Upon his return, he joined the Ministry of Foreign Affairs and was elected to the first

---

6. Agheli, 1380^{SH} a, vol. 3: 1198.

7. Agheli, 1380^{SH} a, vol. 2: 895–6.

8. Agheli, 1380^{SH} a, vol. 2: 1100.

9. Yousefdehi, 1392^{SH}: 136–8.

Majles. He was appointed Minister of Post and Telegraph in Moshir al-Dowleh's cabinet and served in the cabinets that followed.[10]

Deputy Prime Minister: Hosein Samiei Adib al-Saltaneh was a member of the famous Samiei family in Rasht. He studied in Rasht, Tehran, and Kermanshah, and was employed by the Ministry of Foreign Affairs. Later on he joined the constitutional movement. After the Triumph of Tehran, he was transferred from the Ministry of Foreign Affairs to the Ministry of Interior Affairs. He served in the third Majles representing Rasht. After Russian troops advanced on Iran, he joined a group of representatives and political figures who migrated to Qom, Kashan, Isfahan, and Kermanshah. He was Minister of Interior Affairs in Nezam al-Saltaneh Mafi's cabinet-in-exile. He then left for Aleppo and Constantinople before returning to Tehran in 1918 and becoming Deputy Minister of Interior Affairs in Moshir al-Dowleh's cabinet in 1920.[11]

Second Statement of the Prime Minister

Concurrently with naming his cabinet, Sepahdar released a second statement on November 16, 1920, outlining his plans for running the country, as he had promised in his first statement:

> **Prime Minister's Statement**
>
> In the currently overwhelming torrent of horrendous events exposing nations and countries to the threat of extinction at any moment, I have been instructed by His Majesty to form a cabinet. In light of the critical situation dominating our country, there is no need to explain about the burden of the responsibility of running the country in these troubled times. I assume this responsibility only by trusting in God. Needless to say, my only incentive has been to support the nation.

10. Agheli, 1380^{SH} a, vol. 3: 1293–4.

11. Yousefdehi, 1392^{SH}: 17–20.

> Thanks to God and the help of patriotic and upstanding colleagues, I have managed to form my cabinet. I briefly present my agenda for the public to hear about the new policies proposed by the government.
>
> On domestic policy: The current government does not deem it appropriate to give any firm commitment about reforms. Naturally, it will try its best with a view to guaranteeing public welfare and to running state affairs more effectively. It will work toward the inauguration of the National Consultative Assembly so that representatives of the nation would make the necessary arrangements for state affairs.
>
> On foreign policy: In view of the inauguration of the National Consultative Assembly in the near future, the current cabinet will try its best to strengthen ties with all friendly governments, hoping to make arrangements for more promising developments. As far as the Anglo-Persian Agreement is concerned, just as it was decided by the former cabinet, the agreement will be held in abeyance and no action will be taken for its implementation before the inauguration of the National Consultative Assembly.
>
> Dear countrymen, Iran is going through dark days, but a glimmer of hope is still visible. Salvation of our nation and country from the abyss of misery is tied to a sense of unity, duty, self-belief, and the shared endeavor to achieve happiness. Let us rely on God's blessings for Iran to save itself in this tumultuous world.
>
> Fathollah Sepahdar-e Aʿzam, Prime Minister[12]

In his address to the House of Lords on the same day, Lord Curzon, who hoped the new cabinet would ratify the 1919 Agreement, adopted a condescending tone, criticizing the policy of former prime minister, Moshir al-Dowleh, as idiotic, but heaping praise

---

12. *Ra'ad*, Rabi' al-Awwl 7, 1339[AH]; see also: Makki, 1361[SH], vol. 1: 104–5.

on Sepahdar's cabinet and indicating that the British government would extend the hand of friendship to it. Curzon also stated that the new cabinet represented the nascent democratic movement in Iran and would be making important new proposals.[13]

Disclosure of Bribery for the 1919 Agreement

Another issue occupying Sepahdar's mind at this time was a revelation of bribery by three ministers in the Agreement Cabinet, in which he had also served. In the absence of any evidence, the issue was considered just a rumor until the matter was raised by a representative of the UK House of Commons, William Ormsby-Gore, who asked the Chancellor of the Exchequer whether a loan had been paid to the Iranian government while the 1919 Agreement was still in abeyance. The chancellor responded that a small part of the promised loan had been paid, with the rest being subject to the approval of the agreement by the Majles.

Reuters News Agency reported the news about payment of the small loan in its bulletin destined for India and the Near East. The question-and-answer session between the representative and the chancellor was relayed to Tehran and Karachi. In Tehran, due to a careless oversight by Norman, the full report was distributed among journalists. The news was published in the press exactly when Sepahdar was trying his best to convince everyone that the Iranian government had not received so much as a penny from the British. Sepahdar had been totally unaware of the alleged bribery and was assured that nothing had been paid to the Iranian government. He became anxious and asked Norman to deny the Reuters report, but Norman would not comply, and he even acknowledged the accuracy of the report. The said amount had indeed been paid by the Imperial Bank. Vosuq al-Dowleh, then prime minister, had received 200,000 tomans, and Nosrat al-Dowleh, then Minister of Foreign Affairs, and Sarem al-Dowleh, then Minister of Finance, each received 100,000 tomans respectively, totaling 131,000 pounds sterling. Well aware

---

13. Mostofi, 1360^{SH}, vol. 3: 141.

that the revelation would kill any chance of the approval of the 1919 Agreement, Norman suggested that Sepahdar release a press statement, explaining that the sum in question had been drawn on from the loan for calculating interest rates, usury, and other costs.[14] But Sepahdar was experienced enough to know that such an important issue would not remain secret forever. Such a statement would defame him as someone who had been bribed. Therefore, he sent a message to Norman on November 18, 1920, saying he would not accept this solution. He asked for consent to reveal the facts to the press. Since Vosuq al-Dowleh and two of his colleagues had received this sum, without depositing a single penny into state coffers, the British government's payment would be considered a private matter between the three corrupt politicians and the British legation with no relevance whatsoever to the Iranian government. Sepahdar had made the right decision. He was exonerating himself of charges of collaboration with the receivers of the bribe, while at the same time relieving the Iranian government of a new burden.

But Norman imposed a ban on naming the triumvirate. In an exchange of messages, he convinced Sepahdar to note in his statement that the Iranian government had not been informed of the affair, which dated from Vosuq al-Dowleh's cabinet, and that he would soon announce the results of his investigation into the matter. In the end, Sepahdar released the following statement to the press:

> The press report in the capital, based on a Reuters telegram from London, states that the Iranian government has been paid a tranche of the two-million-pound sterling loan set forth in the Agreement. The current cabinet feels obliged to announce that it has not taken any action whatsoever with regard to said loan. Based on investigations carried out, the Government's financial records carry no reference to the receipt of such a sum.
>
> Fathollah Sepahdar-e A'zam, Prime Minister[15]

---

14. Sheikh al-Islami, 1392[SH]: 530–31.

15. *Ra'ad*, Rabi' al-Awwal 8, 1339[AH]

Norman also took the initiative to discuss the affair with Moshir al-Dowleh, convincing him to release a statement declaring that he knew nothing about the sum in question and that no such sum had been paid into the Iranian state coffers during his premiership.[16] In a telegram to Lord Curzon dated November 18, 1920, Norman described the fallout of the affair:

> The Prime Minister [Sepahdar Rashti] is very angry with the triumvirate having been bribed, and proposes that they should return the entire sum. For this purpose, he intends, if need be, to seize the property and real estate of the three ministers, forcing them to return what they have been paid.[17]

Norman goes on to note in his message that the way Sepahdar intended to disclose the affair would make the bribe-takers in question detested and likely to be expelled from the political scene, which would in turn harm the British government's standing. He also suggested that the 400,000-toman sum in question be secured from another source. He wanted it to be associated with the lending rate and other costs, which had been deducted in error from the total, and that the British government would pay the entire 2 million pounds to the Iranian government once the 1919 Agreement had been approved by the Majles.[18] Infuriated by what was happening, Curzon responded:

> As you know, I was opposed to this gesture from the very beginning. I only agreed when your predecessor in Tehran [Sir Percy Cox] relentlessly and frequently wrote to me that the Agreement would not be approved without paying this sum, and subsequently I authorized the payment. The current prime minister was serving as the minister of war in

16. Sheikh al-Islami, 1392^{SH}: 532.

17. Sheikh al-Islami, 1392^{SH}: 532.

18. Sheikh al-Islami, 1392^{SH}: 532–3.

> the same cabinet, which received this money from us, and remained in the post for eight months after. Therefore, I hold him responsible for what has been done in Vosuq's cabinet and he cannot evade the obligation accepted by the former cabinet. You should speak to him very strongly on this issue.
>
> But regarding the proposal you mentioned, in the final part of your telegram, concerning securing this amount from another source, in order to keep the total of the loan intact, I would like to inform you that this proposal is by no means acceptable.[19]

Revelation of this scandal, which delivered a fatal blow to the 1919 Agreement, was completely to the advantage of Iran and to the disadvantage of Britain. Because anyone who had shown support for the agreement now sought to dissociate themselves from it, in a bid to avoid criticism. An overwhelming majority of the thirty-nine representatives due to sit in the fourth Majles whose endorsement was decisive and vital to the ratification of the 1919 Agreement, expressed their opposition to it.[20] Norman's mistake in not suppressing the Reuters report was so bizarre, with such serious consequences, one might think he had done it deliberately.

Years later, in the sixth National Consultative Assembly, when Mirza Hasan Khan Mostofi al-Mamalek, the prime minister at that time, nominated Vosuq al-Dowleh to the Majles as a candidate for the justice portfolio, Dr. Mohammad Mosaddegh delivered a long speech against him on September 21, 1926, hinting at the bribery affair and its revelation by Sepahdar:

> Would it not be better for Mr. Vosuq al-Dowleh to settle accounts with our friends before becoming minister? According to a telegram relayed to Mr. Sepahdar, he had received 200,000 tomans to guarantee the implementation of the Agreement. It may be interesting to know that a friend

---

19. Sheikh al-Islami, 1392^{SH}: 534.

20. Sheikh al-Islami, 1392^{SH}: 534–6.

> of Mr. Vosuq al-Dowleh said a couple of days ago that he [al-Dowleh] had never dipped into this money and had purchased property for the Iranian government. A senior cleric said in response that it would have been better to have said this to the British government. Britain had paid a sum in return for something, but it did not materialize and therefore the sum has to be returned. Vosuq al-Dowleh already shoulders a heavy burden. I ask you not to make it heavier. In those days when he was receiving the money to purchase property for the nation, where was the nation? Now too there's no nation and accepting property would set a bad precedent and an expensive proposition for Iran. If any foreign government pays traitors to achieve their ambitions and then fails, it would remember this precedent and take back money from the impoverished nation of Iran. For God's sake, please leave the nation alone and let Mr. Vosuq al-Dowleh return the money from whomever he has taken it, or transfer the same amount.[21]

During another session of the sixth Majles, on November 21, 1926, representative Ali Dashti made further revelations in much more damning terms.

> This issue was never known and nobody talked about it. Nor did anyone seek to gain information about it, until after Moshir al-Dowleh's cabinet fell and that of Sepahdar took office. Britain's minister, Mr. Norman, wrote a letter to Sepahdar and subsequently Sepahdar's cabinet took action, and a telegram was sent to Vosuq al- Dowleh (who was then in Europe). The telegrammed reply indicated that the Toumanians Trade Center was on the verge of bankruptcy, which was regrettable. [Vosuq] gave 200,000 tomans from his own money to him, in return for Toumanians' property in Mazandaran.

21. The deliberations of the National Consultative Assembly, period 6, session 11, dated Shahrivar 29, 1305[SH]

> Therefore, it is clear that this money was not given to the Iranian government, but rather to a private person.[22]

No further action was taken at the time regarding retrieving the bribe money.

Fourth Legislative Vote

The order for the fourth legislative vote had been issued by the first cabinet of Vosuq al-Dowleh on May 9, 1917. Sepahdar, the then Minister of Interior Affairs, was in charge of holding the election. But the election was delayed due to the political and financial imbroglio and lack of security throughout the country. Three and half years had already passed and liberal-minded politicians feared that a Majles whose election was held by Vosuq al-Dowleh would endorse the 1919 Agreement. Former prime minister Moshir al-Dowleh, whose domestic policy had been vague and at the same time based on following the Constitution, wanted to complete the election properly, and give a lawful appearance to it by referring to public opinion; however, his cabinet did not survive.

The new prime minister pursued the same vague domestic policy as his predecessor, with the exception of the election process. Since Sepahdar had already organized elections for the fourth Majles in his capacity as the Minister of Interior Affairs, he could not call them into question and did not want to. No doubt the reopening of the Majles would be the most important task during this historic period. In the days that followed, Sepahdar did his utmost to clear this political obstruction and fill the legal void caused by the inactive Majles. The clearest evidence of this are the remarks by Mohammad Taghi Bahar (Malak al-Shoara) delivered on December 29, 1921, in the National Consultative Assembly:

---

22. The deliberations of the National Consultative Assembly, period 6, session 11, dated Shahrivar 29, 1305[SH].

> Since the Majles was to be inaugurated as soon as possible, during the tenure of Sepahdar's cabinet, the cabinet insisted on accelerating the voting process to elect representatives sooner. However, the Central Monitoring Association has declined to provide any minutes or verification of credentials …[23]

Furthermore, a telegram sent by Norman to Lord Curzon on December 5, 1920, confirms this:

> The Government of Persia is trying its best to inaugurate the Assembly as soon as possible. For this purpose, it has been communicated to all civil servants who have been elected to the Assembly before, that they would be dismissed from office at their present government positions, in order to join the "Parliament." Therefore, it would be in their own interest to step down, and accept their elected positions as Members of Parliament.[24]

Sepahdar himself repeatedly expressed the following sentiments during his tenure: "I will open the Majles, with whichever representative, no matter how they were elected, without listening to objections because we cannot delay it any further."[25] However, the 1919 Agreement was unlikely to be approved in the fourth Majles, as the opposition to the Agreement by the majority of representatives was clearly indicated and that was exactly why the British government had pressured successive Iranian governments to implement the agreement without waiting for the Majles's vote.

---

23. The deliberations of the National Consultative Assembly, period 4, session 64.

24. Rahimzadeh Safavi, 1362[SH]: 346.

25. Dolatababdi, 1361[SH], vol. 4: 182.

CHAPTER 7

BRITAIN'S ULTIMATUM AND THE COLLAPSE OF THE CABINET

It was no surprise that the British government was unhappy with the way prime minister Sepahdar had kept the 1919 Agreement in abeyance. It was this that inspired the British government and legation in Tehran to consider mounting a military coup against the Iranian government, with the chief purpose of bringing the Cossacks under their own command.

To this end, as reported by Herman Norman to Lord Curzon on November 25, 1920, Norman and General Harold Richard Dickson, the British legation's military attaché, met with Sepahdar and his war minister, Amir Nezam Gharagozlou. At the meeting, the British officials complained about the incompetence of former commanders and lack of discipline in the Cossack ranks. They also noted that the British government was seeking to reduce war expenses and that British troops were unlikely to stay there beyond the following spring. Therefore, the Iranians had to establish a military force as soon as possible to fill the void after the departure of British troops in order to be able to resist a possible Bolshevik invasion. The British also warned that if the formation of a military force was dependent on the fate of the 1919 Agreement, the Iranians would miss this great opportunity to fill that void.

The British negotiators submitted the following six-point plan to the prime minister and his war minister:

1. Full control of Iranian military forces was to be delegated to British commanders.
2. Full control of Iranian financial affairs was to be delegated to British advisers.
3. The Ministry of War's supervision on armed forces was to be via British commanders.
4. Rebuilding the armed forces, to which public opinion was sensitive, was to be carried out in Qazvin instead of Tehran.
5. Iranian officers and troops who were not qualified to be integrated into the rebuilt military force were to be transferred to the Central Brigade, which would be under the command of the Minister of War.
6. All arms, ammunition, and equipment in the Cossack Division's arsenal that had not been used would be transferred to the newly established force.

Norman and General Dickson then explained to Sepahdar and Gharagozlou that the formation of a new military force, whose initial costs the British government would bear, would not be associated with the Anglo-Persian Agreement which required parliamentary approval.[1]

Well aware of the British government's tricks, the seasoned Sepahdar knew that accepting this plan would mean in effect implementing the agreement without approval by the Majles. He did not dismiss the plan outright, pledging to submit it to the cabinet. However, the following day, he sent a rejection of the proposal

---

1. Sheikh al-Islami, 1392[SH]: 540–41.

General Harold Richard Dickson

to Norman on the grounds that the cabinet had examined the plan and, although they agreed in principle with its provisions, they refused to endorse it for fear of how the public would respond. He and the cabinet had concluded that immediate implementation of the plan might incite public outrage and even trigger riots across the country, thereby dashing any hopes of approving the 1919 Agreement by the next Majles. Sepahdar therefore requested a two-week deadline for the cabinet to examine the plan more closely.

Norman, despite being held in low regard by his superiors owing to his successive diplomatic failures, and his inept handling of how the bribery of the former cabinet ministers had been disclosed, would not be fooled either. He rejected Sepahdar's proposal, giving his reasons in a telegram to the Foreign Office:

> I felt that if I surrendered, I would be giving an opportunity to the hesitant supporters of the prime minister and those who are in principle opposed to us to exercise their influence behind the scenes and preclude any endorsement of the proposed plan by the cabinet.[2]

Therefore, the following day, November 27, 1920, Norman and General Dickson, along with General Ironside, attended a meeting with Sepahdar. Referring to the threats posed to Iran, they asked the prime minister to stand firm and save the country. However,

---

2. Sheikh al-Islami, 1392^{SH}: 541.

General Edmund Ironside

after their goodwill gesture, they submitted a strongly worded and threatening note to the Iranian government. While recalling the provisions set forth in the agreement, they issued an ultimatum to the government of Iran citing discontent among British members of parliament and other politicians:

> 1. Cossack forces shall come under the command of British forces.
> 2. On the delivery of money to the Persian government, the House [members of the House of Commons] and other politicians in the British government have protested. Furthermore, regarding the withdrawal of British military forces from Persia, there has been resistance in view of the possible consequences and the possibility of aggression [by the Bolsheviks].
>
> We wish to remind you that, if the Persian government is unwilling to remain on friendly terms with us, or is not in need of our assistance, we shall take the risk and draw back.[3]

The British government raised sensitive issues of particular importance to the Iranian government because a sudden withdrawal of British forces from Iran, and the lack of funds and provisions for the Cossacks, would be tantamount to opening the floodgates and allowing chaos to overwhelm the country. The whole country—from the Shah and the government to the general population—lived in fear of a Bolshevik advance if there was a sudden withdrawal of British troops.

Supreme Advisory Council

Because of public opposition to the 1919 Agreement, neither Ahmad Shah nor Sepahdar were ready to assume the responsibility for its implementation. On the one hand, the Iranian government was waiting for the outcome of talks between Iran's delegate, Moshaver al-Mamalek Ansari, with the Russian government. If these negotiations concluded successfully, it would mean the subsequent withdrawal of the Bolsheviks from Gilan, at which point the British government's pressure on the Iranians would automatically be lifted. On the other hand, the Iranian government was waiting for the outcome of the

3. Makki, 1361^{SH}, vol. 1: 106.

legal action it had taken in London regarding APOC's payment of liabilities to Iran, which could resolve many financial problems. However, the ultimatum issued by the British government could have irreparable consequences. Therefore, the Shah and the prime minister decided to establish an advisory council in order to shift the responsibility for the implementation of the agreement onto the Council. In case of non-implementation, this would at least buy them a bit of time.

Upon the government's request, Ahmad Shah ordered on November 27, 1920, the formation of the Supreme Advisory Council to discuss options for the resolution of the crisis and draft a response to the British government's ultimatum. A meeting of the council was then convened, in which political figures, scholars, ministers, landlords, and a number of representatives due to sit in the fourth National Consultative Assembly participated. The meeting was opened by the arrival of Ahmad Shah, dressed in black, as an indication of the severity of the situation, and accompanied by several princes and courtiers.

After delivering a short inaugural address to explain why the Council had been established, he asked participants to express their views and offer advice in view of the unprecedented crisis facing Iran. Finally, he prayed for the protection of the country, and then left the meeting to return to his residence in Farahabad Palace. After endorsing the Shah's remarks, Sepahdar invited the deputy prime minister, Adib al-Saltaneh Sami'i, to read out a speech on his behalf:

> Hardly have two weeks passed since the current government was formed, to take the helm of the country's affairs. It is now faced with a series of serious problems, before even being fully established. Prior to assuming this responsibility, we were already faced with daily-increasing problems in the country as we sacrificed and accepted to serve our duty. However, we never imagined that the challenging problems would be to such an extent.
>
> Over these two weeks since taking office it is known that governmental bodies have access to various sources

of information. Having received this information, the government informed His Majesty of the state of affairs. His Majesty called for the establishment of the Supreme Advisory Council, comprising the elite of the country. Now, pursuant to His Majesty's decree, the government will briefly explain the current situation.

Our northern, northwestern, and eastern borders are being threatened, and it seems that the threat is growing. Gilan has been the target of this aggression for the past six months, which may expand around the Caspian Sea and other northern borders. If it were possible to unite forces that are scattered around the country, the government would have established a defense force. However, currently the government can only resort to the Gendarmerie and the Cossacks. But these two forces alone cannot ward off threats. The Gendarmerie is busy in the provinces, safeguarding roads and streets and establishing order wherever needed. As for the Cossacks, due to the recent developments in Gilan and two defeats, their morale is very low.

Perhaps you think that the current government has enough authority to organize a new force. To disabuse you of this notion, I call your attention to the current financial conditions, and the delay in the payment of wages. With the existing budget deficit, no reform is possible in the short term, because this cabinet is not receiving the financial aid the previous cabinets received from foreign governments, and the government is faced with a serious budget crisis.

Under such conditions, the British Legation has delivered a note to the government, adding to its concerns and causing new political problems. After receiving this note and learning about the situation, the government realized that it is impossible to be faced with such problems without informing the nation of them. Were the National Consultative Assembly in session, the government would know what to do, and we would have an advisory body. But currently the National Consultative Assembly is unfortunately shut down, and the only way for us is to refer to your opinions as open-minded individuals who are expected to assist the government.

The note from the British Legation will be read out shortly. After preliminary deliberations, if you think that it should be examined, you are requested to name an ad hoc committee to review the note and urgently inform the government of your conclusions.

Fathollah Sepahdar-e A'zam, Prime Minister[4]

Sepahdar initially preferred to keep the issue of the British legation's note secret in order not to trigger panic among the public. He suggested that an ad hoc committee be established to examine it, but some participants insisted that it be read out publicly. Finally, the note was read out by Adib al-Saltaneh. After it was read out, the participants discussed it, and issued the following response:

The Majles did not have the authority to make a decision in this regard;
The elected representatives, who were in the capital, were not legally authorized to approve any law or agreement before their legislative term officially began and their credentials had been approved;
Any approval of the Agreement in question would violate the neutrality of the government which had been enacted by the previous legislative body;
Nothing could be decided before the outcome of negotiations between Iran's delegates to Russia was known;
An accelerated effort for the inauguration of the National Consultative Assembly was necessary to remove legal obstacles;
It was necessary for the government to forcefully repel the northern rebels and seek assistance from the nation or force people to defend their land.

---

4. *Ra'ad*, Rabi' al-Awwl 17, 1339[AH] (November 29, 1920); see also: Sheikh al-Islami, 1392[SH]: 544–6; Makki, 1361[SH], vol. 1: 109–111.

After being presented with the response from the participants of the Supreme Advisory Council, the prime minister announced to the Majles that no solution to the problem addressed by the gentlemen had been found. Therefore, the government would fulfill its duty and responsibility.[5]

Government Actions

After rejecting, in effect, the ultimatum from the British government, Sepahdar's cabinet assumed the British government might move first to cut financial aid to Iran. Therefore, on November 28, 1920, the following note was issued by the Ministry of Finance, highlighting the financial downturn in the country:

> Given the lack of sufficient funds in the coffers of the Treasury, the necessity of settling the government's urgent expenses, as well as the receipt of irregular financial aid (unlike in previous cabinets), the National Audit Office has been ordered to put on hold issuance of some payments to stabilize the Treasury's finances. It is crucial to respect national interests at this critical time. The Ministry of Finance is calling upon creditors to please refrain from referring to related offices during this period of budget crisis, so that the Ministry of Finance is able to address the government's financial deficit.
>
> Ministry of Finance[6]

Sepahdar, who was well aware of Vosuq al-Dowleh's acceptance of a bribe in return for securing the approval of the 1919 Agreement, tried to retrieve the sum in question from the former prime minister in a bid to solve the government's problem. He apparently sent a

---

5. Makki, 1361^{SH}, vol. 1: 111–18; Mostofi, 1360^{SH}, vol. 3: 178–80

6. Makki, 1361^{SH}, vol. 1: 80.

telegram to Vosuq al-Dowleh, who then turned to Lord Curzon. On December 1, 1920, Curzon sent an urgent telegram to Norman, asking him to dissuade Sepahdar from following up on the matter:

> Vosuq al-Dowleh has received a telegram from Sepahdar, in which the latter has accused the former of receiving 250,000 pounds sterling in bribes from the government of Britain. His Excellency wants me to inform you that the sum was deposited with him immediately after the signature of the Anglo-Persian Agreement following insistence by Sarem al-Dowleh and Prince Firouz (Nosrat al-Dowleh), each of whom received 100,000 tomans. However, Vosuq al-Dowleh has not touched this sum and has firmly opposed such deals. His Excellency has allocated the remainder, which was 200,000 tomans, in aid to Toumanians although it failed to save his company from bankruptcy. In return for this payment, His Excellency has mortgaged his land and property in the north of Iran and is now ready to give it all to the government or pay back the sum entirely after returning to Iran. He wants Sepahdar to know that he has not been paid the 250,000 pounds sterling sum.[7]

Vosuq al-Dowleh had bought land in the Soleimaniyeh district of Tehran. Ultimately, when Reza Shah rose to power years later, Vosuq al-Dowleh was finally made to pay the sum back as Taghizadeh describes in his memoirs: "After ascending the throne, Reza Shah said that these bastards took bribes from abroad. They have to pay it back. Because of his strong leadership, these matters could be addressed quickly. As the finance minister, I was assigned to get the bribe back, and I did."[8]

---

7. Rahimzadeh Safavi, 1362^{SH}: 344–5.

8. Taghizadeh, 1391^{SH}: 171.

The Anglo-Persian Political Game

At that time, Sepahdar politely turned down the British government's proposal of establishing a military force under the command of British officers. However, Norman did not sit idly by. On December 4, 1920, he sent Seyyed Zia al-Din Tabataba'i and Abdol-Hosain Khan Sardar Moazzam Teymourtash to pressure Sepahdar into accepting the idea. After intensive talks, during which the pair accused Sepahdar of pushing the country towards insolvency and collapse, they forced him to promise that he would send a note to Norman to announce his agreement to the formation of a centralized army under British command. Sepahdar agreed in principle to send such a note, in which he then included certain stipulations that he must have known would be rejected by Britain:

1. The number of servicemen in the new army should be increased to 15,000 from the current 7,000.
2. The army should remain under command of the Ministry of War of Iran.
3. The British government should give 1 million pounds sterling to the Iranian government for the restoration of the gendarmerie and police.[9]

A telegram sent by Lord Curzon to Norman on December 8,1920, showed that the British government was well aware of the political game being played by the Iranian government:

> The Persian government's financial tactics are highly suspicious. After using up the British government's official financial aid, they are pressuring us, and buying time, in order to receive money from the Anglo-Persian Oil Company and the Imperial Bank. After this is used up, they will sell the Russian concessions, which they have overturned. For this purpose, they have entered into talks with the Bolsheviks

9. Rahimzadeh Safavi, 1362^{SH}: 347.

> with a view to signing an agreement with them. At stake is the Khoshtaria Oil Company. The Persian government is encouraging the Americans to take advantage of this chaos. Besides such tactics, they also did not allow British officers to train the Cossack Division, which proves that I was right to be suspicious of them. The Persian Government is pushing the country towards insolvency and collapse.[10]

In December, more talks were held between Sepahdar and Norman, the results of which Norman telegrammed to Curzon. Referring to the prime minister, Norman notes:

> Sepahdar is honest and not corrupt. He is more under our control than his predecessors were. If he is convinced that we will keep him in office, he will do whatever we want. Former prime ministers would bribe people to cover up their words and deeds, from the 350,000-toman aid we released to them. But Sepahdar has allocated a budget and has refused such payments. He does not hesitate to imprison anyone who is subversive. This policy has proven really effective. Even those supporting the Agreement dare to speak out now.

This telegram indicates that Sepahdar had managed to win the trust of the opposing party, by diplomacy. It also shows that he was financially untainted. But the comment "he will do whatever we want" in the telegram is not factually correct, because despite pressure and threats from the British government, Sepahdar not only never implemented the agreement, but his delaying the ratification process also shows that he was constantly searching for a solution to the country's problems.

In another report to Lord Curzon, dated December 20, 1920, Norman records his full negotiations with Sepahdar:

---

10. Rahimzadeh Safavi, 1362^{SH}: 348.

> **Sepahdar**: Does the British government really want this Agreement to pass the Majles?
>
> **Norman**: All communications and correspondence by the British government indicate that the British government wants the Agreement to pass the Majles.
>
> **Sepahdar**: If the British government really insists on the approval of the Agreement to protect its interests, it has to spend 100,000 pounds sterling or so thereupon, because I have talked to the representatives and I am assured that nothing will go ahead without bribery. Personally, I don't want anything. I'll give you a list of people who could be bribed. You can pay them directly. I don't want to interfere with it at all, and I have no expectations.
>
> **Norman**: The Anglo-Persian Oil Company may do so in order to protect its interests, but such a sum couldn't be paid unless the Agreement has been adopted. Then, it could be paid. The Imperial Bank may release the credit, which would be accessible after the task is done.

Based on this conversation, it is clear that Sepahdar held out the possibility that the agreement would be approved by the National Consultative Assembly, thereby encouraging the British government to oil the wheels of some representatives. But he must have known that such a controversial agreement would not be approved by the Majles. Given the state of the country and the restrictions upon the government, it is likely that Sepahdar might have made these remarks in a gesture of goodwill to Norman. He also was perhaps buying time, until the talks with Russia reached a conclusion. Sepahdar was also trying to prevent a military coup by the British, because he must have been well informed about any behind-the-scenes plotting, via his cousin Mirza Karim Khan Rashti, a member of the Zargandeh Committee, or through other channels.

Lord Curzon

Telegrams by Curzon, sent to Norman on December 8, 9, and 23, show that he was well aware of the games being played by Iranian politicians, stating that first, Moshir al-Dowleh and then Sepahdar formed cabinets with the specific aim of getting the agreement approved by the Majles, and that if Iranians had no interest in the agreement and the Iranian government, due to the opposition of the Majles, was not able to approve the agreement in due time, responsibility for the future of the country rested with the Iranian government, and it could no longer expect any support or assistance from the British government.[11]

Norman in a telegram to Curzon on December 24, 1920, asks:

> Would you please let me know why the Foreign Office is so suspicious of and pessimistic about Sepahdar? This lack of confidence is unfounded, because Sepahdar is definitely the most honest and the best prime minister we have dealt with in Tehran, and he respects our guidance more than his predecessors did. A reliable source has stated that Vosuq al-Dowleh has manipulated Britain's Foreign Office against Sepahdar.[12]

In another report, Norman informs Curzon that he had told Sepahdar to be firm and incisive, reshuffle his cabinet, and reinstate the Majles as soon as possible. He adds that Sepahdar had promised to release a statement on January 26, 1921, to form the Majles one week later, before encouraging a number of representatives to study the agreement. According to Norman, Sepahdar had also noted that people might get a negative impression about hiring British officers, suggesting that they be hired from neutral countries instead. Norman then suggested Belgium as a neutral state. In the same report, Norman also writes about Colonel Henry Smyth's behind-the-scenes activities, with regard to the Cossack regiment's affairs, noting that the latter desperately needed funding to carry out a coup.

In response, Curzon appears to blame Norman, telling him that "Belgian officers are not good [for enforcing British interests]. Don't endorse them." In the same letter, he expresses disappointment about the delay in forming the Majles. Norman responds:

> It's regrettable that you say that the parliament will never be formed. I witness the challenge of reconvening

---

11. Rahimzadeh Safavi, 1362^{SH}: 348–9.

12. Rahimzadeh Safavi, 1362^{SH}: 353.

> representatives. I try to tell the Prime Minister that the representatives should come back, without any fear, and express their views freely . . . I am trying my best to strengthen and preserve the current government.[13]

Nonetheless, the trend of events showed that Curzon was right, and that veteran Iranian politicians were playing games with the British government. Not only was the Majles not reopened on the promised date, but its inauguration also occurred much later. The delay was not caused by the Iranian government, however, but by other political decision-makers in the country.

A telegram sent by Dr. Mosaddegh, the then governor of Fars, to Sepahdar on December 14, 1920 was indicative of the precarious situation in another part of the country.

> His Excellency the Prime Minister
>
> The situation in Fars is such that any official assigned by any ministry is required to be well informed, sincere, and faithful. The former cabinet was expected to send someone from the Ministry of War, subject to my consent, but nothing has happened so far. It is feared that the remaining troops would become useless, as they have no arms or ammunition. For the Finance Department, I have nominated several competent candidates, and I had hoped the most qualified ones would have been appointed quickly. Nothing has occurred so far.
>
> I am here alone, and if no rapid action is taken in such minor issues, how can I fulfill my obligation vis-à-vis the government? As you authorized me, I hereby submit my requests to Your Excellency, in the hope of reaching a conclusion in the shortest possible time. I swear by God, I pursue no other objective but rendering my services. I request once more that special attention be paid to the appointment

13. Makki, 1361^{SH}, vol. 1: 120–22.

> of provincial officials here, because a poorly informed official with a negative attitude had better not be assigned.
>
> Mosaddegh al-Saltaneh[14]

This was just one example of the political problems throughout the country.

Despite every effort, Sepahdar failed to reconvene the fourth Majles. He even threatened to dismiss from public office the elected representatives who refused to step down as required by law. However, owing to more pressing concerns of their own, as in the case of Dr. Mosaddegh, most provincial representatives did not agree to come to the capital to sit in the Majles.[15]

In late December, various worrying rumors were spreading among the people. In a bid to assuage concerns, Sepahdar released a statement on December 29, 1920:

> Although morally speaking, I deem it inappropriate to speak about rumors, however, due to some damaging accounts currently being spread, I feel obliged to inform the public:
>
> 1. It is said that the government has kept secret a telegram received from Mr. Moshaver al-Mamalek [Iran's minister plenipotentiary in Moscow] or has ignored it. First and foremost, such political and national issues could never be ignored by the government. Second, such issues require profound investigation, negotiations, and consultation before being made public. In this particular case, we have not yet responded to Mr. Moshaver al-Mamalek's telegram, and the government shall inform the public, once the matter is final.

---

14. Mossadegh, 1352^{SH}: 39–40.

15. Rahimzadeh Safavi, 1362^{SH}: 347.

2. With regards to the pound sterling's conversion rate, which has caused confusion, it is hereby noted that if the government has received any sum, it has been in the legal tender of the country, and part of royalties, and there has been no conversion.
3. It has been rumored that the government has hired a number of British military officers. It is hereby noted that the government's initial decision holds, and no negotiations have been held to that effect, nor has any action been taken.

December 29, 1920

Fathollah Sepahdar-e A'zam, Prime Minister[16]

Talks with Russia

After two months of talks with the Russian foreign commissioner, Iran's delegate, Moshaver al-Mamalek Ansari finally managed to secure an important and valuable treaty. He dispatched Manshour al-Molk, Iran's consul in Baku, to Astara by ship for talks with Fahim al-Dowleh, acting Minister of Foreign Affairs, and Adib al-Saltaneh, deputy prime minister. The following day, January 3, 1921, Sepahdar himself went to the Telegraph Office and communicated with Manshour al-Molk, quoting him as saying that the government should make up its mind soon. Sepahdar found himself in a dilemma once again. If he refused such an important treaty he would incite the ire of his fellow countrymen, but if he accepted the treaty, he would enrage the British, who had long waited for the implementation of their agreement. Some attribute Sepahdar's hesitation in accepting the Russo-Persian Treaty of Friendship to his suspected bias towards Britain. But that was not the case. Accepting the treaty with Soviet Russia was fraught with risk, and there were a number of drawbacks to signing it:

---

16. *Ra'ad*, Rabi' al-Thani 18, 1339[AH] (December 30, 1920); see also: Makki, 1361[SH], vol. 1: 119–20.

- The Russians expected the Iranian government to expel British-backed anti-Bolshevik White Russians first, and not to replace them with British forces. Accepting such an obligation was impossible for Iran as long as British forces were present in the country.[17]
- Signing a treaty with Soviet Russia might have accelerated the British troops' withdrawal while the Iranian government was not convinced about the trustworthiness of the Russians' pledges, and it was likely that they would push their advance on Iranian territory in the absence of British forces. Therefore, the Iranian government announced to the Russians that this treaty would be signed when the last Russian soldier had left Iranian territory.[18]
- Article 21 of the treaty required Iran not to ban pro-Bolshevik propaganda in the country, which was naturally unacceptable for a monarchy.
- Although the Russo-Persian Treaty of Friendship was deemed to be beneficial to Iran, unlike the Anglo-Persian Agreement, both treaties required approval by the Majles, whose reconvention still had not occurred and was shrouded in mystery.

To address the issue, the Shah and the prime minister decided to reconvene the Supreme Advisory Council, resorting once more to taking the matter to other political figures in the country.

Regarding the Russo-Persian Treaty of Friendship as a threat to their interests, the British government took steps intended to intimidate the Iranian government and people. On January 6, 1921, Britain ordered its nationals in Iran to leave the country and called on depositors of the Imperial Bank to withdraw their money. This gesture by Britain was aimed at undermining Iran's position in the

---

17. Sheikh al-Islami, 1392^{SH}: 554–7.

18. Sheikh al-Islami, 1392^{SH}: 557 and 583–4.

negotiations with the Russians and at killing any chance of finalizing the Russo-Persian Treaty.[19]

Ahmad Shah Plans a Trip to Europe

While all this was going on, Ahmad Shah announced to Sepahdar that he planned to travel to Europe for medical treatment. Sepahdar mentioned this to Norman, who in turn sent a telegram to Curzon on January 3, 1921:

> The Prime Minister recently informed me that the Shah will soon try to win my consent for travelling to Europe. The Prime Minister says, if I reject the Shah's demand at my own discretion, His Majesty may decide to go ahead with his plan, and upon arrival in Europe, he will try to convince the British government that his European trip was necessary. The Prime Minister wants me to tell the Shah that I will forward his request to the Foreign Office. The Prime Minister's view is that you can then reject his demand.[20]

Norman also notes in the same telegram:

> [In the past] after returning to Iran from Europe, the Shah was warmly welcomed by people. Had he shown interest in governance and dealing with state affairs instead of accumulating wealth to be sent abroad, he might have become popular. But since only his personal interests matter to him, people of all social classes now detest him. If he leaves Iran, I don't think he would ever come back. The Shah's exit may not be useless provided that a suitable successor could be found. However, under the present

---

19. Makki, 1361^{SH}, vol. 1: 120–25; Bahar, 1371^{SH}, vol. 1: 55.

20. Rahimzadeh Safavi, 1362^{SH}: 356–7.

> circumstances, any dethroning of the Shah will destabilize the situation and may even cause a mass revolution.[21]

In response, Curzon noted that any decision by the Shah to leave the country, even for medical treatment, would be construed as cowardice and evading responsibility. If he chose to flee Iran, he should not expect any assistance or protection on the part of the British government. Curzon concurred that anyone else chosen as monarch in Iran would be better than the current monarch.[22]

Supreme Advisory Council Reinstated

On January 8, 1921, the Supreme Advisory Council was reconvened to discuss the Russo-Persian Treaty of Friendship. The same individuals who were firmly opposed to the treaty before approved it with some modifications before submitting it to the foreign minister. The main points in the 26-article treaty were as follows:

- Russia would declare as null and void all previous agreements and treaties between Russia and Iran, as well as between Russia and other countries about Iran.
- The two parties would undertake to refrain from interfering with each other's internal affairs and would enjoy equal navigation rights in the Caspian Sea.
- Russia would abandon the continuation of the economic undertakings of the tsarist government, the object of which was the economic subjugation of Iran. Russia would therefore cede to the Iranian government the full ownership of all funds and of all real estate and other property, which the Russian Discount Bank possessed on Iranian territory, and likewise would transfer to it all the assets and liabilities of that bank.

---

21. Rahimzadeh Safavi, 1362^{SH}: 356–7.

22. Rahimzadeh Safavi, 1362^{SH}: 357–8. For more information, see: Sheikh al-Islami, 1362^{SH}: 586–91.

- Russia would cede to Iran all land, property, buildings, and assets in its possession in Iran, including roads, piers, ports, and telegraph lines. Only the Russian legation in Tehran and in Zargandeh and consulate buildings would be deemed to belong to the Russian government, and in turn the Iranian government would assure that it would not transfer to any other foreign governments or subjects what it had obtained from Russia.
- The Ashouradeh and Firouzeh islands would be restored to the Iranian government and a joint committee established to settle border disputes along the Khorasan border.
- Capitulation would be declared null and void and subjects from either country would be subject to local law.
- The Iranian government would undertake to preclude any aggression on the Russian territory by its enemies, and in case of failure to prevent an aggression it would not block intervention by Russian forces. For its part, Russia would undertake to prevent any aggression on Iran by Azerbaijan and Armenia.
- The Fishery Concession would be awarded to a company comprising both Iranian and Russian subjects.
- Russia would undertake to indemnify all damage caused by the presence of Russian troops in Gilan.[23]

The Government Falls

The situation in northwestern Iran (Azerbaijan and in Kurdistan), which had been invaded by a large group of highway bandits, began to deteriorate from the beginning of January 1921. Resistance by Cossack forces and the gendarmerie failed to pay off, and Tabriz was close to falling.[24] The chaos was not limited to the northwest region.

---

23. For the full text of the treaty, see: Makki, 1361^{SH}, vol. 1: 125–128; Mostofi, 1360^{SH}, vol. 3: 183–185 and 189–194; Sheikh al-Islami, 1392^{SH}: 557–559.

24. Makki, 1361^{SH}, vol. 1: 134.

On January 7, Movafagh al-Dowleh, the governor of Qazvin, announced in a telegram to Sepahdar that British forces had withdrawn from Roudbar to Manjil (in Gilan), and that refugees were returning home to Gilan. He added that in case this situation continued, the Cossack troops should be deployed to stop the chaos.[25]

At the same time, Britain was cutting monthly aid to the Iranian government and rumors of the imminent pullout of British forces caused public anxiety and touched off demonstrations in Tehran and other cities.

At the request of the prime minister and the order of the Shah, the Supreme Advisory Council held three other meetings between January 9 and 14 to discuss how to assuage concerns and consider economic and political reforms. The British legation in Tehran now believed that Sepahdar's position as prime minister was untenable, as Norman laid out in a telegram to Curzon on January 13, of which the key points are as follows:

- Sepahdar would no longer be able to control the situation in the country once British forces leave Iran.
- In a bid to win over the people, he had resorted to appealing to populist figures, who believed that the only way to salvage Iran would be to sign an agreement with the Russians.
- The Moscow talks had lent him credence among the public, but the government no longer trusted him.
- Members of the cabinet complained that the prime minister was making arbitrary decisions, and they were taking action against him.
- Even if Sepahdar managed to reconvene the Majles, the representatives would not dare approve the 1919 Agreement.

---

25. Haghani (ed.), 1379^{SH}: 256.

- Sepahdar had been told that, given the current situation, a cabinet reshuffle was essential, and he must firmly resist anyone opposed to a reshuffle.
- A cabinet reshuffle or replacing the prime minister would be discussed after Nosrat al-Dowleh returned to Iran from England.
- The best composition for a future cabinet would be to appoint Mirza Hasan Khan Mostofi al-Mamalek as prime minister and Abdol-Hosain Khan Farmanfarma as his right-hand man.[26]

This telegram from Norman to Curzon reflects the pressure placed on the prime minister by the British government to appoint pro-British ministers like Farmanfarma and his son, Nosrat al-Dowleh Firouz. It also demonstrates Britain's dissatisfaction with the current situation and Sepahdar's refusal to cooperate with the British.

Sepahdar, during his talks with Norman realized the intentions of the British, including their desire to replace him as prime minister with Mostofi al-Mamalek, who enjoyed great prestige nationally. Sepahdar stepped down on January 15, 1921 following the resignation of two of his ministers (Nasr al-Molk and Fahim al-Dowleh). He had been in office for fifty days.

The previous day, January 14, 1921, Sepahdar personally informed the Shah of his intention to resign, which Ahmad Shah did not accept. The following day, the Shah gathered a group of influential figures at Farahabad Palace for negotiations about state affairs. Sepahdar chose not to attend. He was invited anew by telephone, but on the pretext that he was ill, he turned down the invitation and instead sent his letter of resignation to Farahabad Palace before retiring to his summer residence in Tajrish, a suburb in north Tehran.[27]

---

26. For the full text of the telegram, see Sheikh al-Islami, 1392[SH]: 600–601.

27. *Ra'ad*, Jumada al-Awwal 6, 1339[AH] (January 16, 1921); see also: Makki, 1361[SH], vol. 1: 131.

In a telegram to Curzon on the same day (January 15) to the Foreign Office, Norman gives an account of what happened:

> His Majesty said that the Prime Minister has tendered his resignation twice over the past three days. Although his resignation has not been accepted, he has left Tehran to stay in his residence in the country. His Majesty also said that, during a meeting of former prime ministers he had presided over, the participants had unanimously said that, in light of the present conditions in the country, a more proficient person than Sepahdar should be put in charge. His Majesty is now seeking our opinion to see if we still insist on keeping the current prime minister in office.[28]

Noman goes on to note that the Shah agreed with the former prime ministers and suggested Mostofi al-Mamalek for the premiership, and Farmanfarma and Ayn al-Dowleh for membership in the new cabinet.

28. Sheikh al-Islami, 1392[SH]: 601–2.

CHAPTER 8

PRIME MINISTER AGAIN

No sooner had Sepahdar reached his summer residence in Tajrish when Sepahsalar Tonekaboni and a group of influential figures arrived at his house to convince him to reconsider his decision and become prime minister again.

When Sepahdar returned to Tehran from Tajrish later that evening, a group of representatives of merchants, workers' unions, and various social groups also met with him in the hope of persuading him not to tender his resignation and resume the premiership.[1]

Meanwhile, after Sepahdar's departure, the Shah ordered all deputy cabinet ministers to inform him of any important issues, and to report to him via coded telegrams, until a new prime minister was appointed. He also called in Mostofi al-Mamalek, and asked him to assume the premiership. Mostofi al-Mamalek asked for time to discuss the issue with Norman.

The following day, Mostofi al-Mamalek sent a message to Norman, saying that the Shah had asked him to form a cabinet, but he could not submit the 1919 Agreement to the Majles because he

1. *Ra'ad*, Jumada al-Awwal 7, 1339[AH] (January 17, 1921).

Mirza Hasan Khan Mostofi al-Mamalek

knew that, even if it was submitted, it would be rejected. He further stated that he would hire financial and military advisers from any country he desired and suggested that the 1919 Agreement be overturned so that he could reopen the Majles.[2]

Norman, who did not expect this reaction from Mostofi al Mamalek and felt he had been double-crossed, did not accept this proposal, which would have meant the official annulment of the agreement. Mostofi al-Mamalek then returned to the Shah and said that if he became prime minister, the fourth Majles would not open

2. Sheikh al-Islami, 1392^{SH}: 603–6.

immediately. The Shah did not agree with this and his premiership was set aside.

Sepahdar Reinvited

At the same time, amid rumors of Abdol-Hosain Mirza Farmanfarma becoming prime minister, Seyyed Zia al-Din Tabataba'i published an article in support of Sepahdar on January 17, 1921, in the *Ra'ad* newspaper:

> [. . .] About two months have passed since Sepahdar A'zam assumed his role as prime minister, yet nothing has been able to bring about his downfall except for several corrupt princes, reactionary figures, and courtiers. Now that Sepahdar's resignation has been accepted, there are two candidates for the post of prime minister: Mostofi al-Mamalek and Farmanfarma. Should Mr. Mostofi al-Mamalek refuse to accept the post and subsequently Prince Farmanfarma be tasked with forming a cabinet, then, given the country's current situation, his appointment would bode gravely for the country. Handing the reins of the state to a person who has been behind the misery and problems of Iran during various periods will destabilize the very pillars of the country and harm the prestige of the Iranian monarchy.[3]

The irony is that, one week later, Seyyed Zia al-Din Tabataba'i would form a cabinet that is known historically as the "Black Cabinet."[4]

Seyyed Zia was an ambitious man who was aligned with Britain's interest in a potential coup d'état. Farmanfarma's premiership would have undone his plans. Farmanfarma was a firm person with a military background, and he could definitely take control of the country, but,

---

3. *Ra'ad*, Jumada al-Awwal 7, 1339[AH] (January 17, 1921).

4. The families of those arrested by Seyyed Zia's administration organized a political campaign against him and called his cabinet "the Black Cabinet."

as a veteran politician, he would be unlikely to take an ambitious youth such as Seyyed Zia seriously.

Moshir al-Dowleh and Ayn al-Dowleh were separately summoned to Farahabad Palace on January 19. Neither of them accepted the post of prime minister, and Farmanfarma's appointment was ruled out due to public opposition.[5] Via his chief of staff, Moein al-Molk, the Shah informed Norman that appointing Mostofi al-Mamalek as prime minister was out of the question. Instead, Ahmad Shah suggested that Sepahdar become prime minister again and start work after a cabinet reshuffle. The Shah also asked Norman's opinion, but the British Minister did not give any advice. Norman then sent the following telegram to the British Foreign Office on the same day (January 19):

> In response to Moein al-Molk's query about the premiership, I said that, unlike the past, I'm no longer in a position to keep Persian prime ministers in office by granting financial aid. Nor can I accept the moral liability of suggesting someone for prime minister without being able to preclude his downfall. Future cabinets in Persia should absolutely rely on the people themselves. The chief of staff asked me to study the royal message for 24 hours, and I promised to do so.
>
> However, I will not answer differently after the expiry of the deadline, because anyone I suggest will be considered as the British Legation's candidate, and because after the withdrawal of British troops from Persia, I will be losing the authority and the influence which the troops' presence had given me. I will not be able to continue supporting my desired candidate, and even my candidate will have to step down due to opposition, at which point, our damaged prestige will be harmed further.[6]

---

5. *Ra'ad*, Jumada al-Awwal 9, 1339^{AH} (January 19, 1921); Afshar (ed.), 1380^{SH}: 153–5.

6. Sheikh al-Islami, 1392^{SH}: 605–6.

Moein al-Molk went to Sepahdar's residence in Tehran and held two hours of talks with him in an attempt to convince him to become prime minister again. The same day, yet another group of people went to see Sepahdar, consisting of party leaders, scholars, merchants, and other influential figures, in order to try to persuade him to accept the offer.[7]

The timing of all this coincided with good news from Gilan. After the arrival of Soviet Russian agents and the subsequent disarmament of the Soviet Russian forces, the town of Ghaziyan in Bandar Anzali was transferred to the Iranian government. Iranian Bolsheviks and Jangali Movement fighters took refuge in the woods, and some fled to surrounding areas, the Iranian Bolsheviks asking the Soviet Russian government for a guarantee of protection from reprisals from the Iranian government.

Majles Representatives Called In

During the negotiations between the Shah and Sepahdar to take on the premiership again, a meeting of the representatives elected to sit in the fourth Majles was convened at the Baharestan building on January 20 in order to secure their consent for the formation of a new cabinet. It was Prince Shabab al-Dowleh, representing the Shah, who made the opening address to the assembly:

> Following the resignation of Mr. Sepahdar and the urgency of settling the crisis, Mr. Mostofi al-Mamalek was assigned the premiership. However, after he informed His Majesty of his unwillingness to accept the post, Mr. Moshir al-Dowleh was considered. He refused as well. After that, due to the urgency of the matter, Mr. Sepahdar has been asked, once again, to form a cabinet. As the National Consultative Assembly is expected to reopen soon, this matter is presented to the members of the Majles for deliberation

---

7. *Ra'ad*, Jumada al-Awwal 10, 1339[AH] (January 20, 1921).

> at the order of His Majesty. If the members of the Majles agree, Mr. Sepahdar will serve as prime minister again.[8]

Following Shahab al-Dowleh's address, Prince Sardar Mofakham, the representative from Qazvin, chaired the meeting. For two hours, fifteen representatives delivered their speeches, from which two main points emerged. The first was gratitude to the Shah, for asking for their opinion even though their credentials had yet to be endorsed, and the second was the fact that they had been able to reach a majority decision regarding the appointment of Sepahdar. The Shah's endorsement and the majority decision by the representatives granted Sepahdar legitimacy.

The following day, January 21, 1921, Sepahdar was received again by the Shah. Meanwhile, political figures and other influential people kept frequenting his residence in a continued effort to persuade him to accept the post.[9] Finally, on January 22, the Shah issued the second decree for Sepahdar's premiership.

Another reason put forward for the renewed tenure of Sepahdar was that his resignation had elicited a negative response in Moscow, as the Russians believed that his support for the Russo-Persian Treaty of Friendship had led to his downfall. Concerned about the next cabinet's policies vis-à-vis the treaty, the Russians might have been prompted to halt their military withdrawal from Ghaziyan and its transfer to the Iranian Government.[10]

Additional Crises

It was the beginning of a new dilemma for Sepahdar, since it would be difficult to convince new ministers to join his cabinet when the country was in such a state of crisis. In a bid to boost the legitimacy of the government and accelerate the proceedings, Sepahdar engaged

---

8. Makki, 1361^{SH}, vol. 1: 131–3.

9. *Ra'ad*, Jumada al-Awwal 11, 1339^{AH} (January 21, 1921).

10. Dolatabadi, 1361^{SH}, vol. 4: 214.

with some well-known opponents of the 1919 Agreement in the newly formed cabinet.[11]

Meantime, the initiative launched by former prime minister Moshir al-Dowleh for Iran to collect its liabilities from APOC came to fruition and subsequently 600,000 pounds sterling, equivalent of 10 million tomans, were deposited into the account of the Iranian government with the Imperial Bank. But due to arrangements with the British government, the bank refused to let the Iranian government withdraw this money. That is why the state coffers were empty, and the government could only manage to scrape together 100,000 tomans by asking for money from the British legation via its agent Seyyed Zia al-Din.[12]

On January 31, 1921, Sardar Homayoun, commander of the Cossack Division, wrote a letter to the prime minister, warning him about the back wages of the Cossack forces. He noted in the letter that, while the forces based in Tehran had been paid for two months, in Qazvin, the troops had received payment for one month only. He also added that the 50,000 tomans recently supplied would not allow for a significant pay raise and warned that delayed payment would cause problems. Sepahdar wrote in response: "Of [a total of] 100,000 tomans, it was not planned to allocate upwards of 50,000 tomans to Qazvin. However, I will find a solution to send money to Qazvin."[13]

Seyyed Zia al-Din Tabataba'i, later elected to the fourteenth National Consultative Assembly, gave an account of the affair many years afterwards, on March 8, 1944.

> They came and told me about the situation of the Cossack forces. They warned of consequences if no action was taken. This part is a secret, which I do not have to reveal to you. I went to Mr. Sepahdar and talked with him. He said: "The British are withholding our funds. What is one to do?" I said

---

11. Dolatabadi, 1361[SH], vol. 4: 216.

12. Makki, 1361[SH], vol. 1: 153.

13. Haghani (ed.), 1379[SH]: 257–8.

> we should go and negotiate with them. Maybe they would pay him. I went to Mr. Norman and told him the situation was critical, asking him to pay the government of Iran one or two months' pay. Norman said: "I'll pay, provided that government offices have a share." I asked him: "What do you mean? Who else will receive this money?" He said: "The money will be given to the refugee migrants who have come to Tehran." I said: "The migrants are destitute. What should they do?" He said: "The government itself and the people should help them." I went and talked with the late Sepahdar, but he said: "It's impossible! Nobody can give them any aid." Again, I talked to Sepahdar and finally convinced him to allocate a share to the Cossacks if the British government paid any sum regarding the moratorium on backpay. He accepted and finally agreed to pay 50,000 to 60,000 tomans to the Cossacks . . . Now Sardar Homayoun intended to spend these 50,000 tomans entirely on the 500 Cossack forces in Tehran without giving anything to [the troops in] Qazvin. Finally, I convinced him to give two-thirds to Tehran and one-third to Qazvin. At last, Qazvin received 20,000 or 30,000 tomans. The Cossacks soon realized who had arranged their pay, and they referred to me in future. The same situation continued, and the sum was increased each month.

What Seyyed Zia does not mention is that Norman supplied money to the Cossacks through him so that he would make a favorable impression and the Cossacks would be beholden to him as an agent of the British Foreign Office.

Forming a New Cabinet

It took twenty-six days to form a new cabinet. One reason it took so long was the difficulty of persuading some individuals to accept a post as minister. In a bid to give assurances to the country at large, Sepahdar suggested that some celebrated opponents of the 1919 Agreement join the cabinet. Ahmad Shah agreed with this plan, and Sepahdar therefore invited three individuals—Haj Hasan Khan

Mohtasham al-Saltaneh Esfandiari, Mirza Morteza Khan Momtaz al-Molk, and Mirza Sadegh Khan Mostashar al-Dowleh—who had been sent into exile in Kashan owing to their opposition to the agreement during the prime ministership of Vosuq al-Dowleh. According to Malak al-Shoara Bahar, Sepahdar had promised Haj Hasan Khan Mohtasham al-Saltaneh Esfandiari, Mirza Morteza Khan Momtaz al-Molk, and Mirza Sadegh Khan Mostashar al-Dowleh that he would postpone the reconvention of the Majles to provide time for clarifying Iran's foreign policy, though a group of representatives of the Majles urged Ahmad Shah to oppose this decision.[14] Mostashar al-Dowleh explains how he was approached:

> Sepahdar sent me Dr. Amin al-Molk, the then minister of finance, saying national interests require that Haj Mohtasham al-Saltaneh, Mostashar al-Dowleh, and Momtaz al-Molk join the cabinet. I refused. The following day, he [Dr. Amin al-Molk] came and insisted on his demand. He said Sepahdar would come in person. My answer was negative again. Amin al-Molk left. Haj Mohtasham al-Saltaneh Esfandiari came and said: "Sepahdar says 'the problems are not as you imagine. I am counting on you, because I hope that we can spare the country from harm. In fact, I want you to show patriotism for your country; otherwise, we will all burn together'". . . I then realized that Britain's plot was becoming a reality.[15]

On February 5, 1921, Sepahdar took his nominated ministers to Farahabad Palace.[16] After the audience, Mohtasham al-Saltaneh, Momtaz al-Molk, and Mostashar al-Dowleh were summoned again by Ahmad Shah, and some issues were raised that delayed the formation of the cabinet. In this meeting, Ahmad Shah told the trio—the main critics of the 1919 Agreement—that national interests necessitated that the National Consultative Assembly be reconvened as soon

---

14. Bahar, 1371^SH^, vol. 1: 56–9.

15. Mostashar al-Dowleh, 1367^SH^, vol. 1: 134.

16. *Ra'ad*, Jumada al-Awwal 27, 1339^AH^ (February 6, 1921).

as possible. But, worried about the possible approval of the agreement, they opposed reopening the Majles and used the pretext that representatives of Gilan and Azerbaijan were absent. Ahmad Shah indicated that he was unhappy with stonewalling efforts of this kind by political leaders, especially when some of them appeared to favor their own prestige over national interests. Offended by such sarcasm, Mohtasham al-Saltaneh Esfandiari responded sharply: "Your Majesty is apparently worried about our presence in the cabinet. We were sent into exile in Kashan once. Your Majesty can send us into exile again, but he had better banish us this time to somewhere farther away, like Baghdad or India, in order to get rid of us for good."[17]

These exchanges led Mohtasham al-Saltaneh Esfandiari, Momtaz al-Molk, and Mostashar al-Dowleh to think twice about joining the cabinet, thereby delaying its formation once again. Disappointed by the nationalists' hesitancy, Sepahdar once again tendered his resignation, on February 8, which Ahmad Shah once again rejected.

The Putschists Gain Momentum

While Sepahdar was trying to find new ministers for his cabinet, the British were plotting a coup, waiting for the arrival of Firouz Mirza Nosrat al-Dowleh from London, whom they had chosen to lead it.[18]

The political imbroglio and economic downturn in the country had led not only the British government but also Iranians including, Sardar As'ad Bakhtiari, a military leader, who had gathered forces in Isfahan; Seyyed Hasan Modarres (a cleric), who had invited Mirza Kouchak Khan to come to Tehran; and Seyyed Zia (the journalist), who had been building a politico-military alliance with the help of the British for some time, to consider mounting a coup.

Reconvention of the Majles had been delayed due to divisions among the elite and sporadic demonstrations. There were both proponents and opponents of the reopening of the Majles, each

17. Sheikh al-Islami, 1392^{SH}: 606.

18. Makki, 1361^{SH}, vol. 1: 134–5; Dolatabadi, 1361^{SH}, vol. 4: 219–26.

Mirza Hasan Khan Mohtasham al-Saltaneh Esfandiari

group inspired by different political leaders. The proponents wanted the Majles to reopen to unblock the political situation, while the opponents feared it would lead to approval of the 1919 Agreement, as elections for the Majles had started when the Agreement Cabinet was in power. Sepahdar was undoubtedly well aware of the situation in the country and with all the activities of these different factions under way.

Firouz Mirza Nosrat al-Dowleh, the proposed coup leader, arrived in Tehran on February 7, 1921. Meanwhile, General Ironside had won over the Cossack commander, Reza Khan Mirpanj to take on the role as military leader of the coup. But Nosrat al-Dowleh stood aside as soon as he realized that the British legation was planning the mass arrest of princes and political figures in the country, on the pretext that they were his close relatives, friends, and colleagues. His role was transferred to Seyyed Zia al-Din. Ali Akbar Dehkhoda gives an account of the developments behind the rise of Seyyed Zia.

> After Sepahdar became prime minister again, and was busy choosing his ministers, one day I went to see my friend [Dr. Esma'il Khan] Amin al-Molk. His servant told him of my arrival, but strangely I was asked to wait in another room. I waited five or six minutes, but my host didn't appear. I decided to leave. As soon as I left the room, two people left another room before me. One was running ahead and one behind with the latter trying to keep the former from leaving. Finally, the one running ahead left the building. The one who was running after him was Amin al-Molk. He offered his apologies for the delay and said: "I was busy with Seyyed Zia al-Din. This man intends to become minister of interior affairs in the cabinet. I sought in vain to convince him that he lacks the necessary experience. As you saw he left in a fury and he may now be plotting against us."[19]

Years later, Seyyed Zia recounted how angry he had been with Sepahdar:

> When Sepahdar refused to form a cabinet, with me as its mastermind, I was infuriated with him. Later on, I appointed myself prime minister. I found that political leaders in Iran only wore a moustache and hat, without any other sign of manly vigor. If you touch them under the table, you will

19. Makki, 1361^{SH}, vol. 1: 171–2; Mostofi, 1360^{SH}, vol. 3: 205–6.

Firouz Mirza Nosrat al-Dowleh

find them to be castrated eunuchs. I said to myself: a real man is needed for all these eunuchs. Go ahead, Seyyed![20]

---

20. Elahi, 1393^{SH}: 63.

On February 14, 1921, Seyyed Zia travelled to Qazvin with between 70,000 and 80,000 tomans in a bid to bring the Cossacks under control and join the military leader of the coup.

Sepahdar's Second Cabinet

Sepahdar finally nominated his second cabinet, half of whom were from Gilan, on February 16. Members of this cabinet mostly comprised those of the previous one, with the addition of Mohtasham al-Saltaneh Esfandiari and Mirza Issa Khan Feyz and notably without Momtaz al-Molk and Mostashar al-Dowleh, the rest of the aforementioned trio.

Minister of Foreign Affairs: Hasan Esfandiari Mohtasham al-Saltaneh, was born during Naser al-Din Shah's rule. After studying medicine, literature, philosophy, logic, and mathematics at Dar al-Fonoun, he was employed at the foreign ministry and served as an Iranian diplomat in Germany and India. During Mozaffar al-Din Shah's reign, he became the director-general and translator at the foreign ministry. At the beginning of the constitutional period, he was the liaison officer between the prime minister, Mirza Nasrollah Khan Moshir al-Saltaneh, and the first Majles. Under Mohammad Ali Shah, he was acting Minister of Interior Affairs in the cabinet of Amin al-Soltan. He also served as the governor of Urmia, though he did not have much success in the role, managing to antagonize residents and the Russian, British, and Ottoman governments. Later on, he was Minister of Justice in Moshir al-Saltaneh's cabinet. After the end of the Minor Tyranny period, he served in successive cabinets as Minister of Justice, Minister of Foreign Affairs, Minister of Interior Affairs, and Minister of Finance. Firmly opposed to the 1919 Agreement during the tenure of Vosuq al-Dowleh, he was among those sent into exile in Kashan before joining Sepahdar's second cabinet.[21]

---

21. Agheli, 1380[SH] a, vol. 1: 109–14.

Acting Minister of Finance: Mirza Issa Khan Feyz studied finance in Europe, and later joined the Ministry of Finance. He then became comptroller of Gilan. He was promoted to deputy finance minister and then joined Sepahdar's second cabinet.[22]

---

22. Agheli, 1380^{SH} a, vol. 1: 1143–4.

CHAPTER 9

THE COUP

The Cossacks Head to Tehran

On its fourth day in office, the new cabinet faced a challenge: 2,000 Cossack forces were marching towards Tehran under the military command of Reza Khan and the political leadership of Seyyed Zia al-Din Tabataba'i. In his later account of events, Seyyed Zia comments:

> The coup occurred on Saturday night [February 21, 1921]. I was traveling between Tehran and Qazvin as of Thursday. I wanted to assure the Cossack forces that I had special permission from Tehran and specifically make Reza Khan understand that his position as military leader was not under threat. There was a tense atmosphere at the British Legation.[1]

Regarding divisions within the British Legation about the establishment of a powerful government in Iran in order to counter the Bolsheviks, he says:

---

1. Elahi, 1393^{SH}: 68.

> One group believed that it should be carried out through a street uprising to allow Democrats to come to power. Another group maintained that there should be a military attempt, be it the Gendarmerie or the Cossacks. There were also politicians who said that, in a traditional country, princes and aristocrats should handle the affair. Interestingly, those favoring popular uprising were the military staff of the British Legation, led by General Dickson, who was in charge of the Persian Military Commission under the 1919 Agreement. He was not happy with the Gendarmerie, because of their lack of expertise and their European style. He didn't like the Cossacks either, because of their negative political precedent. He believed that motivating freedom seekers would be the best way to block Communists. But the political figures of the Legation, who were more experienced, maintained that Communism was too powerful to be blocked by a democratic government. Some of them backed the Cossacks and Messrs. Smart and Howard were among them.[2]

Smart and Howard were two officials at the British legation who had negotiated a monthly payment to Seyyed Zia from the British government. Zia had used this money to pay the Cossacks' salaries.[3]

In order to transfer Cossack forces from Qazvin to Tehran, General Ironside initiated a plan to reorganize the Cossack Training Camp. For this purpose, he appointed Colonel Smyth, who was to persuade Norman that the Cossacks in Tehran were in a dire state and needed to be transferred to Qazvin to undergo military training, while the Qazvin-based forces would be sent to Tehran to replace them.

On February 19, 1921, the Cossack leader Sardar Homayoun, after hearing from Colonel Smyth, called for the redeployment of the Qazvin-based Cossack regiments to Tehran. Ahmad Shah, feeling

---

2. Elahi, 1393^SH^: 68. For more on the division among British government officials, see: Ghani, 1378^SH^: 203–9.

3. Elahi, 1393^SH^: 68–9.

threatened by this plan, told Norman via his chief of staff, Moein al-Molk, that he did not want this decree to be executed and that gendarmerie and police forces were sufficient for the establishment of order in the capital. However, Norman replied to Moen al-Molk that the Cossack forces were already on their way to Tehran.

Government Countermeasures

Seyyed Zia went to Sepahdar's residence on February 20, 1921. In his own account of the visit to Sepahdar, he states:

> I woke up at 6 in the morning and went to the prime minister's residence. I was sure that he would be sleeping until 9. The prime minister had been wanting to see me for six days, but he couldn't reach me. I went to his house and said: "Is His Excellency sleeping?" The reply was "Yes." I said: "I will leave now, but I'll be back." I had a garden in Zargandeh. I ordered a dinner to be prepared there and asked three Tar playing musicians to join me there by the evening.[4]

Contrary to Seyyed Zia's account, according to family members, Sepahdar usually rose early in the morning and would have been awake, especially on such crucial days before the coup. Most likely, Sepahdar simply refused to receive Seyyed Zia that morning.

The Shah and the government called on Sardar Homayoun to block the Cossacks midway. Sardar Homayoun reported on February 21 that he met with the forerunners of the Cossack forces on the Qazvin–Karaj road, and that they promised to return to Qazvin. But everyone knew that the Cossacks were still advancing on Tehran.[5]

On the same day, at noon, Sepahdar invited his cabinet members to a meeting. Their talks, which went on until the evening, resulted in a call for the dismissal or resignation of Sardar Homayoun as leader

---

4. Elahi, 1393[SH]: 187.

5. Ghani, 1378[SH]: 200.

of the Cossack Division. The government then sent a letter to the Minister of War, Haj Amir Nezam, asking him to stop the Cossack forces heading towards Tehran:

> His Excellency Mr. Amir Nezam, Minister of War
>
> In light of the fact that a group of Cossacks, without receiving any command or permission from the government, have arbitrarily departed from Qazvin and are heading to Tehran and while on their way are harassing passers-by, the government orders an urgent halt to their activities. Your Excellency is hereby authorized to prepare necessary forces from the Central Brigade and Tehran-based Cossacks, among others, to dispatch the necessary equipment for blocking the advance of the Cossack forces. You are granted all necessary authority for this purpose to make any changes in the Cossacks and the Brigade. The Gendarmerie has been ordered to prepare necessary equipment and arrange its forces under the authority of the Ministry of War.[6]

Martial Law Declared

Sepahdar issued the following statement to declare martial law:

> In light of the flood of problems and obstacles that are emerging in different forms on a daily basis in Iran's political scene and given the personal ill intentions of a limited group of opponents, I deemed it right to step down, demanding that His Majesty assign the mission of serving the nation and the country to other persons at the current very sensitive juncture. In spite of my expectations, those who were competent to run the country at this period of time refused to assume responsibility. Therefore,

6. Haghani (ed.), 1379[SH]: 263–4.

> His Majesty who has always made decisions in the best interests of the nation, asked me to form a cabinet.
>
> Obedience to the royal decree forced me to assume the responsibility once again, despite all the difficulties and obstacles, which I hope I can resolve successfully. While offering my gratitude to sympathetic fellow countrymen, I would like to highlight several points:
>
> The current situation in our country necessitates a powerful government to end infiltration by incompetent officials and persons. National interests must not allow opportunist elements to benefit from the current imbroglio for their own ends and subvert public opinion. My devotion to the country obliges me to be sensitive to whatever is against the national interests and adopt a new policy in order not to sacrifice a whole nation for the ambitions of the few.
>
> From this viewpoint, I warn rioters that martial law will remain in effect until the inauguration of the National Consultative Assembly. Police and military officers have been given necessary training and special authority to prosecute and punish anyone posing a threat to national security or attempting to subvert public opinion.
>
> Fathollah Sepahdar-e Aʿzam, Prime Minister[7]

However, news of the Cossacks' advance on Tehran had already made an impact, unsettling the Shah and spreading fear and anxiety among dignitaries and ordinary people alike. In a bid to provoke further anxiety, the British legation dismissed its Iranian employees and, as before, spread rumors that British subjects were leaving Iran. It also spread rumors that the Imperial Bank was closing its branches and called on people to withdraw their money. Norman was spending more time with the Shah in order to keep tabs on him. Ahmad Shah, who feared being dethroned, was planning to move the capital from

---

7. Makki, 1361^{SH}, vol. 1: 139–41.

Tehran to Shiraz, and then to travel to Europe or southern Iran, but a group of his associates dissuaded him from doing so.[8]

The Cossacks Advance on Tehran

Commanded by Reza Khan, the Cossacks were still advancing on the capital and had reached Mehrabad, a few kilometers from Tehran. On February 21, in the afternoon, Sepahdar tasked just six gendarmerie officers with blocking their advance. According to Colonel Georges Alfred Ducros, the French military attaché in Tehran, Sepahdar ordered Colonel Gleerup, the Swedish head of the gendarmerie, to take up only defensive positions in the city. Gleerup ordered his troops to remain in their camp and later instructed the Central Gendarmerie Regiment to move towards the Qazvin road, but without permission to engage.[9]

Following rumors that the Cossacks now had aligned with the Bolsheviks and were planning to capture the capital, Sepahdar sent his deputy, Adib al-Saltaneh, and the Shah's chief of staff, Moein al-Molk, along with two British officers, to negotiate with the Cossacks, but, with Seyyed Zia maneuvering behind the scenes, their negotiations with Reza Khan failed and they along with a few putschist representatives returned to Tehran.[10]

While the delegates were on their way, Ahmad Shah made a phone call to Sepahdar holding him accountable for the crisis to which the Shah received a stern rebuttal from his prime minister: "Sardar Homayoun was bribed by Reza Khan Mirpanj and [in return] he granted him the command of this regiment. Am I to be blamed?"[11]asked Sepahdar.

---

8. Makki, 1361[SH], vol. 1: 142–3.

9. Ayati (trans.), 1380[SH]: 59–60.

10. Makki, 1361[SH], vol. 1: 201–2; Bahar, 1371[SH], vol. 1: 111 Dolatabadi, 1361[SH], vol. 4: 129–227; Elahi, 1393[SH]: 71.

11. Bahar, 1371[SH], vol. 1: 112.

Reza Khan Mirpanj

The Cossacks entered the capital at 11:30 PM, and captured key points in the city. Despite the declaration of martial law and knowing of the arrival of the Cossacks, Sepahdar is said to have refused to order 10,000 gendarmerie and police forces deployed in the capital to block them, strengthening rumors that he had been in alliance with the coup plotters and that he had been told that the Cossacks were coming.[12] In support of this theory, Abdollah Mostofi quotes Seyyed Yahya Naser al-Islam Nedamani, a politician from Gilan, a member of Majles, and a close relative of Sepahdar:

> I used to go to Sepahdar's house every night. We were close friends. On the night of February 21, 1921, unlike other evenings, Sepahdar was wearing a black [suit] and a starched-collar shirt, and it was as if he was waiting for an announcement to go somewhere or receive someone at home. He waited until after midnight. He showed no signs of stress despite the sound of cannon fire in the city. The following morning, his carriage was ready. Nothing happened. Mirza Isa Khan Soroush was sent to learn the news. It was after Mr. Soroush's return that [Sepahdar] realized that he was no longer in power....[13]

Seyyed Zia acknowledged later that he had sent 500 pounds sterling to the Minister of War, Amir Nezam, and two other cabinet ministers to order gendarmerie and police commanders not to resist the Cossacks.[14]

The most intriguing evidence in support of Sepahdar's foreknowledge of the coup, possibly being published for the first time, is his own account, as relayed via his son, Mohsen Akbar, and given in the preface to this book. Years after the coup, Sepahdar told his son that he had met with Reza Khan secretly on several occasions, including on February 20, 1921, and that Reza Khan told him of his plans. This account is supported by Colonel Ducros, the French military attaché in Tehran, who stated that the day before the coup, Sepahdar told him that Tehran would be captured the following night.[15] In addition, Naser al-Islam Nedamani's account is that, on the night before the coup, Sepahdar was formally dressed, as if he were waiting for an

---

12. Mostofi, 1360[SH], vol. 3: 208.
13. Mostofi, 1360[SH], vol. 3: 206–7.
14. Elahi, 1393[SH]: 72.
15. Ayati (trans.), 1382[SH].

announcement directing him to go somewhere, or waiting to receive someone at home. That "someone" was Reza Khan.

With this information as background, Sepahdar's minimal defense measures against the Cossacks can be interpreted as mere staging and show. He had at his disposal the 10,000 gendarmerie forces and refused to dispatch them, presumably to allow for a successful and bloodless coup.

What did and did not happen after the coup further bolsters the argument that Sepahdar was involved. Specifically, the fact that Sepahdar, the prime minister, was one of very few dignitaries who were not arrested after the coup strongly indicates that Sepahdar was complicit. Also, as mentioned in the Preface, he regularly had an audience with Reza Shah during the latter's reign years later. After Sepahdar's death, Reza Shah even received Sepahdar's sons to express his condolences. It is important to note that Reza Shah did not extend the same signs of respect to many other dignitaries.

There is also a possibility that Sepahdar was directly supported by the British embassy in Tehran. Norman's defenses of him in some of his correspondence with Curzon could be a sign of this support.

Dignitaries Arrested

From the night of February 21, 1921, the Cossacks started arresting prominent politicians in the capital, following a list prepared by Seyyed Zia. Scores of people—from princes and aristocrats to constitutionalists and members of the Majles—were arrested and detained by the Cossacks. The detainees included such key figures as Abdol-Hosain Mirza Farmanfarma and his two sons, Firouz Mirza Nosrat al-Dowleh and Abbas Mirza Salar Lashkar (Minister of Justice) despite being British sympathizers; Abdol-Majid Mirza Ayn al-Dowleh, Mohtasham al-Saltaneh Esfandiari (Minister of Foreign Affairs), Amir Nezam Hamedani (Minister of War), former prime minister Sepahsalar Tonekaboni, and Seyyed Hasan Modarres.[16]

---

16. Makki, 1361^{SH}, vol. 1: 236–7.

British legation in Tehran

Sepahdar, who was no longer the prime minister, sought refuge at the British legation. As he would not be arrested, he then left the legation and went home.[17] For three days, the Cossacks ravaged houses and seized large sums of money. Among the detainees, Amir Nezam was among those who agreed to pay money, 250,000 tomans in his case, to secure his release, but others did not agree to pay for their release and therefore were kept in detention.

The Meeting of Seyyed Zia and Sepahsalar Tonekaboni

Mohammad Vali Khan Tonekaboni Sepahsalar-e Aʿzam apparently had been one of the candidates considered by the British legation for the role of prime minister after the coup. Talks had been held with him to that effect, but the British had set a condition for his appointment: Naming Seyyed Zia al-Din as Minister of Interior Affairs. However, persuading Sepahsalar Tonekaboni, the commander of the Triumph of Tehran, and the obstinate former prime minister,

17. Makki, 1361SH, vol. 1: 276.

was not so easy. Finally, Seyyed Zia decided to visit him in person to discuss the issue with him in private. At Sepahsalar's house, Zia first informed him about the arrest and banishment of some dissidents, which Sepahsalar Tonekaboni welcomed. Then, Seyyed Zia raised the issue of the Ministry of Interior Affairs. The following is an account of what occurred, as told by Sepahsalar's secretary, Mohazzeb al-Molk:

> Seyyed said: "But regarding the Ministry of Interior Affairs do you have someone able to implement with precision the orders of his majesty and theirs [Britain's], one who would be accepted by both sides?" Sepahsalar wanted to ignore what Seyyed had said, but Seyyed Zia repeated himself. I was behind the door and I felt that Sepahsalar was getting angry, because I saw him pulling on his cap once or twice.
>
> Finally, he told Seyyed: "If I am to take the interior ministry in hand, it should be unconditional." At which point Seyyed said: "Of course, they have nothing against that, but they want assurances about the interior minister that your excellency might choose." Sepahsalar said: "Name any person they have chosen or recommended. I may be in agreement with them if the candidate is acceptable." Seyyed Zia said: "They have considered me."
>
> As soon as Sepahsalar heard this, he pulled his cap and then tightened it on his head, just like someone who is preparing for a wrestling match. Then he said: "You! You! Never! I'll never accept to lead a cabinet whose minister of interior affairs would be Seyyed Jimbo (sarcastically giving him an English name). This is shameful! This Seyyed wants to become interior minister in a cabinet whose prime minster would be me! Get out of here right now! Hurry up! It's all to be blamed on Mohazzeb al-Molk, who pushed me towards such a dirty business. As the last insults were hurled, Seyyed Zia was already on his way out.[18]

---

18. Mostofi, 1360^{SH}, vol. 3: 203–4.

Seyyed Zia as Prime Minister

On February 23, 1921, at the putschists' request, Ahmad Shah nominated Seyyed Zia al-Din Tabataba'i as prime minister. Ahmad Shah also appointed Reza Khan Mirpanj as the official commander of the Cossack Division by awarding him the title of Sardar Sepah [Commander of Forces]. Sepahdar, who notably was among few dignitaries to have been spared imprisonment, sent the following note to Seyyed Zia in his capacity as former prime minister, requesting to meet with him:

> I would like to offer my sincere congratulations to you for assuming the responsibility to run the country and wish your excellency success in your post. I will be sending you the prime minister's seal with Mr. Mirza Ali Khan. Since I would like to offer my good wishes to you in person and share some issues briefly with your excellency, I would like a short meeting.
>
> Fathollah

In response, Seyyed Zia declined to receive his predecessor.[19]

Seyyed Zia introduced his cabinet to the Shah on March 2, 1921 and remained in power for about three months. During his term in office, the Russo-Persian Treaty of Friendship was signed, and Russian troops pulled out of Gilan. The Imperial Bank unfroze the Anglo-Persian Oil Company's liabilities to the Iranian government, which allowed payment of back wages and hiring top advisers from Sweden, Britain, the United States, and France to work in various ministries. All this was achieved despite the 1919 Agreement being declared null and void by the new government in Iran in consultation with the British government. However, it was practically implemented, as Norman highlighted in a telegram to Lord Curzon:

---

19. For Sepahdar's letter and Seyyed Zia's reply see: Haghani (ed.), 1379^{SH}: 264–5.

Seyyed Zia al-Din Tabataba'i

> It seems that annulment of the Agreement will not change the situation, because our advisers are working at the Ministry of Finance, and British officers are involved in military affairs. Control of South Persia Rifles will be transferred to the government and the Agreement has practically been implemented. Please do not hesitate to agree.[20]

During his tenure, Seyyed Zia, under the guidance of the British legation, supervised the withdrawal of more than 10,000 British troops, as well as embarking on various reforms, including banning opium, helping to prevent the spread of typhus, housing neglected and orphaned children, preventing the further hoarding of provisions by the British and the Russians, and supplying the needs of the

---

20. Makki, 1361^{SH}, vol. 1: 305.

residents of the capital. Seyyed Zia was remarkably successful, thanks to financial and political backing by the British, in contrast to his predecessors who were preoccupied with keeping Iran independent of foreign powers.

However, Seyyed Zia's inclination to support Crown Prince Mohammad Hasan Mirza strained his ties with Ahmad Shah. The Shah, who wanted to support a powerful rival to oppose Seyyed Zia, boosted Reza Khan, now Sardar Sepah, whom he promoted to the post of Commander of the Cossack Division and Minister of War. Differences gradually emerged between the two main coup leaders, and the Shah, who had become weary of Seyyed Zia's conceit, finally dismissed him.

Mohammad Hasan Mirza Qajar, Crown Prince.

CHAPTER 10

THE RISE OF SARDAR SEPAH AND THE FALL OF THE QAJAR DYNASTY

After the collapse of Seyyed Zia's hundred-day Black Cabinet, Mirza Ahmad Khan Qavam al-Saltaneh, Vosuq al-Dowleh's brother, was released from prison and brought to Farahabad Palace, where Ahmad Shah named him prime minister on May 30, 1921. Qavam al-Saltaneh immediately ordered the freedom of all those imprisoned by the putschists.

During Qavam al-Saltaneh's tenure, the country plunged once again into chaos. Various groups—led by Mohammad Tahgi Khan Pesyan in Khorasan; Saed al-Dowleh, son of Sepahsalar Tonekaboni, in Tonekabon; Ehsanollah Khan Doustdar in Chalous; and Amir Moayyed Savadkuhi in Mazandaran—rebelled against the central government, while armed outlaw Haji Baba Ardebili spread lawlessness in the Zanjan area. At the same time, socialists established a Soviet republic in Gilan.

Mirza Ahmad Khan Qavam al-Saltaneh.

Fourth National Consultative Assembly

The interregnum between the third and fourth National Consultative Assembly lasted more than five and a half years. Qavam al-Saltaneh finally managed to convene the fourth Majles, which had been planned by his brother, Vosuq al-Dowleh. Elections were held during

Back row from left to right: Sardar Mohyee (Sepahdar Rashti's cousin), Khalou Ghorban, Ehsanollah Khan, Reza Khajavi, and Alexander Kualov. *Front row: from left to right:* Haji Morad Mogoyev (hands crossed), Moshir Divan, and Karim Khan Bozorg.

Ala al-Saltaneh's tenure, and the first session was held on June 22, 1921, in the presence of Ahmad Shah. However, as representatives were said to have been groomed by pro-British Vosuq al-Dowleh's cabinet, many credentials were not endorsed while, in some areas, no representative was elected due to local unrest. In Gilan, for instance, due to conflict between the Jangali Movement, the Bolsheviks, and government troops, only three representatives were elected: Mirza Sadegh Khan Akbar Sardar Motamed and Sepahdar (for Rasht); and Haj Sheikh Mohammad Hosain (for Tavalesh and Gorganrud). When Haj Sheikh Mohammad Hosain's credentials were rejected for unknown reasons, only Sepahdar, now once again in the role of representative, and his cousin Sardar Motamed represented Gilan in the fourth National Consultative Assembly.

The fourth Majles was therefore convened not long after the February coup. During deliberations about credentials, anti-coup representatives regularly questioned the extent to which certain representatives had been involved in the coup against Sepahdar's cabinet. During discussions on July 27 about the credentials of Soltan Mohammad Khan, a member of the Majles, for instance, Seyyed Hasan Modarres, a cleric, commented:

> First and foremost, you must know that representatives are not biased. I am also not biased vis-à-vis Mr. Soltan Mohammad Khan. I see him as my own son, and he has worked with me for some time. If anyone claims that the current situation is the product of a non-Iranian intervention, we should all refute such allegations. A friend of ours granted authority to someone who acted against the Constitution, national independence, and the monarchy. A group, either knowingly or unknowingly, followed him. We are all Muslims. Of course, Mr. Soltan Mohammad Khan is also a Muslim, and he has to call for an Islamic establishment. Everyone is liable for contributing to the current situation.
>
> If my friend claims that he didn't know the policies, I will deny such claims, because he has been with me for two years. If he really didn't know the legal policies, he is not competent to sit in this Majles. But if he knows the policies, he should no longer do as he did before. Any government has its shortcomings, and yes, a coup might have occurred to reform the country. Our Constitution has many shortcomings, and the shutdowns that occurred were harmful to our national sovereignty. Every reform should be done by relying on a representative from Iran. Of course, all representatives present here liked Soltan Mohamad Khan very much. However, an illegal and anti-constitutional coup occurred. Therefore, my friend should not be sitting at this Assembly, so that everyone would know that anyone doing so should be deprived of representing the nation . . . Even if one day is left from the term of the National Consultative Assembly, any representative acting against the Constitution will be discredited.

In response, Soltan Mohammad Khan said:

What Mr. Modarres was driving at is as follows: due to my participation in anti-government acts, I am not allowed to be an elected representative. I would like to explain several points here, and since parliament is the center of justice, I hope that no decision would be made against justice and truth. He claims that I've been complicit in anti-government actions. Which government does he mean? If he is referring to the cabinet of Sepahdar Aʿzam, I have to remind you that these fellows in the Baharestan building were repeatedly accusing him of being reactionary and expressed the harshest words against him. They have apparently forgotten what spectacle they put up against the cabinet of Sepahdar. If that embodied national sovereignty, this Majles should not be opened because you have forgotten your own words against these representatives.

Now, suppose that Sepahdar's cabinet did embody national sovereignty and a coup was fomented against it. I was neither a putschist, nor was I informed of the coup plot. You can ask the putschists, the same individuals whom you sanctify, ask if I was among them. On the day the coup occurred, it was rumored that all representatives had been arrested. I left my home and went to a friend's house. He can testify. He is Mr. Hakim al-Molk. Three or four days later, a royal decree pasted on the walls indicated that Seyyed Zia al-Din had been named prime minister. Clearly, in the absence of a parliament, appointment of the prime minister is within the exclusive authority of His Majesty. Nobody called into question his premiership and I don't think acquaintance with someone would be interpreted as treason, and amount to an offense.

Seyyed Zia al-Din called me into his office, offering me various posts. I refused. He finally imposed the post of director of the cabinet and then Deputy Minister of Finance upon me. During this period, I've been using all my influence to help people solve problems, and I have managed to secure the release of some prisoners. I sent doctors to treat patients. Mr. Astarabadi, Mr. Garousi, and Mr. Mirza Ali Kazerouni have been witnesses to my activities. Therefore, if you mean that I've participated in the coup, I should say that I had no role in it. I am ready to

> present my evidence, documents, and proof that I did not take part in the coup; rather I even blunted its impact.

Then, Abdol-Hosain Khan Sardar Moazzam Khorasani (Teymourtash), a staunch supporter of Reza Khan Sardar Sepah, spoke against Soltan Mohammad Khan's credentials:

> I decided not to talk about Soltan Mohammad Khan, because I have already raised much more important issues. But he took advantage of freedom of speech and raised unfounded allegations. [. . .]
>
> He raised several issues, which I think need clarification. He said that we should refer to Sepahdar's cabinet as one representing national sovereignty. Mr. Soltan Mohammad Khan must recall that he was very supportive of Sepahdar's cabinet. We were opposed, but you were pro-Sepahdar. Because it was Sepahdar's cabinet that prepared the ground for the coup. The same cabinet set the stage for action against national sovereignty . . . When we say that someone has acted and risen up against national sovereignty, we mean that he has acted against the National Consultative Assembly.
>
> Anybody preparing the ground for the shutdown of the National Consultative Assembly and the Constitution has acted against national sovereignty. It was Seyyed Zia who laid the foundation for opposition to national sovereignty, wasn't it? It was Seyyed Zia who ordered the arrest of representatives in an anti-constitutional move, wasn't it? Of course, it was!
>
> He did act against national sovereignty, against the Constitution, which we believe is sacred while others may not. Seyyed Zia did act against national independence. That is why we intend to deny some representatives a seat in the parliament, not merely for supporting Sepahdar or anyone else . . . We are all aware that preparing the ground for a coup, and any illegal action, requires discrediting opponents first. That is why Seyyed Zia and his predecessor humiliated representatives and the law. They spoke

> critically of them everywhere and insulted them to cause chaos and reach their own objectives for their own ends.
>
> We are well aware that the coup had been prepared long in advance. Therefore, they established these passive governments and kept them in office, spoke poorly of National Consultative Assembly representatives, uttered accusations against them, spread falsehoods and undermined well-wishers. Why? They intended to fish in muddy waters. We knew all this, and therefore we don't believe that Sepahdar's cabinet was synonymous with national sovereignty. When it is established, the Majles is required to decide against anyone who has acted against national sovereignty . . . Your participation in anti-national acts is much more than what Mr. Modarres described.

After Sardar Moazzam spoke, deliberations continued, though Soltan Mohammad's credentials were not endorsed in the end.[1]

Sardar Moazzam's criticism of Sepahdar's hesitation in opening the National Consultative Assembly, should be reviewed given the fact that it was Sepahdar, who, in his capacity as interior minister in the first cabinet of Vosuq al-Dowleh, made necessary arrangements for legislative elections. And when he became prime minister, Sepahdar made several efforts to end political obstruction.

A couple of sessions were also held to discuss the credentials of Nosrat al-Dowleh Firouz, who during the session on August 1, 1921, spoke about the 1919 Agreement. His speech included the following remarks pertaining to Sepahdar:

> I am being criticized for my role in the Vosuq al-Dowleh Agreement. I don't deny it. But what are you insinuating? If you mean that this policy was considered by a group or the general public to be harmful to the nation, the decision-makers and politicians of the time should come and explain whether

1. The deliberations of fourth National Consultative Assembly, fourth session (5 Mordad 1300, 1921).

Fourth National Consultative Assembly representatives, with Sepahdar seated behind the third cleric from left, 1921.

they betrayed the country, or whether they adopted a policy due to circumstances. I don't deny my own involvement, but all my colleagues should be present here in this hearing.

If you want to say that simply signing the Agreement without investigation amounts to action against national sovereignty, it shows misinformation and spitefulness. There was no Majles in office, the reasons for which I don't intend to raise now, and the government made a policy at its own discretion, but subject to parliament approval. . . .

In his address, Mr. Tabataba'i noted some so-called violations of the Constitution during the cabinet of Vosuq al-Dowleh. The sanctity of the Majles and the Constitution bar me from making any comparisons with other cabinets of the interregnum period. I want to ask Mr. Tabataba'i to explain why he and Prince Soleiman Mirza only highlight three names from Vosuq al-Dowleh's cabinet. . . .

Let me say something else too. Liability is not limited to a specific group of ministers. By virtue of the Constitution, all ministers and all groups are equally responsible to the nation.[2]

Interestingly, Sepahdar did not make any comments about the coup and marginal issues of his premiership, and the representatives did not object to his credentials either.

2. The deliberations of the fourth National Consultative Assembly, session 6 (10 Mordad 1300, 1921).

Among the important issues coinciding with the fourth legislature were the growing power of Reza Khan Sardar Sepah and the need to suppress multiple rebellions in various regions of the country. These included the Jangali Movement and uprisings in Azerbaijan and Lorestan. The main pieces of legislation by the fourth National Consultative Assembly included: Annulment of the 1919 Agreement; hiring American advisers; adopting a new education law; discussing Iran's membership in the League of Nations; funding scholarships for students; and enforcing a local dress code for men.[3]

The Growing Power of Sardar Sepah

Assisted by his Minister of War, Reza Khan, Sardar Sepah, a new prime minister, Qavam al-Saltaneh, quashed all the regional rebellions thereby increasing the power of the military. Then, on January 19, 1922, due to disagreements between the government and parliament, Qavam al-Saltaneh stepped down, and with the consent of the Majles, Ahmad Shah appointed Mirza Hasan Khan Moshir al-Dowleh as prime minister, before traveling to Europe. Four months later, Moshir al-Dowleh's cabinet fell against the backdrop of Sardar Sepah's growing influence and power.

Qavam al-Saltaneh became prime minister once again, in June of that year, and Minister of War Sardar Sepah forcefully quashed the unrest in Lorestan and Azerbaijan. A number of representatives who were opposed to Sardar Sepah's growing power spoke out against him in the Majles. In response, Sardar Sepah resigned on October 8, 1922 which resulted in demonstrations by military staff in various cities in support of Sardar Sepah until finally Qavam al-Saltaneh and Crown Prince Mohammad Hasan Mirza persuaded him to return to office.

Ahmad Shah returned to Iran on November 30, 1922 and Qavam al-Saltaneh stepped down once again in February the following year,

3. Cheknaji and Yousefdehi, 1394^{SH}: 28.

due to strong criticism of him by socialist representatives. This time, Mirza Hasan Khan Mostofi al-Mamalek became prime minister, though with a weak majority Majles, and Sardar Sepah remained in his post as war minister. However, in June 1923, Mostofi al-Mamalek faced impeachment, after some agents of Sardar Sepah were found to have swayed the elections for the fifth National Consultative Assembly which took place on April 2, 1923. Two of the impeachers were Seyyed Hasan Modarres and Qavam al-Saltaneh. Sepahdar, Haerizadeh, and two or three others who were in the majority in the Majles then broke ranks to join the minority. As a result, the censure motion worked and Mostofi al-Mamalek was dismissed from the premiership.[4] He was succeeded by Mirza Hasan Khan Moshir al-Dowleh, who in turn quit in October. Finally, Ahmad Shah named Reza Khan Sardar Sepah prime minister as he had grown popular among both military and political figures. The Shah himself then departed again for Europe on December 3, 1923.

Fifth National Consultative Assembly

The elections for the fifth National Consultative Assembly were ordered on April 2, 1923. The Tehran election was held during the term of this Majles, but elections for other constituencies of Iran were held during the seven-month pause between the fourth and fifth assemblies. It was this pause that empowered pro-Sardar Sepah army generals to interfere with the election results and send their desired members to parliament, leading to the aforementioned impeachment of Mostofi al-Mamlek. Interestingly, Sardar Sepah was among the candidates in various constituencies, including Rasht and was the top elected official with the most votes everywhere.

The fifth Majles was inaugurated on February 12, 1924, overseen by Crown Prince Mohammad Hasan Mirza. The representatives of Gilan included Sepahdar (for Rasht).

---

4. Makki, 1361[SH], vol. 1: 316.

After the Ottoman Empire fell and the Republic of Turkey was established in November 1923, pro-Sardar Sepah representatives started talking about the establishment of a republic in Iran. In March 1924, Tehran and other cities witnessed mass demonstrations in favor of establishment of a republic. Government offices were closed. As those not in favor of a republic also held their own demonstrations, heavy scuffles broke out between pro- and anti-republic groups around Baharestan Square on March 22, with heavy casualties. Bowing to pressure from religious scholars, merchants, and others, Sardar Sepah reconsidered establishing a republic and announced his decision in an official statement on April 1, 1924.

Three days later, Ahmad Shah sent a telegram from Europe dismissing Sardar Sepah and demanding that the Majles name Mostofi al-Mamalek as prime minister again. Sardar Sepah stepped down and went to settle in Rudehen outside Tehran, whereupon military groups demonstrated in support of him by marching in the streets and sending threatening telegrams to members of the Majles, giving them two days to reinstate Sardar Sepah. The Majles then held an extraordinary session on April 10, 1924, and reinstated Sardar Sepah. A group of representatives, including Dr. Mosaddegh, went to Rudehen to bring back Sardar Sepah to Tehran, after which, the Majles deliberations on the credentials of representatives resumed.

Sepahdar's credentials were approved by the Majles during the May 16, 1924 session. However, shortly afterwards, he fell ill and requested sick leave. The Majles endorsed his request on June 29, during its thirty-second session. According to the medical report confirming Sepahdar's illness, he stayed in Shemiran during the one-month period of sick leave, and donated his salary to the library of the Majles.

Meanwhile Sardar Sepah brought Khuzestan under full control in December 1924, disarming local nomads and exiling tribal sheikhs. Sardar Sepah and his supporters then embarked on making arrangements for the fall of the Qajar dynasty.

During the Majles session of December 28, Sepahdar once again requested leave of absence, this time for forty days to tend to his properties in Gilan. It was announced:

> Mr. Sepahdar-e A'zam has requested forty days of leave of absence to visit his properties in Gilan. The Commission agrees with his request.
>
> **Vice-Speaker**: Mr. Agha Seyyed Yaqoub.
>
> **Agha Seyyed Yaqoub**: I agree, but since Mr. Sepahdar-e A'zam has always been a generous philanthropist, his paid salary should be used for charitable purposes in the Majles Library.
>
> **Vice-Speaker**: Mr. Sardar Motamed.
>
> **Sardar Motamed**: Since Mr. Sepahdar is ailing and absent, we had better wait until he returns and responds to Mr. Agha.
>
> **Kazerouni**: I do not see his request to be illegitimate. It depends on the Majles to agree or disagree with his request. If he isn't entitled to using his paid salary, that is clear, but if he is entitled to receiving his salary, waiting for him would be a good idea.
>
> **Vice-Speaker**: We put it to vote. Please rise if you agree [majority of members agreed].[5]

After the end of Sepahdar's forty-day absence, the issue of extending his leave of absence was raised during the session of March 14, 1925. Only one representative opposed this. Sepahdar finally returned to the Majles, after over two months of absence, in April 1925.

The following summer, a law was adopted banning titles and making family last names obligatory. Sepahdar chose the family name "Akbar," which was derived from the name of his famous uncle Akbar Khan Biglarbeigi. Most of his relatives adopted similar

---

The deliberation of the 5th National Consultative Assembly, session 112 (7 Dey 1302, 1924).

names, such as Khan Akbar, Naeimi Akbar, and Haghighi Akbar, while some also adopted Omshei as their family name.

The Fall of the Qajars

In late October 1925, Tehran and most cities in the country became the scene of widespread demonstrations against the Qajar monarchy. The National Consultative Assembly, in its session of October 31, 1925, voted 80–85 to declare the end of the Qajar monarchy in Iran. Reza Khan Sardar Sepah was named provisional ruler until the Constituent Assembly was established.[6]

Fathollah Khan Akbar (Sepahdar), who neither wanted to vote in favor of the end of the Qajar monarchy, nor wanted to oppose Sardar Sepah, was among eighteen members absent in the historic session. By the end of the term of the fifth Majles, the Constituent Assembly was established during an election on December 6, 1925. On December 13, 1925, the National Consultative Assembly declared Sardar Sepah, now Reza Shah Pahlavi, as monarch of Iran. The tenure of the fifth National Consultative Assembly ended on February 11, 1926, thereby ending the mandate of all the representatives, including that of Sepahdar.

---

6. The Assembly of 260 seats convened on December 6, 1925.

Reza Shah Pahlavi, 1926.

CHAPTER 11

FINAL YEARS

Isolation

With Reza Shah Pahlavi in power, Sepahdar, like many other Qajar-era politicians, chose to live in isolation. He lived mainly at his residence in Tehran, the house located in a vast garden on Jaleh Avenue.[1] For him, this building brought back memories of the lively years of the constitutional movement, when constitutional leaders and freedom seekers came to his house, enjoying lavish spreads and the generosity of the host, while discussing plans for the constitutional movement. Now, the house was the home of a veteran and weary politician, visited only by the Qajar-era old guard, who spent hours there, reminiscing about past times. What the old statesmen witnessed was the grand modernization of the country. Every aspect of the corrupt and ailing society was changing for the better. Education was on the forefront of Reza Shah's agenda, as was the country's infrastructure. Roads were being built rapidly. A cross-country railway was being implemented. The University of Tehran was established. A new modern healthcare system was developed to counter the vast opium addiction and various deadly epidemics. Suddenly it appeared that

1. Azaramsa, 1378^{SH}: 179.

the country was being led by a leader who cared for the people and not only for the elite. But these faithful old friends who gathered at Sepahdar's famous home also often spoke cautiously about the emergence of a modern dictatorship, as well as the speedy progress visible all around them. So much in the country was changing, and reforms were taking place all over Iran.

Gone were the horse-drawn carriages. Now, Sepahdar had a car and a chauffeur of Belarussian origin. During his retirement, he continued his travels to Europe and on two occasions lived there for short periods. During his time in Europe, he developed friendly ties with Aga Khan III.[2]

Sepahdar during the final years of his life.

Sepahdar was known as a man of faith who performed his daily prayers. He financed the first dome for the mausoleum of Agha Seyyed Jalal al-Din Ashraf in the city of Astaneh Ashrafieh in Gilan.

In the final years of his life, Sepahdar built a family mausoleum in the Ibn Babawayh Cemetery in Ray, south of Tehran. Other prominent families, including the Amini, Foroughi, and Sami'i families, are also laid to rest in this famous cemetery.

2. Ghanei and Elmi, 1391[SH]: 191. His father had been born in Kerman, and he became the forty-seventh Imam of the Nezari Isma'ili Muslims. He went to the University of Cambridge. Despite his close relations with the British and primary interest in Indian affairs, the Aga Khan retained some consciousness of his Iranian ancestry. He claimed always to have followed "an Iranian-Muslim pattern" in his home life (*Memoirs*, p. 30), and even considered himself a member of the Qajar family (*Memoirs*, p. 93), both his father and mother being of Qajar descent. *Encyclopaedia Iranica Online*, © Trustees of Columbia University in the City of New York. Consulted online on February 26, 2023.

Death

Fathollah Khan Akbar Sepahdar died on March 25, 1937, in Tehran. He was eighty-two years old. The same day, a funeral service was held for him in the presence of Mahmud Jam (Modir al-Molk), then prime minister; Hasan Esfandiari (Mohtasham al-Saltaneh), Speaker of the Majles at that time; and numerous other politicians, as well as the entire Akbar clan. The following day, the *Ettelaat* daily newspaper published the following account of the funeral:

> **Funeral for the late Mr. Akbar**
>
> Yesterday, at 3 PM, a funeral service was held for the late Fathollah Akbar (Sardar Mansur—Sepahdar-e Aʿzam) with a massive presence of political and influential figures. The coffin was draped in flowers. The Prime Minister, the Speaker of the National Consultative Assembly, a number of Majles representatives, politicians and former ministers carried the casket from his residence to Baharestan Square, before transporting his coffin by car to the mausoleum of Shah Abdol Azim. After which, a large number of participants proceeded to Ibn Babwayeh Cemetery to attend the burial ceremony, which took place in Sepahdar's private mausoleum.
>
> At the memorial service, which was held at Majd al-Dowleh Mosque before noon today, the Prime Minister, the Speaker of the National Consultative Assembly, and a number of politicians and influential figures were all in attendance.[3]

The family mausoleum was located at the entrance of the cemetery, but there is no remnant of it today, following its destruction during the first few months of the Islamic Republic. A simple, new black tombstone has replaced the grand mausoleum.

Sepahdar was survived by his two wives, Begum Khanum and Bemani Khanum, his daughter Khanum Makhsous, and three sons:

3. *Ettelaat*, 1316[sh] (March 26, 1937).

The family mausoleum in the Ibn Babawayh Cemetery of Tehran where Sepahdar was interred before the mausoleum was destroyed.

Mohamad Ali Khan Akbar, titled Amir Mansur; Gholam Hosain Khan Akbar, titled Biglarbeigi; and Mohsen Khan Akbar.

Iran in a Time of Crisis

As this book is being written, Iran is once again experiencing significant turmoil. Gross mismanagement by its governing bodies, corruption within the system, foreign interference, and sanctions have increased inflation and poverty to unprecedented levels and left the Iranian people struggling to survive. How this crisis will play out is anyone's guess.

Just over a hundred years ago, Iran was also in turmoil. The government was bankrupt and dependent on foreign payments. A looming bread crisis was threatening the return of a great famine and people were desperate and restless. The Russian Bolshevik army was present in Rasht and an attack of the Bolsheviks on the capital was imminent, causing refugees to flee the northern cities. Iran was plunging into chaos. During such a time, Sepahdar, risking his safety, and mindful of the fact that accepting the highest executive post in the country would earn him neither status nor wealth, stepped forward to serve his country once more.

Even though his term as prime minister was short, he played an understated but pivotal role in the years leading up to the coup d'état of 1921 and the rise of Reza Shah. Sepahdar evolved from a dominant feudal landowner who ruthlessly profiteered off the working class to a patriotic constitutionalist who became one of the major financial supporters of that movement, and someone who ultimately put his country above his own interests.

Whether quietly standing his ground against the 1919 Anglo-Persian Agreement, secretly giving refuge to an opposition newspaper publisher, or covertly enabling a bloodless coup, Sepahdar intentionally chose to contribute to his country in subtle ways that kept him in the background, rather than in the spotlight.

The following is an excerpt from one of Sepahdar's statements to the Iranian people in 1920. His message of hope and unity, from over a century ago, seems to reflect the sentiments of many Iranians today.

> Dear Countrymen,
>
> Iran is going through dark days, but a glimmer of hope is still visible. Salvation of our nation and our country from the abyss of misery is tied to a sense of unity, duty, self-belief, and the shared endeavor to achieve happiness.
>
> Fathollah Sepahdar-e Aʿzam
> Prime Minister of Iran
> November 6, 1920[4]

---

4. Makki, 1361[SH], vol. 1: 104–5; see also *Ra'ad*, Rabi' al-Awwl 7, 1339[AH].

APPENDIX

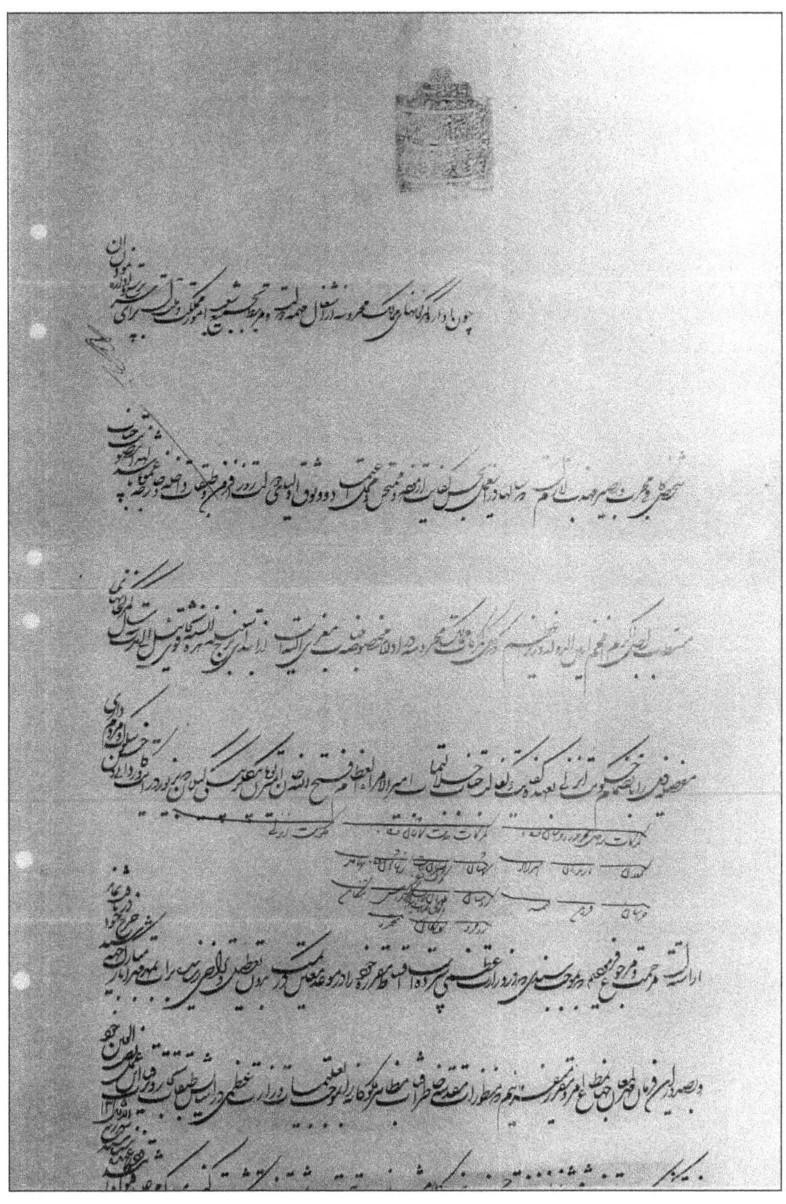

The first Royal Decree appointing Fathollah Khan Sepahdar as Prime Minister. (Mr. Manuchehr Akbar's personal archives)

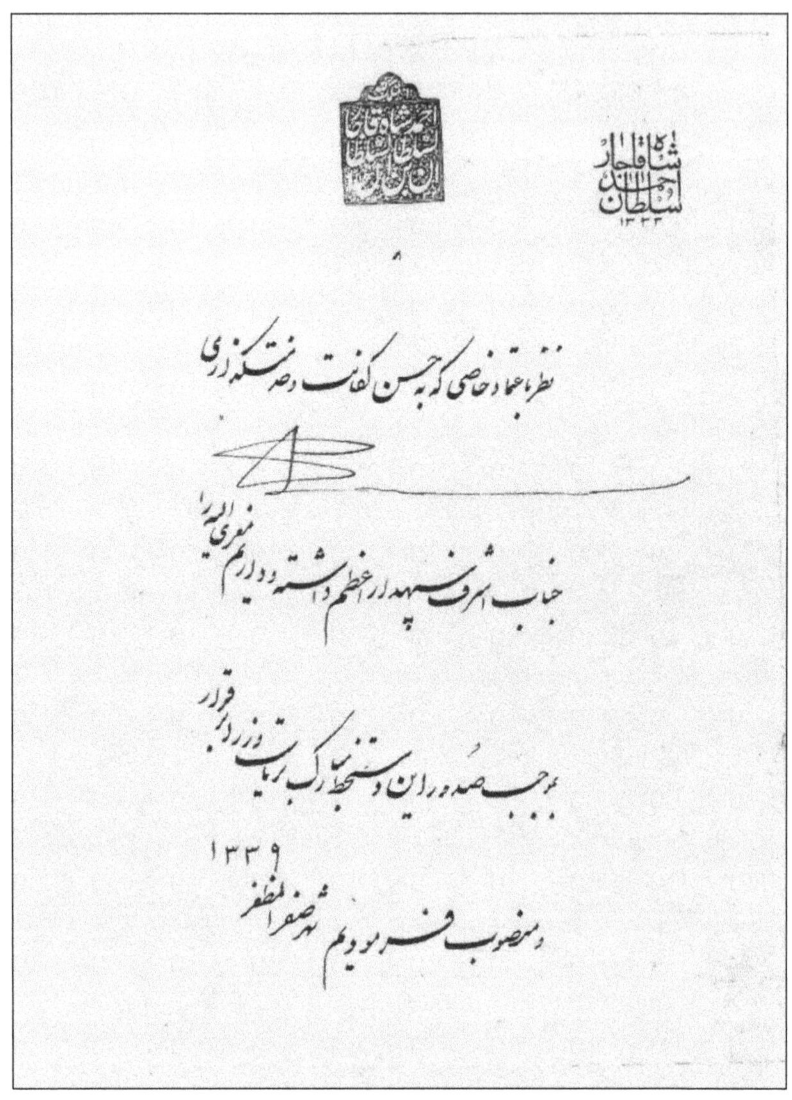

سلطان احمد شاه قاجار ۱۳۳۳

نظر به اعتماد خاصی که به حسن کفایت و صداقت خدمتگذاری

جناب اشرف سپهدار اعظم داشته و داریم معزی الیه را

بموجب صدور این دستخط مبارک به ریاست وزراء برقرار

و منصوب فرمودیم شهر صفر المظفر ۱۳۳۹

The first Royal Decree appointing Fathollah Khan Sepahdar as Prime Minister. (Mr. Manuchehr Akbar's personal archives)

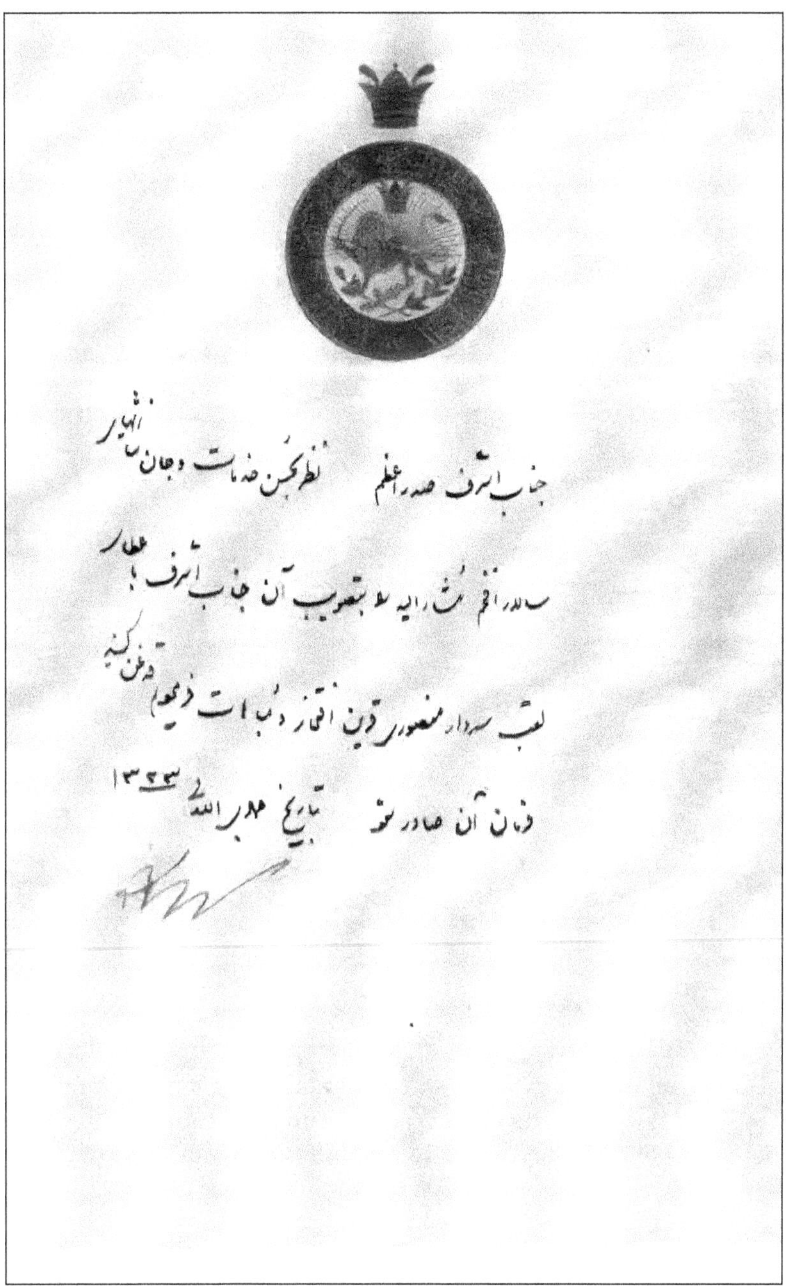

جناب اشرف صدراعظم   نظر بحسن خدمات و جان‌نثاری اظهار
سالار افخم نشان داده‌اند بتصویب آن جناب اشرف با عطاء
لقب سردار منصوری قرین افتخار و مباهات فرمودیم قدغن کنید
فرمان آن صادر شود   تاریخ [illegible] ۱۳۲۳

Royal Decree awarding the title Sardar Mansur to Fathollah Khan Salar Afkham. (Mr. Manuchehr Akbar's personal archives)

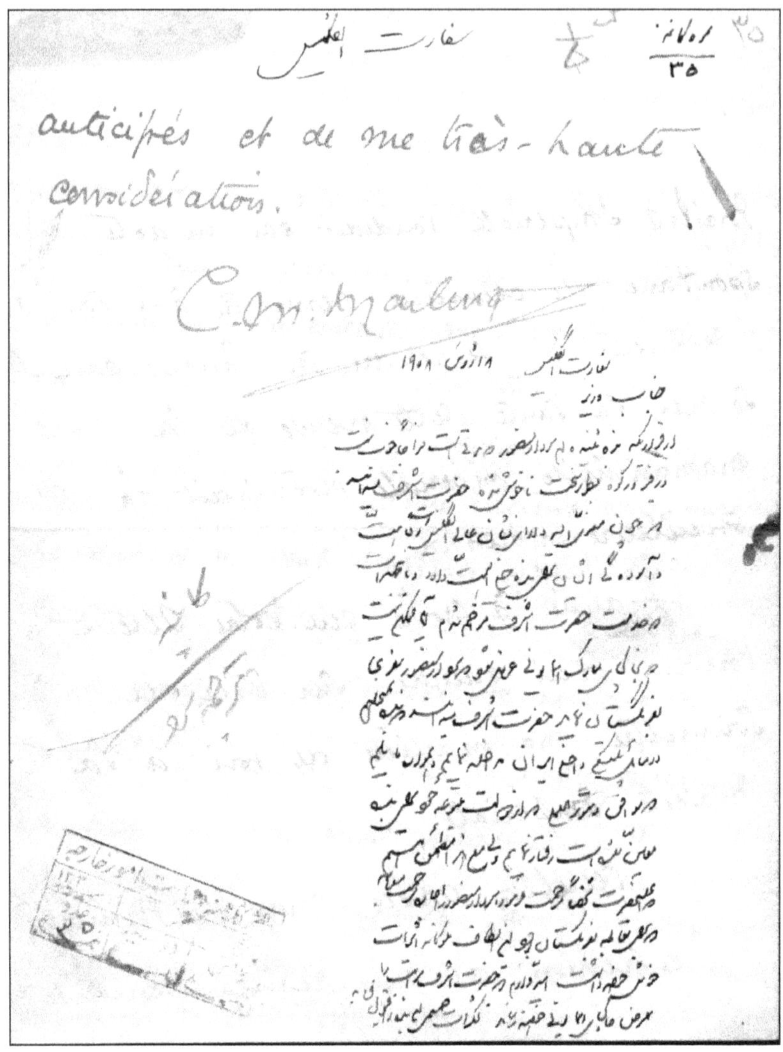

سفارت انگلیس

۳۵

anticipés et de ma très-haute considération.

C. M. Marling

British minister Sir Charles Murray Marling's note to Iran's Ministry of Foreign Affairs about Sardar Mansur.
(Document No. GH1326-K3.1P2-A6.2, Foreign Ministry Archives)

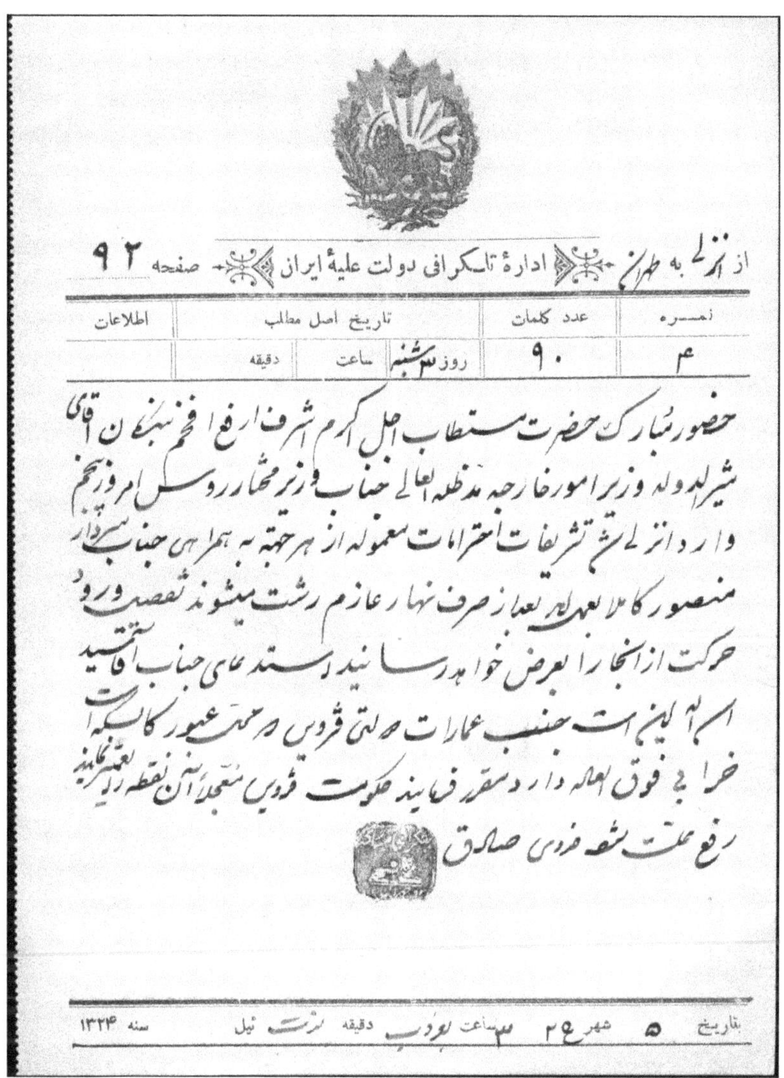

از انزلی به طهران — اداره تلگرافی دولت علیهٔ ایران — صفحه ۹۲

نمره	عدد کلمات	تاریخ اصل مطالب			اطلاعات
۴	۹۰	روز سه‌شنبه	ساعت	دقیقه	

حضور مبارک حضرت مستطاب اجل اکرم اشرف ارفع افخم بندگان آقای
مشیرالدوله وزیر امور خارجه مدظله العالی جناب وزیر مختار روس امروز پنجم
وارد انزلی شد تشریفات احترامات معموله از هر جهت به همراهی جناب سردار
منصور کاملاً معمول بعد از صرف نهار عازم رشت میشوند تفصیل ورود
حرکت از انجا را بعرض خواهد رسانید مستدعی است جناب آقا سید
اسدالله امین است جنب عمارات دولتی قزوین در مدت عبور کالسکه
خرابی فوق العاده دارد مقرر فرمایند حکومت قزوین مستعجلاً این نقطه را تعمیر نمایند
رفع زحمت شد قزوین صادق

بتاریخ ۵ شهر ۲۴ ساعت ۳ دقیقه ... سنه ۱۳۲۴

Sardar Mansur's report on hosting Russia's minister plenipotentiary, 1906. (Document No. GH1324-K28-P1052, Foreign Ministry Archives)

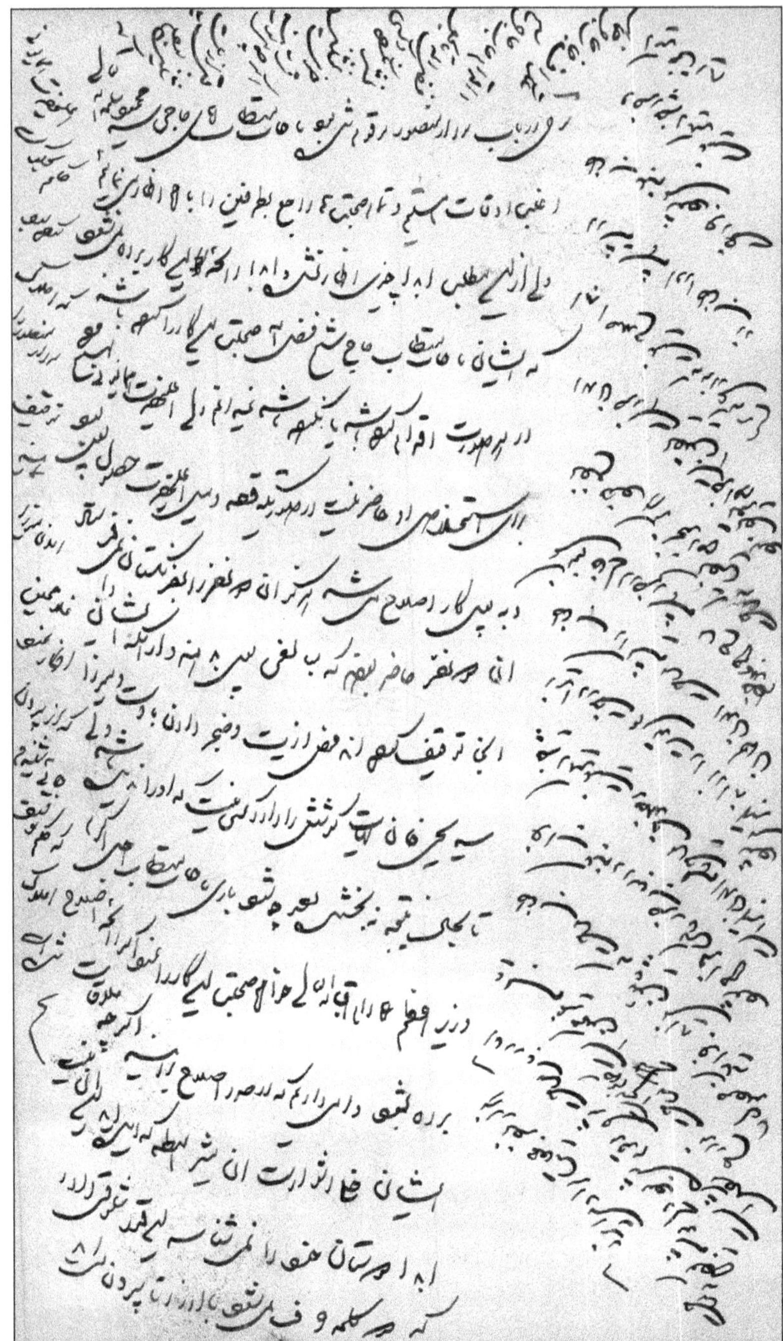

A letter attesting to Mohammad Ali Shah Qajar's opposition to the release of Fathollah Khan Sardar Mansur and ordering confiscation of his property in 1908. (Document No. 296-9154, Iran National Archives)

نمره ۵۱

جناب مستطاب اجل اکرم سردار منصور دام اقباله

نظر بکمال کاردانی و کفایت و حسن مراقبت در انجام تکالیف و مراتب لیاقت که از آنجناب

در ترتیب و اداره کردن تلگرافخانه و پستخانه مبارکه مشاهده و معلوم

بجهات مذکوره و نیز بعد ملاحظه سابقه بصیرت و اطلاعات آنجناب

خدمت وزارت تلگراف و پست ممالک محروسه بعهده کفایت

و کاردانی شما مرجوع و واگذار میگردد که در اولین [illegible] تقدیم

و کاردانی آنجناب است در تنظیم امنیه و خدمت مهم شرط [illegible]

کفایت و امانت را بظهور رسانیده [illegible] ۲۹ جمادی الاولی ۱۳۲۷

Manuscript on appointment of Fathollah Khan Sardar Mansur as Minister of Post and Telegraph in the 1909 Cabinet.
(Mr. Manuchehr Akbar's personal archives)

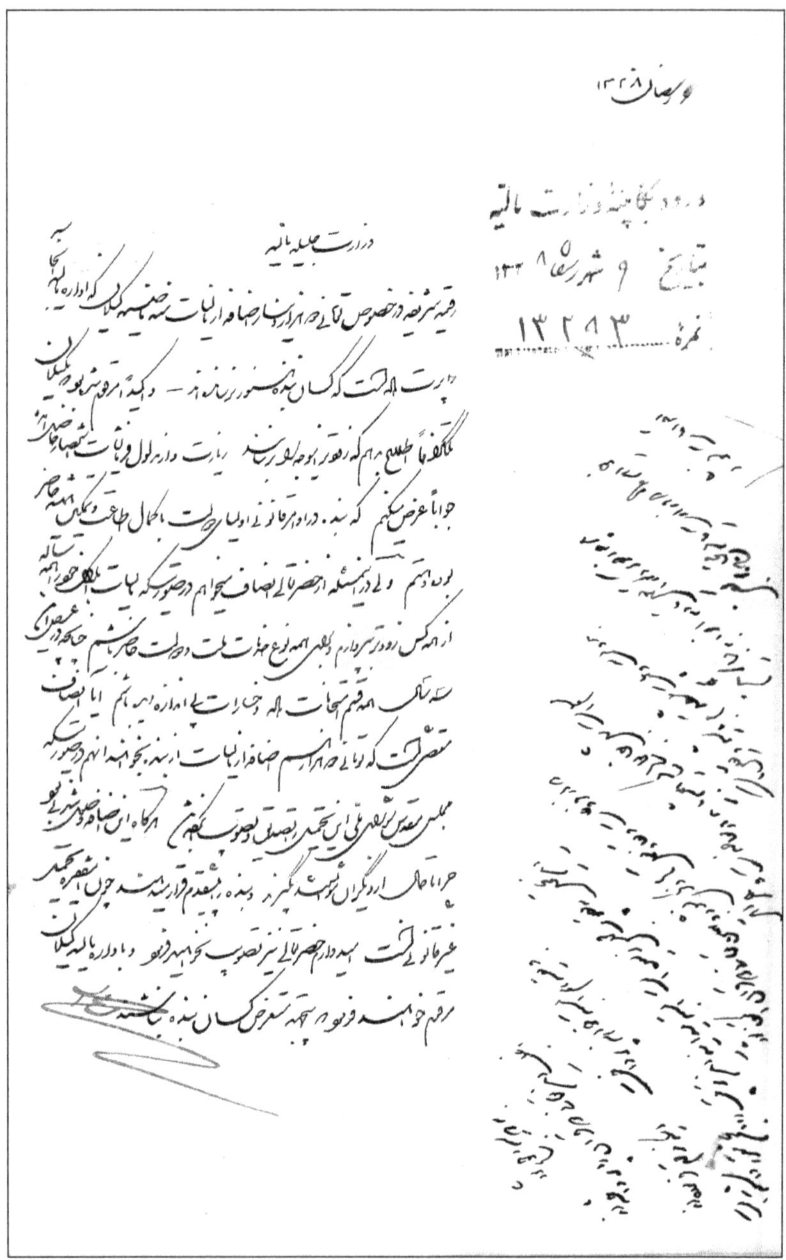

Fathollah Khan Sardar Mansur's handwriting and signature.
(Document No. 240-9154, Iran National Archives)

از وزارت امور خارجه

— رفع اشتباه —

اداره روزنامه مجلس

چون در یکی از نمرات جریده استقلال ایران مندرج است که آقای سردار منصور تشبث به تبعیت روس نموده و از سفارت روس اورا با چند نفر قزاق برشت فرستاده اند لازم میداند توضیحاً اظهار دارد که جناب وزیر مختار روس در جواب سئوال اینجانب اظهار داشتند که سردار منصور هیچوقت تشبث به تبعیت روس ننموده و حق چنین خواهشی هم نکرده است

در باب همراه فرستادن مستحفظ از طرف سفارت که در روزنامه مندرج است در جواب ایراد اینجانب از جناب وزیر مختار اظهار داشتند که ابداً از طرف سفارت مستحفظ فرستاده نشده و فقط حرکت ایشان با عزیمت غلام سفارت که حامل کاغذهای سفارت بوده مصادف شده بدینجهة سردار منصور باتفاق غلام سفارت از طهران حرکت نموده و این ترتیب نیز همه وقت معمول بوده است محض رفع اشتباهی که در اذهان مردم شده لازم دانست که این تفصیل در روزنامه گرامی درج شود که هموطنان ایشان بدانند جناب سردار منصور هیچ وقت بفکر تغییر تابعیت نبوده و تبعه مسلمه دولت ایران بوده و هستند

حسینقلی (وزیر امور خارجه)

Ministry of Foreign Affairs statement denying Majlis newspaper report about Sardar Mansur.
(Document No. GH1327-K25-P14-5, Foreign Ministry Archives)

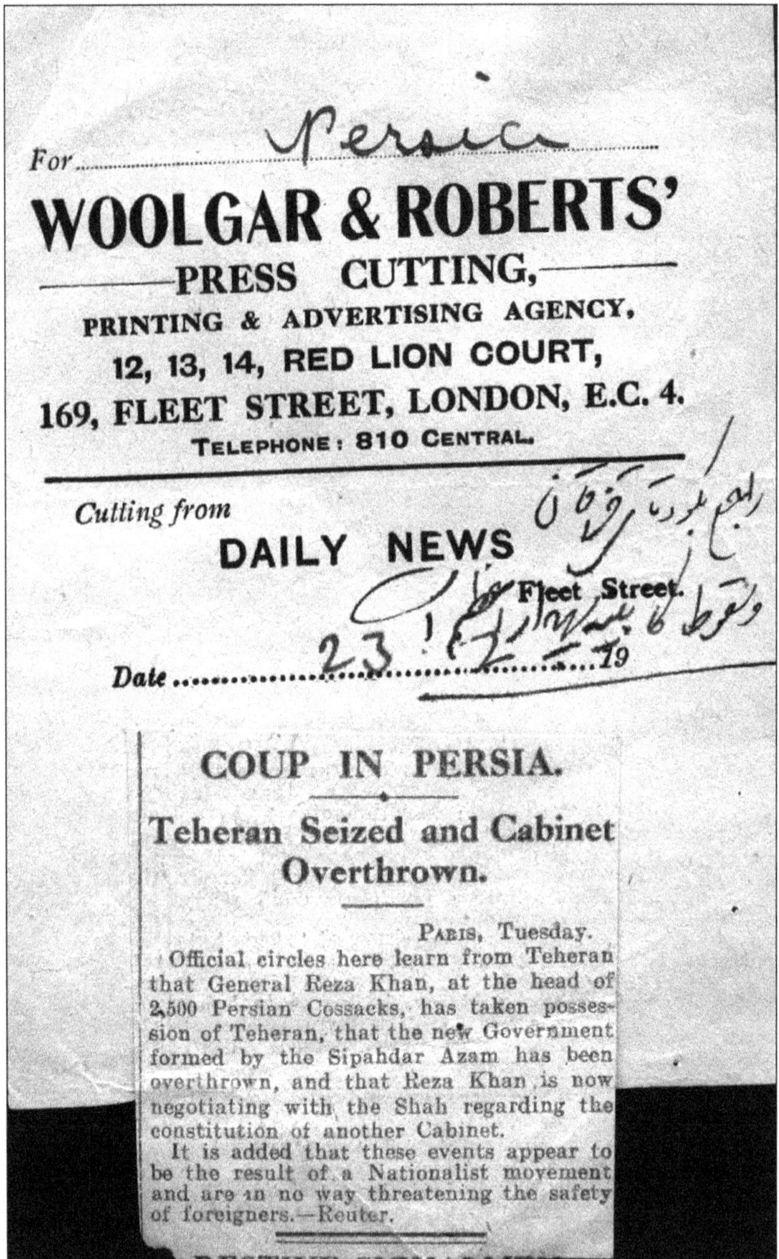

For ....Persia........

WOOLGAR & ROBERTS'
PRESS CUTTING,
PRINTING & ADVERTISING AGENCY,
12, 13, 14, RED LION COURT,
169, FLEET STREET, LONDON, E.C. 4.
TELEPHONE: 810 CENTRAL.

Cutting from
DAILY NEWS
Fleet Street.

Date ....23 ! 19

COUP IN PERSIA.

Teheran Seized and Cabinet Overthrown.

PARIS, Tuesday.

Official circles here learn from Teheran that General Reza Khan, at the head of 2,500 Persian Cossacks, has taken possession of Teheran, that the new Government formed by the Sipahdar Azam has been overthrown, and that Reza Khan is now negotiating with the Shah regarding the constitution of another Cabinet.

It is added that these events appear to be the result of a Nationalist movement and are in no way threatening the safety of foreigners.—Reuter.

A short news item by Reuters regarding the Coup, 1921.
(Document No. GH1339-K63-P16-18, Foreign Ministry Archives)

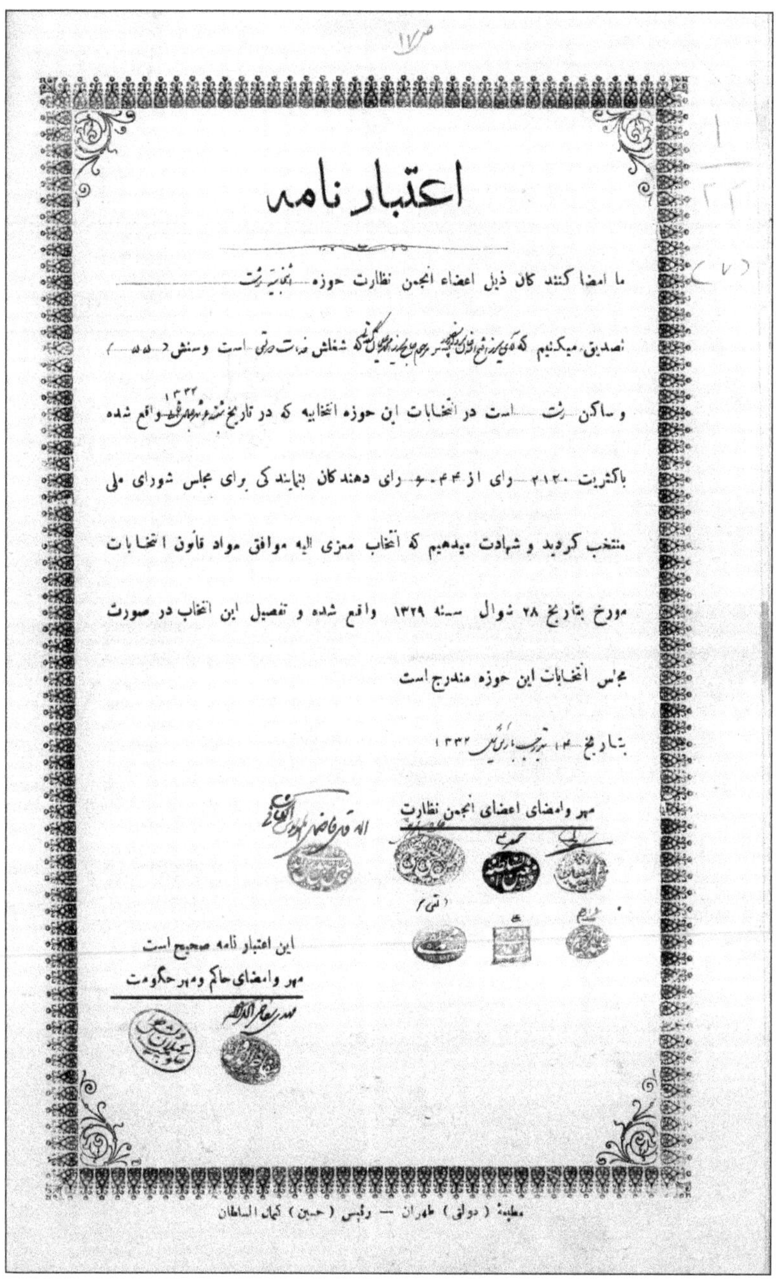

اعتبار نامه

ما امضا کنندگان ذیل اعضاء انجمن نظارت حوزه انتخابیه رشت

تصدیق میکنیم که آقای [illegible] که شغلش [illegible] است وسنش [illegible]

و ساکن رشت است در انتخابات این حوزه انتخابیه که در تاریخ [illegible] ۱۳۳۲ واقع شده

باکثریت ۲۱۲۰ رای از ۴۴۰۰ رای دهندگان بنمایندگی برای مجلس شورای ملی

منتخب گردید و شهادت میدهیم که انتخاب معزی الیه موافق مواد قانون انتخابات

مورخ بتاریخ ۲۸ شوال سنه ۱۳۲۹ واقع شده و تفصیل این انتخاب در صورت

مجلس انتخابات این حوزه مندرج است

بتاریخ [illegible] ۱۳۳۲

مهر وامضای اعضای انجمن نظارت

این اعتبار نامه صحیح است

مهر وامضای حاکم ومهر حکومت

مطبعهٔ (دولتی) طهران — رئیس (حسین) کمال السلطان

Sardar Mansur's credentials for the 3rd National Consultative Assembly, which were not debated on the floor. (Islamic Consultative Assembly Documents Center)

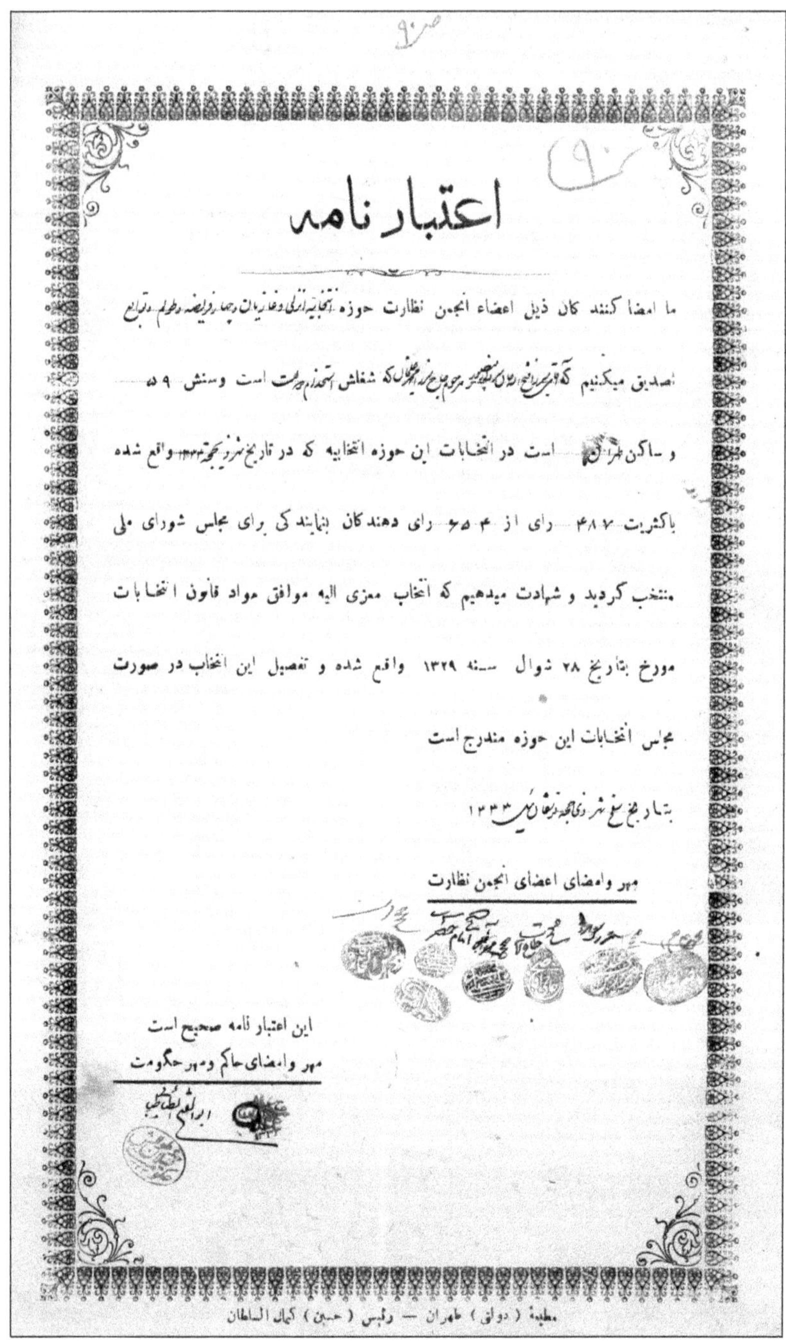

اعتبار نامه

ما امضا کنندگان ذیل اعضاء انجمن نظارت حوزه انتخابیه اراک و غیره ... تصدیق میکنیم که ... که شغلش ... است وسنش ۵۹ و ساکن طهران است در انتخابات این حوزه انتخابیه که در تاریخ ... واقع شده باکثریت ۴۸۷ رای از ۴۵۶ رای دهندگان بنمایندگی برای مجلس شورای ملی منتخب گردید و شهادت میدهیم که انتخاب معزی الیه موافق مواد قانون انتخابات مورخ بتاریخ ۲۸ شوال سنه ۱۳۲۹ واقع شده و تفصیل این انتخاب در صورت مجلس انتخابات این حوزه مندرج است

بتاریخ ... ذیحجه ... ۱۳۳۳

مهر و امضای اعضای انجمن نظارت

این اعتبار نامه صحیح است

مهر و امضای حاکم و مهر حکومت

مطبعهٔ (دولتی) طهران — ... (حسین) کمال السلطان

Sardar Mansur's credentials for the National Consultative Assembly. (Islamic Consultative Assembly Documents Center)

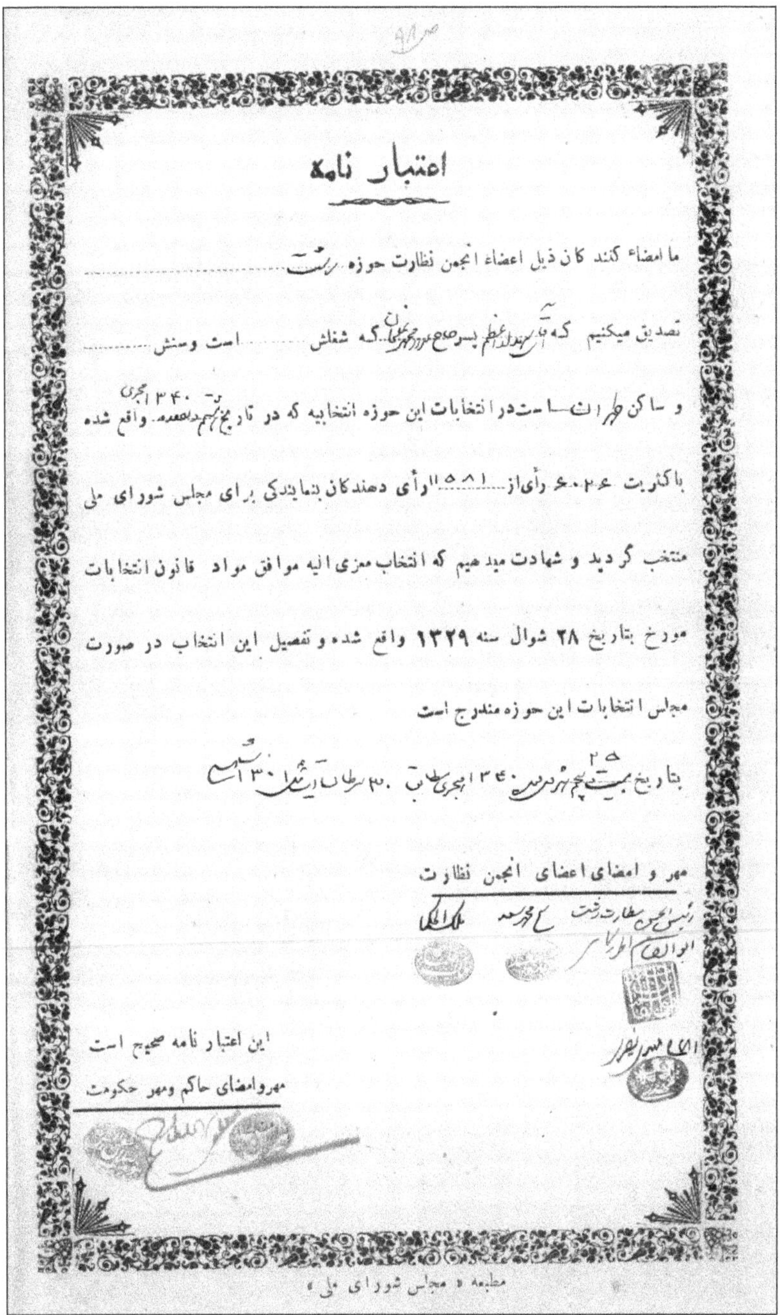

اعتبار نامه

ما امضاء کنندکان ذیل اعضاء انجمن نظارت حوزه رشت

تصدیق میکنیم که آقای سپهدار اعظم پسر [illegible] که شغلش .... است وسنش ....

و ساکن طهران است در انتخابات این حوزه انتخابیه که در تاریخ [illegible] ذیقعده ۱۳۴۰ هجری واقع شده

باکثریت [illegible] رأی از ۵۸۱ رأی دهندکان بنمایندکی برای مجلس شورای ملی

منتخب گردید و شهادت میدهیم که انتخاب معزی الیه موافق مواد قانون انتخابات

مورخ بتاریخ ۲۸ شوال سنه ۱۳۲۹ واقع شده و تفصیل این انتخاب در صورت

مجلس انتخابات این حوزه مندرج است

بتاریخ بیست و پنجم شهر [illegible] ۱۳۴۰ هجری مطابق ۳۰ سرطان [illegible] ۱۳۰۱

مهر و امضای اعضای انجمن نظارت

[illegible]

این اعتبار نامه صحیح است

مهر و امضای حاکم و مهر حکومت

مطبعه « مجلس شورای ملی »

Sepahdar's credentials for the 4th National Consultative Assembly. (Islamic Consultative Assembly Documents Center)

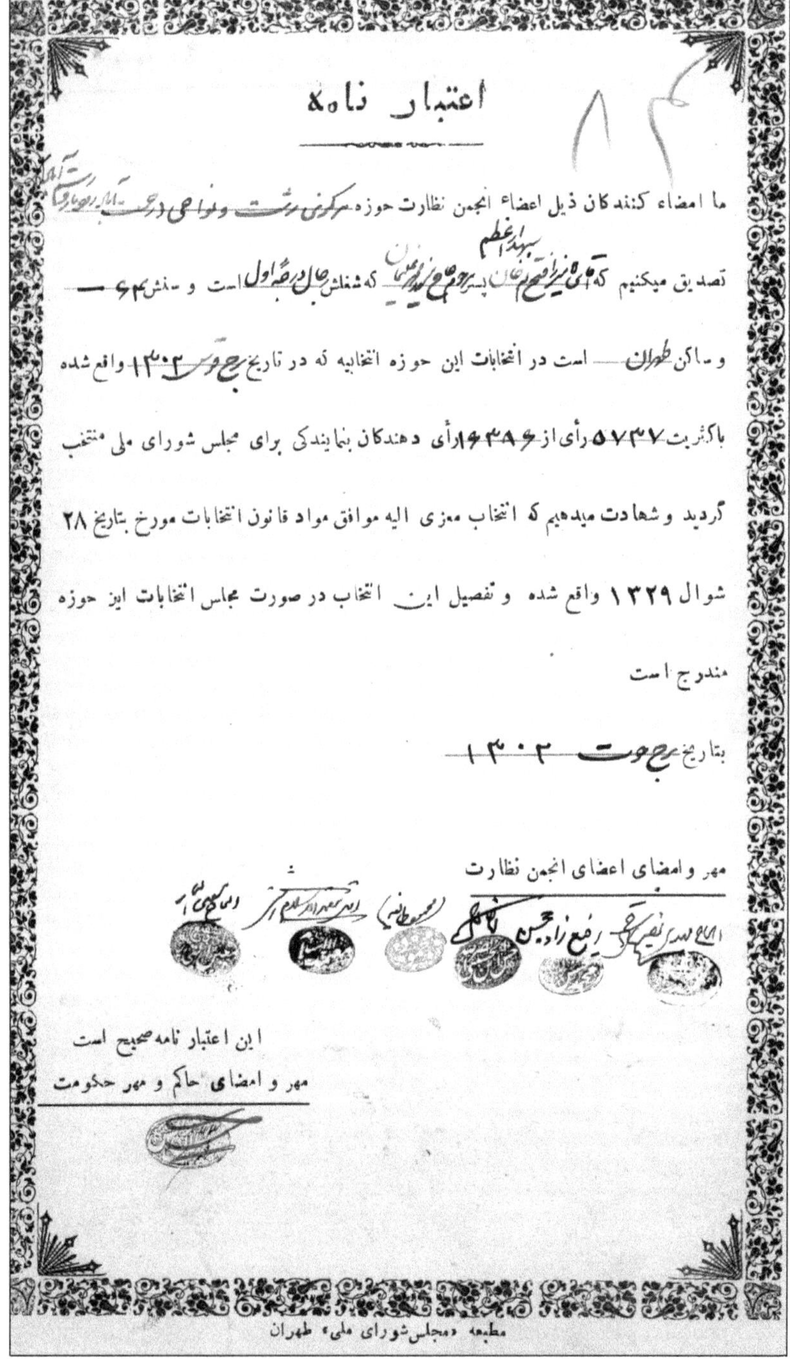

اعتبار نامه

ما امضاء کنندگان ذیل اعضاء انجمن نظارت حوزه مرکزی رشت و نواحی [illegible]

تصدیق میکنیم که آقای میرزا فتح‌الله خان سپهدار اعظم پسر مرحوم حاج [illegible] که شغلش جلیل درجهٔ اول است و سنش ۶۴

و ساکن طهران است در انتخابات این حوزه انتخابیه که در تاریخ [illegible] ۱۳۰۲ واقع شده

باکثریت ۵۷۳۷ رأی از ۱۶۳۸۶ رأی دهندگان بنمایندگی برای مجلس شورای ملی منتخب

گردید و شهادت میدهیم که انتخاب معزی الیه موافق مواد قانون انتخابات مورخ بتاریخ ۲۸

شوال ۱۳۲۹ واقع شده و تفصیل این انتخاب در صورت مجلس انتخابات این حوزه

مندرج است

بتاریخ [illegible] حوت ۱۳۰۲

مهر و امضای اعضای انجمن نظارت

این اعتبار نامه صحیح است

مهر و امضای حاکم و مهر حکومت

مطبعهٔ مجلس شورای ملی، طهران

Sepahdar's credentials for the 5th National Consultative Assembly. (Islamic Consultative Assembly Documents Center)

BIBLIOGRAPHY

Primary Sources

Unpublished Archival Documents

Documents Center of the Iranian Foreign Ministry (DCIFM): CH1324-K23-P7-138; GH1324-K23-P7-83; GH1329-K49-P2-43; GH1326-K3.1-P2-16.2; CH1324-K23-P1-4.5; GH1326-K33-P17-4; GH1326-K33-P17-7; GH1326-K33-P17-9; GH1326-K33-P17-1; GH1326-K58-P10-3; GH1326-K58-P10-1; GH1326-K58-P10-5; GH1326-K58-P10-9; GH1326-K38-P8-72; GH1326-K38-P8-3; GH1326-K33-P17-8; GH1326-K33-P17-6; GH1327-K40-P9-13; GH1327-K40-P9-4; GH1327-K25-P14-4; GH1327-K25-P14-5; GH1326-K25-P14-1.1; GH1332-K59-P1-51.

Great Britain, Imperial War Cabinet, Committee of Imperial Defence, 23/41, no. 20/5, p. 24.

Institute for Iranian Contemporary Historical Studies, Tehran, the testament of Ardeshir Reporter, no. 47305 to 47325.

National Documents Center of Iran, no. 296-9154.

Published Archival Documents

Ayati, Ata (trans.) (1380SH), "Tazehaie az Koudetaye 1299" ["New Documents on the 1299 Coup"], *Iranian Contemporary History Quarterly* 19–20: 47–80.

——— (trans.) (1382^{SH}), “Naghshe Smart dar Koudetaye 21 February 1921” [“Smart’s Role in the Coup d’État of February 21, 1921”], *Iranian Contemporary History Quarterly* 28: 86–79.

Bashiri, Ahmad (ed.) (1363^{SH}), *Blue Book: Secret Reports of British Foreign Ministry About Iran’s Constitutional Revolution*, vol. 1, Tehran: Farhang-e Nashr-e-No Publications.

——— (1368^{SH}), *Orange Book: Political Reports of Tsarist Russia Foreign Ministry about Iran’s Constitutional Revolution*, vol. 1, trans. Hosain Ghasemian, 2nd edition, Tehran: Khousheh Publishing Organization.

Haghani, Mosa (ed.) (1379^{SH}), “Iran az Gharardade 1919 ta Kodataye 3 Esfande 1299 Bar Asase Asnad” [“Iran from the 1919 Agreement to the 1299 Coup d’État According to the Documents”], *Iranian Contemporary History Quarterly* 15–16: 229–325.

Sheikh al-Islami, Javad (trans. and ed.) (1365^{SH}), *Secret Documents of the British Foreign Ministry Regarding the 1919 Anglo-Persian Agreement*, Tehran: Keyhan Publications.

Daily Newspapers

Adab, Jumada al-Thani 23, 1323^{AH}.

Chehre Nama, Rabi’ al-Thani 15, 1323^{AH}; Dhu Qadah 1, 1323^{AH}; Jamada al-Awwl 1, 1323^{AH}.

Daily News, September 11, 1919.

Ettelaat, Farvardin 6, 1316^{SH}.

Habl al-Matin (Tehran), Shawwal 24, 1325^{AH}.

Habl al-Matin (Calcutta), Dhu Hijjah 6, 1324^{AH}.

Iran Soltani, Dhu Hijjah 12, 1309^{AH}; Rabi’ al-Thani 23, 1310^{AH}; Dhu Hijjah 14, 1310^{AH}; Dhu Hijjah 15, 1311^{AH}; Dhu Hijjah 1, 1313^{AH}; Safar 1 and 14, 1319^{AH}, Rabi’ al-Awwl 29, 1323^{AH}; Rabi’ al-Thani 23, 1323^{AH}; Rajab 23, 1323^{AH}; Sha’ban 28, 1323^{AH}; Rabi’ al-Thani 21, 1324^{AH}; Rajab 23, 1324^{AH}.

Jangal, Sha’ban 26, 1335^{AH}; Ramadan 6, 1335^{AH}.

Liverpool Post, September 11, 1919.

Manchester Guardian, August 17, 1919.

Nasim-e Shomal, Moharram 24, 1327^{AH}.

Parvaresh, Sharivar 3, 1309^{SH}.

Ra'ad, Aban 9, 1299^{SH}; Safar 19, 1339^{AH}; Rabi' al-Awwl 2, 1339^{AH}; Rabi' al-Awwl 7, 1339^{AH}; Rabi' al-Awwl 8, 1339^{AH}; Rabi al-Awwl 17, 1339^{AH}; Rabi' al-Thani 18, 1339^{AH}; Jumada al-Awwl 6, 1339^{AH}; Jumada al-Awwl 7, 1339^{AH}; Jumada al-Awwl 9, 1339^{AH}; Jumada al-Awwl 10, 1339^{AH}; Jumada al-Awwl 11, 1339^{AH}; Jumada al-Awwl 27, 1339^{AH}; Jumada al-Akhar 1, 1339^{AH}; Jumada al-Akhar 8, 1339^{AH}.

Sobh-e Sadegh, Sha'ban 24, 1325^{AH}.

Memoirs, Personal Records, and Books

Afshar, Iraj (ed.) (1359^{SH}), *Oraghe Tazeyabe Mashroutiat va Naghshe Taghizadeh* [*New Papers* on *Constitutionalism and Taghizadeh's Role*], Tehran: Javidan Publications.

——— (ed.) (1368^{SH}), *Ghabaleye Trarikh* [*Deed of History*], Tehran: Talaye Publications.

——— (ed.) (1380^{SH}), *Oraghe Jangal: Namehaye Rasht va Asnade Nehzate Jangal* [*The Jangal Papers: Rasht Letters and Documents of the Jangal Movement*], Tehran: Farzan-e Rouz Publications.

Afzal al-Molk, Gholam-Hossein (1361^{SH}), *Afzal al-Tavareikh* [*Best History*], ed. Mansoureh Ettehadie and Syrous Sa'advandian, 1st edition, Tehran: Tarikhe Iran Publications.

Aga Khan III, Soltan Mohammad Shah Hosayni (1954), *Memoirs: World Enough and Time*, London: Cassell and Company.

Amir-Ahmadi, Ahmad (1373^{SH}), *Khaterate Avvalin Sepahbode Iran, Ahmad Amir-Ahmadi* [*Memoirs of the First Lieutenant General of Iran, Ahmad Amir-Ahmadi*], ed. Gholam-Hosain Zargari-Nejad, Tehran: Institute for Research and Cultural Studies.

Amlashi, Bahauddin (1352^{SH}), *Goushehaie az Tarikhe Gilan* [*Corners of Gilan History*], ed. Mohammad-Hadi Mizan, [Tehran]: Bahman Publications.

Bahar, Mohammad Taghi (1371^{SH}), *Tarikhe Mokhtasare Ahzabe Siasie Iran* [*A Brief History of Iranian Political Parties*], vol. 1, Tehran: Amir-Kabir Publications.

Bibesco, Marta (1373^{SH}), "Rasht der Hasht Behesht" ["Rasht in Eight Heavens"], trans. Abolfazl Mosafi, *Golcharkh* magazine (3)10: 13–20.

Dolatabadi, Seyyed Yahya (1361^{SH}), *Hayate Yahya* [*Life of Yahya*], 4 vols, Tehran: Ibn Sina Publications.

Emad al-Kottab (1384^{SH}), *Komiteye Mojazat va Khaterate Emad al-Kottab* [*The Punishment Committee and Memoirs of Emad al-Kottab*], ed. Mohammad-Javad Moradinia, Tehran: Asatir Publications.

Eskandari, Abbas (1361^{SH}), *Ketabe Arezou: Tarikhe Mofassale Mashroutiate Iran* [*Book of Desire: A Detailed History of Iran's Constitutionalism*], Tehran: Ghazal Publications.

Foroughi, Mohammad Ali (1396^{SH}), *Yaddashthaye Mohammad Ali Foroughi az Safare Konfranse Solhe Paris* [*Mohammad Ali Foroughi's Diary of His Trip to the Paris Peace Conference, December 1918–August 1920*], ed. Mohammad Afshin-Vafaie and Pejman Firouzbakhsh, Tehran: Sokhan Publications.

Fortescue, L. S. (1379^{SH}), *Rejale Tehran va Barkhi Iyalate Shomale Gharbe Iran* [The *Dignitaries of Tehran and Some Northwestern Provinces of Iran*], trans. Mohammad-Ali Kazembeigi, Tehran: Ministry of Foreign Affairs Press.

Ghazvini, Mohammad (1363^{SH}), "Vafiat al-Moaserin" ["Deaths of Contemporaries"], in: Iraj Afshar (ed.), *Yaddashthaye Ghazvini* [*Notes of Ghazvini*], vols 7–8, Tehran: Elmi Publications.

Hedayat, Mehdi-Gholi Khan (1363^{SH}), *Khaterat va Khatarat* [*Memories and Dangers*], Tehran: Zovvar Publications.

Kamarei, Seyyed Mohammad (1382^{SH}), *Rouznameye Khaterat* [*Diary*], 2 vols, ed. Mohammad-Javad Moradinia, Tehran: Shirazeh Publications.

Kasmaei, Haj Ahmed (1383^{SH}), *Yaddashthaye Ahmad Kasmaie az Nehzate Jangal* [*Ahmed Kasmaie's Notes on the Jangal Movement*], ed. Manouchehr Hedayati, Rasht: Katibeye Gil Publications.

Kasravi, Ahmad (1369^{SH}), *Tarikhe Mashrouteye Iran* [*History of the Iranian Constitutional Movement*], 15th edition, Tehran: Amir-Kabir Publications.

Mahallati, Haj Mohammad-Ali (1359^{SH}), *Khaterate Haj Sayyah* [*The Memoirs of Haj Sayyah*], ed. Hamid Sayyah, Tehran: Amir-Kabir Publications.

Malekzadeh, Mehdi (1382^{SH}), *Tarikhe Enghelabe Mashrotiat dar Iran* [*History of the Constitutional Revolution in Iran*], vol. 3, 6 vols, 3rd edition, Tehran: Elmi Publications.

Mosaddegh, Mohammad (1352^{SH}), *Namehaye Doctor Mosaddegh*, [*Dr. Mosaddegh's Letters*], ed. Mohammad Torkman, Tehran: Hezaran Publications.

Mostashar al-Dowleh, Sadegh (1367^{SH}), *Khaterat va Asnade Mostashar al-Dowleh* [*The Memoirs and Documents of Mostashar al-Dowleh*], vol. 3, 3 vols, ed. Iraj Afshar, Tehran: Talaye Publications.

Mostofi, Abdollah (1360^{SH}), *Sharhe Zendeganie Man* [*My Biography*], 3rd edition, vol. 3, Tehran: Zovvar Publications.

Mozaffar al-Din Shah Qajar (1362^{SH}), *Dovvomin Safarnameye Mozaffar al-Din Shah be Farang* [*Mozaffar al-Din Shah's Second Travelogue to Europe*], Tehran: Kavosh Publications.

——— (1390^{SH}), *Safarnameye Sevvome Mozaffar al-Din Shah be Farang* [*Mozaffar al-Din Shah's Third Travelogue to Europe*], ed. Mohammad Nasiri Moghadam, Tehran: Islamic Consultative Assembly Press.

Rahimzadeh Safavi, [Ali Asghar] (1362^{SH}), *Asrare Soghote Ahman Shah* [*Secrets of the Fall of Ahmad Shah*], ed. Bahman Dehgan, Tehran: Ferdosi Publications.

Roshdieh, Shams al-Ddin (1362^{SH}), "Gharardade Vosoug al-Dawaleh va Havadese Marbout be An" ["The Vosouq al-Dowleh Agreement and Incidents Relating to It"], in: *Khaterate Siasi va Tarikhi* [*Political and Historical Memoirs*], Tehran: Ferdosi Publications.

Salour, Ghahraman Mirza Ayn al-Saltaneh (1378^{SH}), *Rouznameye Khaterat* [*Diary*], ed. Masoud Salour and Iraj Afshar, vol. 7, Tehran: Asatir Publications.

Sepehr, Ahmad-Ali (1374^{SH}), *Khaterate Siasi* [*Political Memoirs*], ed. Ahmad Sami'i, Tehran: Namak Publications.

Shuster, W. Morgan (1912), *The Strangling of Persia*, New York: Centory Co.

Taghizadeh, Seyyed Hasan (1379^{SH}), *Tarikhe Enghelabe Mashroutiate Iran* [*History of the Iranian Constitutional Revolution*], ed. Azizullah Alizadeh, Tehran: Ferdos Publications.

——— (1391^{SH}), *Zendegie Toufani* [*A Stormy Life*], ed. Iraj Afshar, Tehran: Tous Publications.

Wright, Denis (1977), *The English Amongst the Persians: During the Qajar Period 1787–1921*, London: Heinemann.

Yeghikian, Gregory (1363^{SH}), *Shoravi va Nehzate Jangal* [*The Soviet Union and the Jangali Movement*], Tehran: Novin Publications.

Zahir al-Dowleh, Ali Khan (1367^{SH}), *Khaterat va Asnad* [*Memoirs and Documents*], ed. Iraj Afshar, Tehran: Zarrin Publications.

Online

Encyclopaedia Iranica Online, © Trustees of Columbia University in the City of New York. Consulted online on January 21, 2023.

Secondary Sources

Abadian, Hosain (1390^{SH}), *Tarikhe Siasie Moasere Iran az Jange Jahanie Avval ta Koudetaye 1299* [*Contemporary Political History of Iran from the World War I to the 1299 Coup*], 2nd edition, Tehran: Political Studies and Research Institute.

Adamiyat, Fereydun (1379^{SH}), *Majlese Avval va Bohrane Azadi* [*The First Majles and the Crisis of Freedom*], Tehran: Roshangaran Publications.

Afshari, Parviz (1383^{SH}), *Nokhostvazirane Selseleye Qajar* [Prime Ministers of the Qajar Dynasty], Tehran: Documents Center for Research Services.

Agheli, Bagher (1380^{SH}), *Rouzshomare Tarikhe Iran az Enghelabe Mashroutiat ta Enghelabe Eslami* [*Chronology of Iran's History from the Constitutional Revolution to the Islamic Revolution*], vol. 1, Tehran: Goftar and Elm Publications.

——— (1380^{SH} a), *Sharhe Hale Rejale Siasi va Nezamie Moasere Iran* [*Biography of Contemporary Iranian Politicians and* Military Leaders vol. 3, Tehran: Goftar and Elm Publications.

Akbar, Abd al-Rahim (1395^{SH}), *Khandane Akbar* [*Akbar's Family*], Mashhad: Mohaghegh Publications.

Azramsa, Mahindokht (1378^{SH}), "The Most Important Houses of Tehran in the Constitutional Era," *Contemporary History of Iran Quarterly* 3(10): 171–93.

Bamdad, Mehdi (1371^{SH}), *Sharhe Hale Rejale Iran* [*Biography of Iranian Dignitaries*], 4th edition, vol. 1, Tehran: Zovvar Publications.

Barzegar, Kayhan (1377^{SH}), "October Revolution and Its Effect on Reza Khan's Coming to Power," *Political-Economic Etelaat Journal* 137–138: 34–41.

Cheknaji, M. P., and Houman Yousefdehi (1394^{SH}), *Namayandegane Gilan az Enghelabe Mashrote ta Engelabe Eslami* [*Gilan's Representatives from the Constitutional Revolution to the Islamic Revolution*], Rasht: Farhang Ilya Publications.

Chaqueri, Cosroe (1386^{SH}), *Milade Zhakhm: Jonbeshe Jangal va Jomhourie Shoravie Sosialistie Iran* [*The Soviet Socialist Republic of*

Iran, 1920–1921: Birth of the Trauma], trans. Shahriar Khajian, Tehran: Akhtaran Publications.

Churchill, George Percy (1391^{SH}), *Rejal va Diplomathaye Asre Pahlavi* [*Statesman and Diplomats of Qajar and Pahlavi Era*], Persian trans. Gholam-Hossein Mirzasaleh, Tehran: Moien Publication.

Elahi, Sadr al-Din (1393^{SH}), *Seyyed Zia Amele Kodeta* [*Seyyed Zia, the Coup Agent*], Tehran: Ferdos Publications.

Ettehadie, Mansoureh (1381^{SH}), *The Emergence and Evolution of Political Parties During Constitutional Movment: The 1st and 2nd Periods of the National Consultative Assembly*, Tehran: Siamak Publications.

Fakhraei, Ebrahim (1371^{SH}), *Gilan dar Enghelabe Mashroutiate Iran* [*Gilan During the Constitutional Revolotion*], 3rd edition, Tehran: Enghelabe Eslami Publications.

Floor, Willem (2018), *Salar al-Dowleh: A Delusional Prince and Wannabe Shah* (Washington DC: Mage Publishers, 2018).

Ghanei, Saeed, and Mohammad Ali Elmi (1391^{SH}), *Nokhostvazirane Iran az Sadre Mashrote ta Froupashie Dolate Bakhtiar* [*Prime Ministers of Iran from the Beginning of the Constitution to the Collapse of the Bakhtiar Cabinet*], Tehran: Asone and Elmi Publications.

Ghani, Cyrus (1378^{SH}), *Iran: Baramadane Reza Shah, Baroftadane Qajar va Naghshe Ingilisiha* [*Iran and the Rise of Reza Shah*], trans. Hasan Kamshad, 2nd edition, Tehran: Nilofer Publications.

Gilak, Mohammad-Ali (1371^{SH}), *Tarikh-e Enghelab Jangal* [*History of the Jangal Revolt*], Rasht: Gilkan Publishers.

Golban, Mohammad (1383^{SH}), "Seyyed Hasan Kashani and *Habl al-Matin* Daily Newspaper and His Trial," *Peike Nour Magazine*, Winter: 73–80.

Hasani, S. (2013), "Research on 'The Position of Northern Fisheries in Iran–Russia Relations' Based on Archival Documents (1828–1953 AD)," *History of Islam and Iran*, 23(17): 69–97.

Hoseini, Mohammad (1378^{SH}), "Society of Humanity and Its Branches: The Beginning and Completion of a Political Association During the Constitutional Era," *Contemporary History of Iran Quarterly* 3(10): 7–64.

Katouzian, Homa (2000), *State and Society in Iran: The Eclipse of the Qajars and the Rise of the Pahlavis*, London and New York: I. B. Tauris.

Majd, Mohammad Gholi, *The Great Famine & Genocide in Iran, 1917–1919*, 2nd edition, Lanham, MD: University Press of America, 2013.

Makki, Hosain (1357^{SH}), *Zendeganie Siasie Soltan Ahmad Shah Qajar* [*The Political Life of Soltan Ahmad Shah Qajar*], Tehran: Amir-Kabir Publications.

——— (1361^{SH}), *Tarikhe Bist Saleye Iran* [*20-Year History of Iran*], vol. 1, Tehran: Nasher Publications.

Nikoyeh, Mahmud (1387^{SH}), *Rasht: Shahre Baran* [*Rasht: The City of Rain*], Rasht: Farhang Ilya Publications.

Nozad, Reza (1398^{SH}), *Akhbare Gilan dar Matboate Asre Qajar* [*Gilan News in the Press of Qajar Era*], vol. 1, Rasht: Farhang Ilya Publications. vol. 1, 3 vols.

Parto, Afshin (1377), "Peimane 1919 va Vakoneshhaye Barkhaste az An" ["The 1919 Agreement and the Reactions Against It"], *Political-Economic Ettelaat Journal* 129–130: 86–101.

Rabino, E. L. (1357^{SH}), *Velayate Darolmarze Gilan* [*The Border Provinces of Gilan*], trans. Jafar Khomamizadeh, Rasht: Ta'ati Publications.

——— (1368^{SH}), *Mashroteye* Gilan [*The Constitutional Movement in Gilan*], ed. Mohammad Roshan, Rasht: Ta'ati Publications.

Raeen, Esma'il (1357^{SH}), *Faramoush-khane va Freemasonry dar Iran* [*Freemasonry in Iran*], 3 vols, Tehran: Amir-Kabir Publications.

Sheikh al-Islami, Javad (1359^{SH}), "Etaye Neshane Zanouband Be Mozaffar al-Din Shah" ["Awarding the KCMG to Mozaffar al-Din Shah"], *Ayandeh* magazine (6)1–2: 55–64.

——— (1366^{SH}), *Ghatle Atabak va Shanzdah Maghaleye Tahghighie Digar* [*Atabak's Murder and Sixteen* Other Investigative Stories Tehran: Kayhan Publications.

——— (1392^{SH}), *Simaye Ahmad Shah Qajar* [*A Portrait of Ahmad Shah Qajar*], Tehran: Mahi Publications.

Soleymannejad, Farhad (1401^{SH}), "Liberal Constitutionalist: An Introduction to the Political Thought of Seyyed Hasan Taghizadeh," in: Farhad Soleymannejad (ed.), *Founding Fathers of Modern Iran*, vol. 1: *Seyyed Hasan Taghizadeh*, Tehran: Agar Publications.

Yousefdehi, Houman (1392^{SH}), *Rejale Mashroteye Gilan* [*The Constitutionalists of Gilan*], Rasht: Farhang Ilya Publications.

INDEX

Italicized page numbers indicate photographs and images.

A

Abdol-Hosein Khan, Sardar Moazzam Khorasani (Teymourtash), 89, 159, 212, 213
Abdol-Hosein Sheibani Vahid al-Molk, 139
Abol Fath Mirza Salar al-Dowleh, 71
Abol Qasem Khan Naser al-Molk, regency of, 70, 72
Abolfazl Mirza Azod al-Soltan, Prince, 16, 20, 21, ***21***, 32
Accounting and Loan Bank of Persia, 57–59
Adamiyat, Fereydun, 33
Adib al-Saltaneh Hosein Samiei (deputy prime minister), 140, 154, 166
Afshar, Iraj, 6
Afzal al-Molk, Gholam-Hossein Khan, 10–11
Aga Khan III, xxii, 223
Agha Bala Khan, Sardar Afkham, 48, 53, 53–54
Aghasi, Haj Mirza, 4
Ahmad Shah Qajar
- Akbar, Fathollah Khan (Sepahdar) and, x, xi
- appointment of Vosuq al-Dowleh as prime minister, 79
- dismissal of Samsam al-Saltaneh Bakhtiari, 85
- European trip amid crisis, 168–169
- imposition of martial law, 100
- installation as king, 55, ***57***, 73
- negotiations with Soviets, 106–108
- photograph, ***108***
- Reza Shah Pahlavi and, 204
- Russian officers expelled, 123
- Supreme Advisory Council, convening of, 154
- Vosuq al-Dowleh resignation and, 103–104, 118

Akbar, Fahimé Yamin Esfandiary (compiler & editor's mother), xxi
Akbar, Fathollah Khan (Sepahdar)
- background/early career:
  - about, x–xi, xxix–xxx, 2–3

abuses of power by, 26–31, 40, 64–67
accolades and titles, 1, 3–4, 9–12, 19–20, 76, 126
customs offices appointments, 10–11, 19
death and burial, xxvii–xxix, 224–226, ***226***
early career, 7–8
father, 2
final years, 223–224
hosting the shah, 13–15
legacy, 226–227
lifestyle and philanthropy, xv–xvii, xxiii, 20, 21, 22
literary mentions, xxiii–xxiv, xxv, xxvii
marriages, xi–xii, 1, 4, 7, 225
Mirza Mohammad Ali and, 6–9
Persian language fluency, x–xi
photographs, ***12***, ***14***, ***21***
portrait photograph, ***xxvi***

Akbar, Fathollah Khan (Sepahdar) government appointments:
assassination plot to kill, xvii, 53–54
bank loan recall, 57–59
Bank Melli and, 33, 38
cabinet resignation, 103–104
constitutional cabinets, cooperation with, 61–67
Constitutional Revolution and, x, 31–40, 48–49
constitutionalism, support for, xviii, xxiii, 31–32, 38–39
contempt for government deceit, 89–90
exploitative business practices, 26–31
fifth National Consultative Assembly and, 217
Fishery Authority controversy and, 26–31, 40
house arrest, 17–18, 41–55
interim governorship, 22, 30
interior minister position, 87
involvement with Soviets, 106–109
Kashani incident and, 62–63
loyalties, xv
Majles and, 219, 220, ***231***
minister in successive cabinets, 64, 73–75, 90
ministerial foreign relations, 69–70
Mohammad Ali Shah and, 55–56
Mozaffar al-Din Shah Qajar and, 19–20, 22
Post and Telegraph Office appointment, 27–28
Qajar monarchy, end of and, 220
Rasht governor's office, ***21***
Russian citizenship allegations, 67–70
Vosuq al-Dowleh and, 76–77, 79, 107

Akbar, Fathollah Khan (Sepahdar) prime ministerships:
action list (1920), 135
aid to Gilanis, 130
Anglo-Persian Agreement political maneuverings, 159–166
bribery scandal resolution, 142–147
Britain's ultimatum to, 149–153
cabinets, 137–140, 182–184, 188–189
Cossacks' back wages crisis, 181–182
Cossacks march on Tehran and, xiv, 191, 194–198
coup, foreknowledge of, xiv, 198–199

financial aid pursuant to Anglo-Persian Agreement and, 93–94, 115, 133
government collapse, 170–173
martial law declared, 194–195
photographs, ***119***
post-coup developments, 200–201
prime ministerships, 115–123, 175, 177–180
rejection of British six-point plan, 149–153
Reza Shah Pahlavi, audiences with, xv
second statement as prime minister, 140
secret meetings with Reza Khan, xiii–xiv
Seyyed Zia al-Din Tabataba'i's collaboration with, 129–130
statements on Anglo-Persian Agreement, 125–126, 140–141
Supreme Advisory Council speech, 153–157
Vosuq al-Dowleh and, 138, 163, 213–215

Akbar, Gholam Hosain Khan, Biglarbeigi-e-Rasht (son), ***xxviii***, 226

Akbar, Mirza Sadeq Khan, Sardar Motamed (cousin), 32, 139

Akbar, Mohammad Ali Khan, Amir Mansur (eldest son), xix, ***xxviii***, 11, 46, 226

Akbar, Mohsen Khan (youngest son), xi, xxii, ***xxvii***, 198, 226

Akbar Family Tree, ***xxxi***

Akhtar al-Saltaneh, 53

Ala al-Dowleh, Mirza Ahmad Khan, 41–43, 46

Ala al-Saltaneh, 58–59, 64, 66, 209

Amin al-Dowleh, Mirza Ali Khan, 10, 11

Amin al-Molk Marzban, Esma'il Khan, ***14–15***, 32, 87, 138, 183, 186

Amin al-Soltan, Mirza Ali Asghar Khan
assassination of, 34–35
cabinet of, 188
in Iran's state customs office, 3
political transformation of, 33–34
portrait photograph, ***14–15***
reception of Shah and, 13

Amin al-Zarb, Haj Hossein Agha, 51

Amir A'zam, Nosratollah Mirza, 41

Amir-Ahmadi, Lieutenant General Ahmad, 112

Amjad, Sardar, 39–40

Amo-Oghli, Haydar Khan, 40

Anglo-Persian Agreement of 1919
annulled, 202
bribes to government officials, 93–94, 142–147, 157–158
British interests and, xv, 96
financial aid pursuant to, 93, 109, 115, 121–123, 133, 150, 155, 157–159, 178, 204
international opposition to, 100–103
Iranian nationals' opposition to, 94–103, 129, 148, 227
pressure from Great Britain and, 134–135
Sardar Mansur (Sepahdar), 70, 125–126
Sepahdar's statements on, 125–126, 140–141
support for, 90–97, 129
terms of, 92–93, 93–94

Vosuq al-Dowleh's demands, 98–100
Anglo-Persian Oil Company (APOC), 122, 159, 181, 202
Anglo-Russian Agreement, 24–25
Anglo-Russian Convention (1907), 71, 97
Ardebili, Haji Baba, 207
assassinations, xvii, 9, 34–35, 87–88
Association of Sardars, bill in support of parliament, 35–36
Ayn al-Dowleh, Abdol-Majid Mirza, 17–19, 28, 73–74, ***74***, 75, 173, 178, 199
A'zam, Prince Nosratollah Mirza Amir, 32
Azerbaijan Democratic Party, 104, 111
Azod al-Molk, Ali Reza Khan
Accounting and Loan Bank of Persia loan, 58
arrest by Shah, 43
Constitutional Revolution and, 41–42
death, 70
as regent, 56, 61–62

B

Baha al-Din Amlashi, 88–89
Bahador, Amir, 51–52
Bahar, Mohammad Taghi, Malak al-Shoara, xxiii, 147–148, 183
Bahr al-Oloum, Haj Sheikh Mirza Ali (Sepahdar's son-in-law), 89
Bakhash, Shaul, xxv, xxvii
Bakhtiari, Sardar As'ad, 184
Bakhtiari tribe, 70, 71
Banan al-Molk, 53
Bank Melli (National Bank), 33, 38
Baratov, General, 77
Begum Khanum (second wife), 4, 7, 49, 225.
Behbahani, Seyyed Abdollah, 29, 37, 64
Bemani Khanum Behzad (Khanum Joon) (third wife), xi-xii, 7, 225
Bibesco, Prince George-Valentin (Romania), 16
Bibesco, Princess (Romania), xxi, xxi–xxii, 16–17, ***16***
Biglarbeigi, x, 1, 7. *see also* Akbar, Fathollah Khan (Sepahdar)
Biglarbeigi, Akbar Khan (uncle), 2-4, ***5***
Blondelle, Mademoiselle, xxiv
Bolshevik forces
occupation of Gilan, 105–109, 111–113, 179
occupation of Rasht, 49, 113, 128, 130, 134–135
opposition to 1919 Agreement, 101–102
talks with, 159–160, 166–168
threat posed by, 84, 94–96, 149, 153
Bonin, Charles (French ambassador), 101
bribes to government officials
1919 Agreement and, 93–94, 142–147, 157–158
cabinet ministers and, 198
British legation
bribes to government officials, 142–147, 157–158
constitutionalists and, 69
Cossacks' advance on Tehran and, 191, 194–198
coup d'état, role in, 186, 191–193

interference with prime ministership, 171
monthly payments to Iranian government, 192
photograph, ***200***
supervision of Iranian affairs, 120, 123, 129, 203
ultimatum to Iran, 155–156

C

Chelmsford, Lord Viscount, 102
Chicherin, Georgy, 105
Churchill, George Percy, 118
Churchill, Winston, 135
constitutional decree, 33
constitutional government
constitutional cabinet, 56–59, 61–62
moderate faction members, 63–64
oath in support of, 37
radical faction members, 33–34, 63–64
Constitutional Revolution
abuse of power and, 26–31
Anglo-Russian Agreement spheres of influence, 24–25
base camp for, 49
Gilan Constitutional Corps, 50
goals of, 23, 26
Mohammad Ali Shah Qajar and, 35–38, 40–47
Sardar Mansur (Sepahdar) and, 38–40, 50–55, 64–67
Sattar Committee, 6, 47–49
Sepahdar Tonekaboni (Sepahsalar) cabinets and, 64–67
support for constitutionalism, 31–36, 46
Constitutionalist Commission, 44
corruption, 17–19, 93–94, 142–147, 157–158, 198
Cossack forces
back wages crisis, 109, 111, 121, 130, 181–182
battle with Jangali troops, 80
British authority over, 127–128, 149–150, 153
coup plot and, 163, 186, 188, 191–194
dismissal of Russian officers and, 123–127
Iranian Cossack Brigade, 89
Khiabani riot, 111–112
march on Tehran, 191, 194–200
Reza Khan as commander of, 188, 202
Russian legation and, 68, 77
Shah and, 40–43, 46
coup d'état (1921), xiv, 104, 177, 184, 185–188, 191–193, 196, 198–199
coup plot, xiv, 104, 177, 184, 185–188, ***187***
Cox, Sir Percy (ambassador), 87, ***87***, 101, 102
credentialing, 154, 156, 208–215, 218, ***237***, ***240–242***
Curzon, Lord, 102–103, 121–122, 133, 148, 158, ***162***
customs offices appointments, 10–11, 19

D

Daily News newspaper, 102
Dashti, Ali, 146–147
Dawnay, Hugh Richard, 11–12
Dehkhoda, Ali Akbar, 186
Dickson, General Harold Richard, 149–153

Dolatabadi, Seyyed Yahya, 120, 129
Doustdar, Ehsanollah Khan, 207
Ducros, Colonel, 198

E

Edward VII, King (United Kingdom), 11–12
Emad al-Kottab, 87–88
Esteghlal (Independence) newspaper, 67–68, 69
executions, 62

F

famine (Great Famine, 1917-1919), xv–xvii
Farmanfarma, Abdol-Hosain Mirza (prime minister), 76, 115, 172–173, 177–178
Farmanfarmaian, Abbas, Salar Lashkar, 139
Fathollah Khan Sepahdar A'zam. *see* Akbar, Fathollah Khan (Sepahdar)
Fazlollah, Haji Sheikh, 47
financial status of Iran
  Anglo-Persian Agreement of 1919, 97–103
  financial aid, 93, 109, 115, 121–123, 133, 150, 155, 157–159, 178, 204
  Shuster appointment and, 71, 72, 96–97
Firouz, Nosrat al-Dowleh, 98, 101, 172, 184, 185–188, ***187***, 213–215
fishing rights and contracts, 26–31, 40
Foroughi, Mohammad Ali, 85, 104, 106

G

German activity in Iran, 77, 79
Ghahreman Mirza Ayn al-Saltaneh, 113
Gholam Hossein, Mirza, 47
Gilan Constitutional Corps, 50
global political landscape, 74–75, 84–85, 91–92, 94–95
Great Britain. *see also* British Legation; coup d'état
  anti-British sentiment, 100
  Curzon's 1919 Agreement proposal, 97
  Iranian government, pivotal role in, 85
  occupation of Iran (Britain and Russia), x, xiv
  oil interests in Iran, 84, 95
  pro-British Majles representatives, 209
  Russian and British tug-of-war, 74–75
  ultimatum to Iran, 149–153
Great Famine (1917-1919), xv–xvii
Grey, Sir Edward, 43, 101, 102–103

H

Habl al-Matin (Strong cord) newspaper, 30, 38, 39, 62–63
Hajeb al-Dowleh, Mostafa Qoli Khan Qajar Davallu, 17–18, ***18***, 41
Haji Khan, 1
Hakim al-Molk, Mirza Ebrahim Khan, 56
Haneke, Monsieur, 67
Hardinge, Arthur Henry, 17, ***18***
Hartwig, Nicholas, 43

Hasan Ali Kamal Hedayat, Nasr al-Molk, 139
Hasan Ali Khan, 30
Hasan Khan A'zam al-Vozara Qodsi, 51
Hazrat, Sani, 54
Homayoun, Amid, 28, 31
Homayoun, Sardar (Cossack leader), 123–125, ***124***, 192–194
Hosayni, Soltan Mohammad Shah, xxii
Hosein Gholi Khan Gharegozlou Hamedani, Amir Nezam, 138
Hossein Pasha Khan, Amir Bahador Jang, 50–51

I

Imperial Bank, 159, 202
international relations
- occupation of Iran (Britain and Russia), 76, 79, 84
- Russia and Germany peace treaty, 84
- Russian and British tug-of-war, 74–75
- withdrawal of foreign troops, 84

Iraj Mirza, xxiii
Iran, Malakeh (Naser al-Din Shah daughter), 46
Iranian Cossack Brigade, 89
Iranian nationalists, 76, 90, 100
Ironside, General William Edmund
- Bolshevik withdrawal from Rasht and, 128, 134–135
- British forces and, 111
- Cossack forces, repositioning of, 192
- coup plot and, 185–186

Islamic Revolution (1979), xxix
Islamic Unity Committee, 89

J

Jalal al-Dowleh (son of Zell al-Soltan), 41, 43, 46
Jangali (Jungle) Movement and Jangali fighters, 49, 76, 79–82, 84, 88, 105, 179
Javad Sheikh al-Islami, 35

K

Karim Khan, Mirza (cousin), 6, 47, 50, 129, 161
Kashani, Mirza Mehdi Khan Qaem Maqam, 42
Kashani, Mirza Seyyed Hasan, 62–63
Kasmaei, Agha Sheikh Mahmud, 88–89
Kasmaei, Haj Ahmad, 88, 89–90
Kermani, Mirza Reza, 9
Khaghan, Shokrollah Khan Motamed, 42
Khalkhali, Amir Ashayer (interim governor), 84
Khanum Joon *see* Bemani Khanum Behzad
Khanum Mansur al-Saltaneh (aunt to author), xxi
Khanzadeh Khanum (aunt and first wife), 4
Khiabani, Sheikh Mohammad, 104, 111
Khomami, Haji, 47
Khorasani, Akhound Molla Mohammad Kazem, 62
Khoshtaria Oil Company, 160

Kouchak Khan, Mirza, 105, 111, 184

L

Lahovary, Marthe Lucie, 16, ***16***
Landor, Arnold Henry Savage, xxiv
Liakhov, Colonel, 45–46
Lianozov, Stepan Martinovic, 26, 28–30
Lianozov Concession, 30, 40
Liverpool Post newspaper, 102

M

Maghazei, Agha Mohammad Ali, 38
Mahallati, Haj Sayyah, 50–51. *see also* Mohammad Ali, Mirza
Mahmud, Haji Seyyed, 46
Majles. *see also* National Consultative Assembly
  Association of Sardars petition to, 35–36
  bombing of, 46, 49
  consent for new cabinet, 179
  credentialing process, 154, 156 ***237***, 208–215, 218, ***240–242***
  first, 27, 33
  fourth, 90, 147, 208–216, ***209***, ***214–215***
  Moshir al-Dowleh prime ministerships and, 85, 109–114, 147, 178, 216–217
  radical faction of, 33–34, 63–64
  reconvention delay, 135, 141, 155–156, 184–185
  Russian ultimatum to Iran and, 72
  Shuster approval by, 71, 72, 96–97
Makhsous, Khanum, 225
Manchester Guardian newspaper, 102
Mansur, Sardar (Sepahdar). *see also* Akbar, Fathollah Khan (Sepahdar)
  house as base for Constitutionalists, 49, ***49***
  seizure of properties, 47
  title, 19–21
Mansur al-Molk, 106, 166
Marling, Sir Charles (British minister), 43, 45–46, 87, ***87***
martial law, 100
Ministry of Foreign Affairs, 118
Mirza Malkam Khan, Nazim al-Dowleh, 32
Mirza Kouchak Khan, 76, 79, ***81***,88, ***105***, 107,111,184,
Modarres, Seyyed Hasan, 97, 107, 115, 127, 184, 217
Moein al-Molk, Mirza Mohsen Khan, 11, 41, 178, 179, 192
Moez al-Soltan, Abdol-Hossein Khan, 32
Mofakher al-Molk, 54
Mohammad Ali, Mirza, 6, 7
Mohammad Ali Shah Qajar
  anti-constitutionalist sentiments, 36, 37, 40–43
  assassination of Amin al-Soltan, 34–35
  attempted assassination of, 40
  confiscation of Sardar Mansur's (Sepahdar's) property, 51-52, ***234***
  intrigue to regain government control, 40–41, 71–72
  Mohammad Hasan Mirza Qajar, Crown Prince, 204, ***205***, 216

national crises in new reign, 33–34
plot to kill Sardar Mansur (Sepahdar), 53–54
portrait photograph, 42
Sardar Mansur's (Sepahdar's) arrest, 41–47, 70
tyranny of, xxix–xxx, 6, 40–41, 43–46
unseating of, 55–56
uprising against, 47
Mohammad Vali Khan Sepahdar Tonekaboni (later Sepahsalar Tonekaboni)
Akbar, Fathollah Khan (Sepahdar) and, 61, 77, 175
arrest, 199
bank loans, 57–59, 66–67
cabinets of, 64–67
Constitutional Revolution and, 36, 53, 64–67
hosting the shah, 13
installation at Rasht (Sepahdar's property), xviii–xix
photographs, ***xviii***, ***14***, ***65***
as post-coup prime minister candidate, 200–201
prime ministerships of, 70–71, 76–77
Rasht Revolution and, 49–50
Seyyed Zia al-Din Tabataba'i, meeting with, 200–201
Mohtasham al-Saltaneh Esfandiari, Mirza Hasan Khan,183-184, ***185,*** 188, 199, 225
Mohyee, Sardar (cousin), 53
Mojalal, 54
Mokhber al-Dowleh, 41, 67
Mokhber al-Saltaneh Hedayat, Haji, 111
Mokhber al-Saltaneh Hedayat, Mehdi Gholi Khan, 72
Montague, Edwin, 102
Mosaddegh al-Saltaneh, Mohammad, 130–131, ***131***, 145–146, 164–165
Moshaver al-Mamalek Ansari, 111, 166
Moshir al-Dowleh, Mirza Hasan Khan
Anglo-Persian Oil Company and, 181
bribery of government officials and, 144
cabinet of, 73, 121–122, 139–140, 141–142, 162
Constitutional Revolution and, 53
Fathollah Khan Akbar (Sepahdar) and, 6
fourth Majles election, 147
Khiabani riot, 111
portrait photograph, ***110***
prime ministerships of, 85, 109–114, 147, 178, 216–217
resignation, 114, 115
status as democrat, 64
Moshir al-Dowleh, Mirza Mohsen Khan, 7
Moshir al-Dowleh Pirnia, Hasan, 62
Moshir al-Saltaneh, Mirza Ahmad Khan, 41
Mostafa Gholi Kamal Hedayat Fahim, al-Dowleh, 138, 166
Mostofi, Abdollah, 115–117, 137, 198
Mostofi al-Mamalek, Mirza Hasan Khan
British support for, 172–173, 175–176
as Court Minister, 56
portrait photograph, ***176***

prime ministerships of, 70–71, 73, 75, 177–179, 217–218
Sepahdar and, 115
Vosuq al-Dowleh and, 145
Motamed, Sardar Sadegh Khan, 50
Movafagh al-Dowleh, 171
Mozaffar al-Din Shah Qajar, 11–15, ***14***, 19, 33
Mozaffari Era, 10–22

N

Naser al-Din Shah Qajar, 2, ***8***, 9, 11–12, 123
Naser al-Dowleh, 89
Naser al-Islam Nedamani, Seyyed Yahya, 198
Naser al-Molk, 72
Naseri era, 3
Nasim-e Shomal (Breeze from the north) newspaper, 47
Nasr al-Saltaneh, Mohammad Vali Khan Tonekaboni. *see* Mohammad Vali Khan Sepahdar Tonekaboni
National Consultative Assembly. *see also* Majles
Association of Sardars petition to, 35–36
bill to depose Mohammad Ali Shah Qatar, 55–56
bombing of, 44
fifth, 217–220
first, 27, 33
fourteenth, 181–182
fourth, 82–83, 208–216, ***209***, ***214–215***
Moshir al-Dowleh shut down of, 109, 111
radical faction of, 33–34, 63–64
reconvention delay, 135, 141, 155–156, 184–185
Sardar Sepah election interference and, 217
second, 62
Sepahdar's delay in forming, 135, 213
sixth, 145
third, 73–77
uprising against Qajar Shah, 43–45
nationalization of property, 111, 120
Naus, Joseph, 19, 27
Neda-ye Islam (Voice of Islam) newspaper, 129
Neda-ye Vatan (Voice of the homeland) newspaper, 38–39
Nezam, Haj Amir, 194
Nezam al-Saltaneh Mafi, 41, 140
Norman, Herman (British minister, Tehran), 109, 117–118, 121, 159–166, 202–203. *see also* bribes to government officials
fourth legislative vote, 148
on Mosaddegh al-Saltaneh resignation, 132
pressure on Sepahdar, 159
on prime minister appointment, 178
on Sepahdar's capabilities, 120–121
Nosrat al-Saltaneh, Hasan Ali Mirza, Prince (Ahmad Shah's uncle), 130
Nour al-Din Kharghani, Seyyed, 62

O

Om al-Khakan (Queen Mother), 53–54
Omshaei, Haji Aghajani (paternal grandfather), 2

Omshaei, Haji Mirza Mohammad-Ali Khan, 1
Omsheh settlement, 1
Ormsby-Gore, William (representative, UK House of Commons), 142
Ottoman Pan-Turks, 84–85
Ottomans in Iran, 33, 77, 79, 84–85, 88

P

Pahlavi era, 6
Paris Peace Conference, 98, 101
Pasha, Midhat, 9
Persian Socialist Soviet Republic, 49
Pesyan, Mohammad Tahgi Khan, 207
political landscape in Iran
  occupation by Britain and Russia, 76, 79, 84
  Ottoman troop withdrawal, 88
  protests in Tehran, 127
  upheavals, 84
pseudo-Masonic Society of Humanity, 32
Punishment Committee terrorist group, 84, 87

Q

Qajar monarchy. *see also* Mohammad Ali Shah Qajar
  abolition speculation, 107
  fall of, 218, 220, ***221***
  Shah deposed, 55–56
Qavam al-Dowleh, Shokrollah Khan, 115
Qavam al-Saltaneh, Mirza Ahmad Khan, 115, 207, 208, ***208***, 216–217
Qazvini, Abbas Qoli Khan, 32

R

Ra'ad (Thunder) newspaper, 100–101, 123, 129, 177
Rasht (city)
  about, 1–2
  Bolshevik occupation of, 49, 113, 128, 130, 134–135
  recapture from Soviets, 128
  revolutionary activities in, 47–48
Rashti, Mirza Karim Khan (cousin), 6, 47, 50, 129, 161
Rashti, Mirza Mohammad Khan Moin Homayoun, 32
reforms
  British role in, 97
  economic and political programs, 85, 88, 171
  judiciary, 23, 26
  Mirza Mohammad Ali and, 6–9
  Reza Shah Pahlavi and, 223–224
  Sepahdar and, 126, 141, 155
  Seyyed Hasan Modarres and, 210
  Seyyed Zia al-Din Tabataba'i and, 203
  Society of Humanity and, 32
religious establishment, xxii, 23, 26, 62–63, 218
Reporter, Sir Ardeshir Ji, 102
Reza Khan Mirpanj. *see* Reza Shah Pahlavi
Reza Khan (Sardar Sepah). *see* Reza Shah Pahlavi
Reza Shah Pahlavi

appointed prime minister, 217
Bolsheviks in Gilan and, 112
Commander of Cossack Division, xiii, 188, 202
coup plot and, 186
exile, 6
march on Tehran, 191–192, 194–198
as monarch of Iran, 220
political activity during fifth Majles, 218
portrait photograph, ***197***, ***221***
promotions by Shah, 204
quashed unrest and, 216
recovery of bribe money, 158
rise of, 49, ***49***
Sepahdar and, xxx, 199
Shah's dismissal of, 204
Russian legation
Mohammad Ali Shah Qajar's refuge at, 54–56
photograph, ***55***
Sardar Mansur's (Sepahdar's) refuge at, 51–55
Russo-Persian Treaty of Friendship, 166–170, 180, 202

S

Sa'd al-Dowleh, 53
Sadegh Khan (cousin), 3, 4
Saed al-Dowleh, 207
Safa Ali Shah. *see* Zahir al-Dowleh, Mirza Ali Khan
Safavi, Ali Asghar Rahimzadeh, 106
Salar Afkham, Fathollah Khan. *see* Akbar, Fathollah Khan (Sepahdar)
Salar al-Dowleh, Abolfath Mirza, 33
Samsam al-Saltaneh Bakhtiari, Najafgholi Khan, 30, 71, 85
Sardar Mansur (Sepahdar). *see also* Akbar, Fathollah Khan (Sepahdar)
house as base for Constitutionalists, 49, ***49***
seizure of properties, 47
title, 19–21
Sardar Moazzam, 213
Sarem al-Dowleh, 103–104
Sattar Committee, 6, 47–49
Savadkuhi, Esma'il Khan Amir Moayyed, 46, 207
Sepahdar-e-A'zam. *see* Akbar, Fathollah Khan (Sepahdar)
Sepahdar-e-Rashti. *see* Akbar, Fathollah Khan (Sepahdar)
Sepahsalar Tonekaboni. *see* Mohammad Vali Khan Sepahdar Tonekaboni
Shabab al-Dowleh, Prince, 179–180
Shams al-Din Roshdieh, Brigadier General, 104
Shargh (*East*) newspaper, 129
Shariatmadar, Haj Molla Mohammad Mehdi, 28
Shikak, Simko, 33
Shoa al-Saltaneh, Malek Mansur Mirza (brother to deposed Shah), 71, 72
Shopshal (Seraya), 54
Shuster, William Morgan, 71, 72, 96–97
Simitgou, Esma'il Khan, 33
Smirnov, Captain, 56, 58
Smith, Armitage (financial adviser), 122, ***122***, 128
Social Democratic Labor Party (Russian), 47
Socialist Soviet Republic of Gilan, 49, 105–109, 111, 128, 207

Solat al-Dowleh Ghashgha'i, 130–132
Soltan Hossein Mirza Jalal al-Dowleh, 41–42
Soltan Mohammad Khan, 210–213
Soroush newspaper, 32
Soroush, Mirza Isa Khan, 32
sovereignty, 97–103, 104, 204
SPR forces, 76
spying, xii–xiii
Starosselsky, Colonel Vsevolod, 89, 111–114, ***112***, 123
Stokes, Major Richard (diplomat), 71, 87
Supreme Advisory Council
  Ahmad Shah and, 154
  Anglo-Persian Agreement of 1919 and, 153–157
  bill to depose Mohammad Ali Shah Qatar, 55–56
  emergency meetings, 171–172
  financial deficit, 157–158
  origins, 90
  Russo-Persian Treaty of Friendship and, 166–170, 180, 202
  Sepahdar opening speech, 154–157
surnames, obligatoriness of, 219–220
Sykes, Brigadier-General Percy Molesworth, 76

T

Tabataba'i, Agha Mirza Seyyed Mohammad, 29
Tabataba'i, Seyyed Zia al-Din
  about, 101, 129
  Black Cabinet, 177–178
  bribery of Amir Nezam, 198
  as British Legation agent, 181, 182, 192
  coup d'état and, xiv, 191–193, 196, 198–199
  coup plot and, 104, 177, 184, 185–188
  participation in government affairs, 129–130
  portrait photograph, ***203***
  pressure on Sepahdar, 159
  as prime minister, 201–204
  Sepahdar, article about, 177
  Sepahsalar Tonekaboni, meeting with, 200–201
  in Teimourtash's words, 212
Tabriz, occupation of, 104–105, 170
Tabriz State Association newspaper, 30
Taghizadeh, Seyyed Hasan
  on Herman Cameron Norman, 118
  memoir and papers of, 6, 38, 48, 58, 72
  opposition to Russian interference, 69
  as radical constitutionalist, 33–34, 63
  recovery of bribe money, 158
  role in assassination, 33
  Sardar Mansur's (Sepahdar's) relationship with Russia, 70
Taghvi, Seyyed Nasrollah, 62
Taj al-Moluk Khanum Om al-Khakan (Shah's mother), xvii
Taj al-Moluk (daughter-in-law), xix–xxi, ***xx***
Talesh, Sardar Amjad Khan, 35
Taleshi, Mohammad Hossein Khan Salar As'ad, 32
Triumph of Tehran, xviii–xix, 55, 140
tsarist Russian state, 69, 84, 85

V

Vakil al-Tojjar, Mohammad, 38–39
Vali, Qasem Khan, 127
Vazir Akram, Mirza Saleh Khan, 22, 28, 41, 51. *see also* Asef al-Dowleh
Vosuq al-Dowleh, Mirza Hasan Khan
  "Agreement Cabinet," 90–94, ***91***
  Anglo-Persian Agreement of 1919 and, 90–101
  Bolshevik occupation of Gilan, 105–109, 111–113, 179
  bribe money, 142–143, 145–147, 157–158
  cabinets of, 157–158
  Jangali Movement suppression efforts, 79–82, 88–90
  portrait photograph, ***110***
  post-World War I plans, 88–89
  prime ministerships of, 79, 85, ***86***, 109
  resignation as prime minister, 103–104, 118
  Russian ultimatum to Iran and, 72
  Sepahdar, relationship with, 76, 79, 84, 107, 138, 163, 213–215
  in Sepahsalar Tonekaboni's cabinet, 64
  Seyyed Zia al-Din Tabataba'i and, 129

W

World War I, 84, 88

Y

Yahya Khan, Seyyed, 47
Yazdi, Seyyed Ali Agha, 129
Yeghikian, Gregory, 113

Z

Zahir al-Dowleh, Mirza Ali Khan, ix, 39–40
Zahra Khanum (wife of Sadegh Khan), 4
Zargandeh Committee, 129, 161
Zell al-Soltan, 35, 43, 44

www.ingramcontent.com/pod-product-compliance
Lightning Source LLC
Chambersburg PA
CBHW030312100426
42812CB00002B/680
* 9 7 8 1 9 4 9 4 4 5 6 4 0 *